Propaganda, Lies and False Flags: How the U.S. Justifies Its Wars

Propaganda, Lies and False Flags: How the U.S. Justifies Its Wars

Robert Fantina

Red Pill Press
2020

ISBN 978-1-7349074-0-7

Published by Red Pill Press (www.redpillpress.com)
295 Scratch Branch Rd.
Otto, NC 28763
USA

First edition.

Cover art and design by Travis Fantina

For Edwina, Travis, Vivian and Ruby

Contents

Foreword

A good journalist must ask five questions: who, what, when, where and why. In this book, those questions are asked and then answered in detail.

Who: The US government.

What: Imperial war for profit, based on manufactured evidence and nationalist propaganda.

When: From the nation's founding.

Where: Around the World.

Why: To maintain hegemony for maximum profit.

Sixteen years ago at the writing of this piece, my son Casey, a soldier in the American Imperial Army was killed in Iraq.

April 4th, 2004, was a terrible day for my family, but our tears were like a drop in the ocean compared to what millions in many other nations around the planet have suffered for more than two centuries under the crosshairs of U.S. war profiteers.

The U.S. war against the people of Iraq was a major conspiracy to commit mass murder. As shown in this book, this is nothing new. There have been many exposés of the lies and mass-marketing propaganda which led to the 2003 'Shock and Awe' invasion. This book exposes those lies and the lies of the U.S.'s earlier wars.

I fear that the active violence still happening in Iraq and so many other places is being ignored or forgotten. The stain of the Bush and Obama regimes are fading into the Memory Hole, as did those of all their predecessors. Few blink an eye at this injustice, while some of us still blink at it through our tears.

It seems to be that in the 2020 election, the candidates of the two-winged war bird will be Donald Trump and Joe Biden. Of course, since Joe Biden was a major supporter of the invasion of Iraq and, during his time in the Congress, never objected to any war, and Donald Trump has done nothing but make things worse around the world, neither are saying that the people of Iraq, Yemen, Palestine, Libya or any other nation victimized by the U.S. deserve justice, reparations, and finally an end to the U.S. War of Terror against them and so many other nations. In fact, when Obama was vying to be the Big Boss of the U.S. Crime Mob (aka

President of the United States), he said that those responsible for all the crimes of the previous murder regime would not be prosecuted because we had to "look forward."

Remember that? I wonder how many more U.S. citizens have gone to prison in the last dozen years or so, not knowing that the Boss said that we were now "looking forward?" I know that not one of those people who have been incarcerated were members of the Bush Crime Mob. When will a sitting Crime Boss ever seek accountability for his predecessor, when he/she will be looking for the same professional courtesy from future Bosses?

I miss Casey so much, especially around holidays, his birthday and the beginning of April, which brings emotional agony to me. This heartbreak is compounded by the fact that I know that each and every day more mothers and families will unnecessarily feel the same unending anguish. And I can barely comprehend the amount of suffering caused by U.S. wars throughout history.

Currently, the world is also in the midst of a pandemic, and most people have fallen in line with the accepted establishment narratives about it, but with the long history of riling people up for war, or for regime change, as in the Obama regime's murder of Moammar Qaddafi in Libya, who can really blame some of us for questioning the propaganda? What is more surprising to me is that every fledgling journalist should be asking more questions, and they simply aren't. Business as usual for the U.S. media. Propaganda isn't new in the U.S., as shown so clearly in this book.

To end this Empire of Death, we the people need to wake up and fight back, and our number one "weapon" is truth and enlightenment.

I am glad that my friend Bob Fantina has written this book which makes a valuable contribution to demonstrating the obvious viciousness of U.S. foreign policy throughout its history—not just since Donald Trump was (s)elected. It exposes for all to see the lies and propaganda that have fueled the U.S. war machine from the nation's earliest days.

Cindy Sheehan
Vacaville, Ca, April 2020

Executive Producer and Host of 'Cindy Sheehan's Soapbox'
www.cindysheehanssoapbox.blogspot.com
Coordinator of Women's March on the Pentagon
www.marchonpentagon.com

Introduction

It is a rare day that passes that the United States doesn't somehow proclaim its moral superiority. It is the "leader of the free world," an "exceptional" nation. But whatever causes Americans and their leaders to believe this, the fact remains: the United States has been at war for the vast majority of its history. It is responsible for the killing of millions of innocent people around the world, more often than not based on flimsy evidence, questionable motives, and outright lies.

The irony of this is lost on government leaders, who hold aloft the flag of U.S. 'exceptionalism', that heady concept that, in its sanitized form, says that the U.S. is superior to all other countries, and therefore has a leading role on the global stage, but that in reality simply means that it has the power to ignore any international laws it doesn't like. This is one of the few countries that is not a signatory of the Rome Statute of the International Criminal Court (ICC), because it greatly fears, with good reason, that its governing officials could easily find themselves in The Hague on charges of war crimes. Its strong ally, Israel – a brutal, apartheid regime, and another habitual violator of international law – also refuses to join, for the same reason.

But the lemming-like citizens fall into line as the government they are seemingly so proud of takes them over the cliff. There are always large portions of the public who 'support the troops', even as those troops kill countless innocent men, women and children. If they 'see something' they 'say something,' as the woman did who reported the odd, exotic-looking writings of a dark-complexioned seatmate on a plane, only to learn, after causing a two-hour delay for a 30-minute flight, that he was a mathematics professor, and his 'mysterious writing' consisted of math equations.[1] War hysteria is not just a thing of the past. Whether it is the Chinese, the Japanese, the Russians – or any other enemy du jour – public opinion can be counted on to rally behind the cause and support the government's military objectives.

---

[1] https://www.washingtonpost.com/news/rampage/wp/2016/05/07/ivy-league-econo
mist-interrogated-for-doing-math-on-american-airlines-flight/?utm_term=.5166a
403a6fb

This is the nation that has been at war for 225 of its 243 years in existence. This is the country that spends more on its military than the military expenditures of the next eight countries combined. Yet 21% of U.S. children live in poverty;[2] nearly 15% of all families do.[3]

Why is it that the common man and woman don't see this? Why are they satisfied with the U.S. bombing of Yemen, Syria, Afghanistan, Pakistan and other Middle Eastern countries, knowing that this is creating starvation and refugee crises of catastrophic proportions? How can it not be seen that killing people does not endear their loved ones to the killers?

The term 'false flag' has come into vogue in recent years. Initially a 'false flag' referred to the practice of pirate ships flying another nation's flag while attacking another ship. Doing so had several advantages. Not only would flying a false flag convince the intended victims of their peaceful intentions, thus preventing their victims from preparing for battle, or from fleeing; after an attack, the flag would sometimes remain in place, thereby falsely indicating the guilt of the nation whose flag it displayed. This is akin to the relatively common practice of committing a crime and framing another to take the fall by falsifying evidence pointing in their direction. It is not just common criminals who engage in such behavior; governments do it, too.

For the purposes of this book, a false flag can be defined as follows: An event, real or artificial, that appears to be a violation of international law, human rights, or another widely accepted standard of behavior, that if *real* is blamed on a source other than the actual source, and if *artificial*, is blamed on whatever country may conveniently be accused of it. It is sometimes perpetrated covertly by a nation that will then condemn it as an act of war, and will then sanction, invade, or otherwise violate the freedom and sovereignty of the accused nation. In the process, the country that is making the accusation will use it to curtail the freedoms of its own citizens. In other situations, a nation will seize upon an event, or non-event, that it has *not* arranged, for the same purposes, simply by taking advantage of the opportunity presented by such an event.

Today, the U.S. uses the same method to start many of its wars. Following the attacks on the U.S. on September 11, 2001, the U.S. government exploited the fears of many of its citizens by stating to the world that Iraq was involved in those attacks, and had 'weapons of mass destruc-

---

[2]http://www.nccp.org/topics/childpoverty.html. Accessed June 5, 2018

[3]https://www.children.org/global-poverty/global-poverty-facts/facts-about-poverty -in-usa. Accessed on February 25, 2019.

tion' which threatened the very existence of the United States. Based on these statements, the U.S. invaded Iraq, killing millions of people and displacing millions more, destroying the infrastructure of the country, and re-igniting factional rivalries that had been dormant for years. Despite some quite massive anti-war demonstrations, the citizenry basically supported the Iraqi invasion. Yet no weapons of mass destruction were ever found, and a bi-partisan Congressional report stated clearly that there was no evidence of Iraq involvement in the September 11 terrorist attacks.

What, then, was the real reason for the invasion and occupation of Iraq by the United States? Alan Greenspan, who served as Chair of the Federal Reserve from 1987 to 2006, explained it concisely in his memoirs; said he: "I am saddened that it is politically inconvenient to acknowledge what everyone knows: the Iraq war is largely about oil."[4] But even that isn't the whole story, as we will see in Chapter 24. Nearly seventeen years after that ill-conceived invasion, U.S. troops remain in the country, and conditions for the populace are far worse than they ever were under Saddam Hussein.

Today, false flags come in a variety of forms, often involving atrocities – real or imagined – or the modern bogeyman of terrorism, which has largely replaced that of communism. Recent examples include accusations that Syria has used chemical weapons against its own people (see Chapter 26), or that Iran is exporting terrorism (see Chapter 28). In these cases, some suspected event is seized upon as fact, blown out of proportion, and the U.S. decrees that it must act, before there has been time for any actual investigation and evidence to come to light. But as early as the War of 1812 (see Chapter 2), the government, supported by the popular press, either used suspected incidents, or simply invented them, to get the citizenry to support a new war.

Adolf Hitler first defined the 'big lie' in his book *Mein Kampf*, although it had been in use for centuries. He wrote this:

> ... that in the big lie there is always a certain force of credibility; because the broad masses of a nation are always more easily corrupted in the deeper strata of their emotional nature than consciously or voluntarily; and thus in the primitive simplicity of their minds they more readily fall victims to the big lie than the small lie, since they themselves often tell small lies in little matters but would be ashamed to resort to large-scale falsehoods.

---

[4]https://www.theguardian.com/world/2007/sep/16/iraq.iraqtimeline. Accessed on September 16, 2019.

It would never come into their heads to fabricate colossal untruths, and they would not believe that others could have the impudence to distort the truth so infamously. Even though the facts which prove this to be so may be brought clearly to their minds, they will still doubt and waver and will continue to think that there may be some other explanation. For the grossly impudent lie always leaves traces behind it, even after it has been nailed down, a fact which is known to all expert liars in this world and to all who conspire together in the art of lying.[5]

It's ironic that Hitler, in identifying the 'big lie' and describing how it is used by Jews, used it himself – habitually. And by accusing Jews of perpetrating big lies, he was actually telling big lies about Jews himself. It was a stunning example of political and psychological projection: accusing his enemies of what he himself was doing.

But Hitler was not only a master practitioner of the big lies he accused the Jews of perpetrating; he was also willing to use false flags to his advantage. In January of 1933, Hitler become chancellor, but without a majority. With his election, the government was dissolved; March 5 was the date set for new elections. A month later, on February 27, 1933, the German government building, the Reichstag, was set on fire. Hitler accused the communists of being responsible, a state of emergency was declared and freedoms of speech and assembly were suspended.

A Dutch communist was tried for the crime and executed. But was he, in fact, guilty? Historian David R. Beisel said: "It's well known how, just after the Nazis came to power, Hitler opportunistically used the Reichstag fire to outlaw the Communist Party, a first step in eventually outlawing all political parties except the Nazis."[6]

The question remains of whether or not Hitler simply took advantage of the fire, or was more instrumental in it. According to historian Paul Farhi, "Historians have long debated, for example, whether the fire that destroyed the German parliament building, the Reichstag, in 1933 was set by the Dutch communist executed for the crime or was really a false-flag operation by Adolph Hitler's Nazi party to further entrench its power."[7]

The Nazis leadership seemed to have an instinctive understanding of how to get the citizens of any nation, regardless of the type of government,

---

[5]https://en.wikipedia.org/wiki/Big_lie. Accessed November 5, 2018.

[6]David R. Beisel, "Building the Nazi Mindset," *The Journal of Psychohistory* 37, no. 4 (2010).

[7] Paul Farhi, "Caught in Conspiracy Crosshairs," *Winnipeg Free Press*, December 10, 2016.

to support war. General Herman Goering, President of the German Reichstag and Nazi Party, Commander of Luftwaffe during World War II, and one of the most savage men to have walked the planet, said this during the Nuremburg Trials:

> Naturally the common people don't want war: Neither in Russia, nor in England, nor for that matter in Germany. That is understood. But, after all, it is the leaders of the country who determine the policy and it is always a simple matter to drag the people along, whether it is a democracy, or a fascist dictatorship, or a parliament, or a communist dictatorship. ... Voice or no voice, the people can always be brought to the bidding of the leaders. That is easy. All you have to do is tell them they are being attacked, and denounce the peacemakers for lack of patriotism and exposing the country to danger. It works the same in any country.[8]

In this book, the use of the 'big lie' by U.S. government officials, from before the War of 1812 to the bombing of Syria in 2017, and including ongoing threats against Iran, will be detailed. In each war in which the U.S. has been involved, a big lie of one sort or another has been instrumental in rallying support from the citizenry, including several false flags in all their varieties. In all such cases, however, the real purpose of the war was always far from the one stated. (Please note that the scope of this book is only the United States; this is not meant to imply that the U.S. is the only nation to create or exploit false flags, although it could be argued that it does so most successfully).

Accompanying 'false flags', and very closely aligned with them, is propaganda. Once meaning only persuasion, it has evolved significantly over the centuries. As Ross Collins defines it: "Propaganda is concerned with the management of opinions and attitudes by the direct manipulation of social suggestion."[9] How could the U.S. have justified the invasion of Iraq without creating in the minds of the populace an association between that country and the 9/11 attacks on the U.S.? Even according to a bipartisan Congressional report, there was no involvement by Iraq, but by the time Bush began beating the war drums, Muslims had been vilified and, conveniently, Iraq was a mostly-Muslim nation. The populace had allowed the 'management of opinions and attitudes' to be manipulated by 'social suggestion'. Once a war is started by a false flag, propaganda is a useful tool

---

[8]http://www.globalissues.org/article/400/media-propaganda-and-iraq. Accessed on November 7, 2018.

[9]Ross F. Collins, *Children, War and Propaganda* (Peter Lange, Inc., 2011), 5.

in maintaining the enthusiasm of the citizenry for the far-off slaughter of innocents.

Propaganda was first used officially in the U.S. during World War I. This was the first 'total' war, a war in which every man, woman and child in the U.S. was to be involved, and which they were to support. Collins writes: "Total war demanded the energies of a whole nation, the children not exempt, and if the literal truth about combat zones were told, it was feared morale would plummet and the country would lose."[10]

During World War I, the Commission on Public Information was established as the official propaganda arm of the government; during World War II, it was the Office of War Information. Since then, the corporate-owned media has taken its talking points from the U.S. government, telling the public what matters, and which lives – mainly but not always those of European descent – it should care about.

As Tim Anderson writes in *The Dirty War on Syria: Washington, Regime Change and Resistance*,: "War propaganda often demands the abandoning of ordinary reason and principle".[11] Further, he states, "A belligerent party always has a vital interest in discrediting and delegitimising its opponent. For that reason, we must always view belligerent party 'evidence' against an opponent with grave suspicion."[12]

This is how the U.S. operates. The government first determines which nation it wants to control, either for its natural resources (Iraq in 2003; see Chapter 24), its strategic importance (Syria in 2011–2020; see Chapter 26), or for political expediency (not wanting to appear 'weak' on communism, as in Vietnam in the '60s and '70s; see Chapter 15). Then it unfurls a 'false flag', such as weapons of mass destruction and involvement in 9/11 for Iraq, chemical attacks by the government of Syria, or the Gulf of Tonkin non-incident in Vietnam. Using effective propaganda, it either frightens the populace (Iraq's non-existent WMDs), appeals to their sense of moral outrage (innocent children dying in a chemical attack), or appeals to their over-inflated sense of nationalism, as when North Vietnam was accused of firing on U.S. warships in the Gulf of Tonkin, where those warships had no legitimate reason to be. The corporate-owned media parrots the presidential lies, quotes 'unnamed sources' or bogus organizations (such as was done frequently in relation to Syria; see Chapter 26), and does its part to manipulate public opinion. The president then appears on

---

[10]Ibid., 28.

[11]Tim Anderson, *The Dirty War on Syria: Washington, Regime Change and Resistance* (Global Research Publishers, 2016), 11.

[12]Ibid.

national television or in front of the United Nations Security Council, filled with righteous indignation, demanding that whatever he says has occurred be redressed. Congress members then surround him, putting aside their usually nebulous political differences, and support his call for war, the one topic on which they are usually united. And then, death and carnage at an unspeakable level begins, all in the name of the glory of the mighty U.S.

And what does all this war mean in terms of human life? Just since World War II, it is estimated that the U.S. has killed at least 20,000,000 people in its various wars, in over 37 nations.[13]

This is how the U.S. fights 'terrorism': by unleashing terrorism of its own that dwarfs anything any ragtag group, or even any other nation, would ever conceive of, let alone perpetrate. In response to the killing of 3,000 U.S. citizens on September 11, 2001, the U.S. killed at least 1,000,000 Iraqis who, along with their government, had nothing to do with the 2001 attacks on the U.S.[14]

During her campaign for the 2008 Democratic presidential nomination, former Secretary of State Hillary Clinton said that if Iran were to attack Israel, she, as president, would 'obliterate' Iran. Never is there talk of negotiations, diplomacy, mutual understanding and goals; it is always war, innocent bystanders be damned.

This is a tried and true pattern, and the only way it can ever be changed is by recognizing it. Hopefully, this book will assist in that goal.

This book is divided into three main sections. The first covers the "First Century," the United States' wars between its founding in 1776 and the start of the twentieth century, including the colonists wars on the Native Americans, the War of 1812, and Mexican-American and Spanish-American wars.

The second section, "Becoming a World Power," covers the first half of the twentieth century: Cuba, the Philippines, Nicaragua, Haiti, the World Wars, Korea, and others.

The third section, "Global Killing Fields," takes us from 1955 to the present, including the "anti-communist" wars of the Cold War, and the modern ones in the Global War on Terror.

Although this book is divided into three main sections, there is overlap; for example, the U.S. has interfered in Cuba multiple times since the

---

[13]https://www.globalresearch.ca/us-has-killed-more-than-20-million-people-in-37-vic tim-nations-since-world-war-ii/5492051. Accessed on October 10, 2018.

[14]http://www.nbcnews.com/id/5223932/ns/us_news-security/t/panel-sees-no-link-b etween-iraq-al-qaida/#.Wn2ngK6nG00. Accessed on October 10, 2018.

1898, and the chapter on Cuba, in the Section B, covers information to the present day.

While the U.S. is not the only country to lie to the world to start imperial wars, only U.S. wars will be covered herein. While other nations do the same, none has the military power of the United States, nor have any caused anywhere near the death and suffering that the U.S. has caused.

It is hoped that by recognizing the 'big lies' that the U.S. government tells, people will begin to believe them with less ardor and less frequency. This will be the first step toward changing the centuries-long U.S. policy of constant war-making.

Section A: The First Century (1755–1899)

The U.S. gained its independence after having been a colony of Britain for many years. During that time, it learned valuable lessons in colonizing, occupying, stealing natural resources and killing anyone who got in its way. Its murders of indigenous people began long before the seeds of independence were planted, and continue to this day.

But as early as the U.S. Revolution, propaganda was rampant.

> All newspaper narratives concerning the 'barbarity and insults' of the British in America sought to convince colonials of the cruelty and degeneracy of the British and instill in Americans a hatred for the British. Aimed at destroying any reputation the British may have once held, the *Virginia Gazette* described the colonials' former countrymen as 'royal thieves,' 'savage brutes,' 'uncivilized banditti,' and 'pirates and bloodsuckers.' In 1775 [*Virginia Gazette* publisher John] Pinkney declared that 'the repeated insults which this distressed country has suffered call aloud for everything tending to its preservation and protection.' All wartime efforts on the part of the Williamsburg printers to picture the British as cruel, depraved, and undeserving of American support aimed at ensuring that Virginians answered Pinkney's call.[15]

In addition to the press stirring up hostility towards the British, "... it also set a positive agenda concerning the war by emphasizing the certainty of American success."[16]

This section focuses on the period of time from shortly before the birth of U.S. in 1776, to the start of the twentieth century. It includes information about the Colonists' unspeakable genocide of Native Americans, which, of course, began prior to 1776.

---

[15]Louis Chiasson Jr., *The Press in Time of Crisis* (Westport: Greenwood Publishing Group, 1995), 10.

[16]Ibid., 2.

Chapter 1: Native Americans

Volumes have been written about the horrific, unspeakable abuses that were perpetrated on Native Americans by the U.S. government.[17] No attempt is made here to detail these abuses, but a small sampling of 'false flags' and government and corporate propaganda will be detailed.

That the Native Americans fighting with the British were on the losing side prepared the U.S. to justify the ongoing, horrific abuses it would perpetrate on the Natives for generations, continuing to the present day.

Native Americans felt the brunt of U.S. imperial violence before, during and after the Revolutionary War. Attacks against various tribes were nearly constant, from long before the Declaration of Independence was signed.

The U.S. government was more than willing to tame the land for profit. If this meant killing the millions of people whose ancestors had lived on it from time immemorial, so be it. After all, they were only 'savages,' little better than the animals with whom they shared the land. Historian Dr. Gayle Olson-Raymer commented as follows:

> During the era of Manifest Destiny, Indian people across the continent continued to be the object of stereotypes – savage men and women who had no legitimate rights to land – land they could not and would not tame for profit. Those stereotypes have been slow to diminish. As western novelist Larry McMurtry explains, 'Thanks largely to the movies, the lies about the West are more potent than the truth.'[18]

And these lies continue. These stereotypes have also been perpetuated by our textbooks which tell us that Indians massacred good, strong, Protestant pioneers moving across land that was theirs for the taking. But similar to the stereotypes put forth by Hollywood, there are few facts

---

[17]For detailed information about the U.S. government's treatment of Native Americans, please see *The Great Father: The United States Government and the American Indians* by Francis Paul Prucha and "A Suppressed Chapter in History of American Capitalism: The Conquest of the Indians," *Fourth International* 10, no. 1 (January 1949), by William F. Warde.

[18]http://gorhistory.com/hist110/unit3/indians.html. Accessed September 5, 2018.

to back this up. Indeed, during the 17 years of the largest westward movement – 1842 to 1859 – of more than 400,000 pioneers crossing the Great Plains, less than 400 – or less than 0.1% – were killed by Native Americans.[19]

While the numbers of Native Americans killed by white settlers is unknown, it is estimated to be in the millions. When the first European explorers landed in what is now the United States, it is estimated that there were at least 10,000,000 Natives living there. By 1900, only about 300,000 remained.[20] How the white settlers were able to see the Natives, who initially were friendly and welcoming to them, as less than human is difficult to comprehend. White hostility towards Natives was savagely manifested, even against those who assisted the settlers. A Native American Cayuga leader known only as Logan restrained his tribe's members from attacking white settlers in Ohio. He ceased all friendly relations with the settlers following a settler attack against his tribe in 1774. Among those killed were his entire family. He then began raiding white settlements, but the Cayuga were eventually defeated. He refused to attend the meeting to determine peace terms, but sent a message to be read at the meeting. It has come to known as 'Logan's Lament'.

Logan's Lament

I appeal to any white man to say, if ever he entered Logan's cabin hungry, and he gave him not meat; if ever he came cold and naked, and he clothed him not. During the course of the last long and bloody war 'the French and Indian War, 1755–1763', Logan remained idle in his cabin, an advocate for peace. Such was my love for the whites, that my countrymen pointed as they passed, and said, 'Logan is the friend of white men.' I had even thought to have lived with you, but for the injuries of one man. Col. Cresap, the last spring, in cold blood, and unprovoked, murdered all the relations of Logan, not sparing even my women and children. There runs not a drop of my blood in the veins of any living creature. This called on me for revenge. I have sought it; I have killed many: I have fully glutted my vengeance. For my country, I rejoice at the beams of peace. But do not harbour a thought that mine is the joy of fear. Logan never felt fear. He will not turn on his heel to save his life. Who is there to mourn for Logan? Not one.[21]

---

[19] J. W. Loewen, (2010) Teaching What Really Happened: How To Avoid The Tyranny Of Textbooks And Get Students Excited About Doing History (New York: Teachers College Press, 2010), 69.

[20] http://endgenocide.org/learn/past-genocides/native-americans/

[21] http://www.ohiohistorycentral.org/w/Logan%27s_Lament_(Transcript). Accessed

Here is an example of a Native leader who only wanted to live in peace, and was willing to share the land with the white settlers. But that was not enough for them; the 'savages' had to be removed, and the fact that innocent men, women and children by the millions were among their number had no importance to the blood-thirsty and profit-motivated whites. The betrayal of an ally, one who had worked to prevent violence against them, meant nothing.

Native Americans had one advocate among the future revolutionaries:

> Beginning in 1736, [Benjamin] Franklin published Indian treaty accounts on a regular basis until the early 1760s, when his defense of Indians under assault by frontier settlers at Lancaster cost him his seat in the Pennsylvania Assembly.[22]

Franklin's concern for the Natives lasted for decades. One 'false flag' attack that he was highly critical of concerned the Conestogas, one of the few tribes with whom the white settlers co-existed peacefully.

Yet like all Native Americans, they needed to be removed from their lands so the invading white settlers could have it. Therefore, in the town of Paxton, a group of settlers proclaimed, without any evidence, that the Conestogas were in league with more hostile tribes, and needed to be destroyed.

Over a two-day period, more than 50 men, referred to as 'The Paxton Boys,' attacked and killed more than twenty Conestoga Indians, who had been living for years in peaceful coexistence with the settlers. On the first night they killed six people and burned their cabins; on the second, they killed and scalped six adults and eight children.

> Franklin was the first to demand proper evidence of the Conestogas' supposed complicity with hostile Indians. 'I call thus publickly on the Makers and Venders of these Accusations to Produce their Evidence,' he wrote in his *Narrative*. 'Let them satisfy the Public that even *Will Soc*, the most obnoxious of all that Tribe, was really guilty of those Offences against us which they lay to his Charge.' Even if Sock was guilty, Franklin asked, 'ought he not to have been fairly tried?' Like all the Conestoga Indians, he 'lived under our Laws, and was subject to them; he was in our Hands, and might easily have been prosecuted.' The same applied to 'Shehaes [Sheehays], the women, and the boys and girls hatcheted in their parents'

September 22, 2018.

[22] Bruce Elliott Johansen (editor), *The Encyclopedia of Native American Legal Tradition* (Greenwood Press, 1998), 102.

arms.' If there was evidence that they had done something wrong, they ought to have been treated within the framework of the law.[23]

Although the term 'Manifest Destiny' wasn't coined until 1845, the concept was firmly embedded in the minds of the Colonists. First stated by John O'Sullivan, the cofounder and editor of The United States Magazine and Democratic Review (generally called the *Democratic Review*) the term signified "the mission of the United States 'to overspread the continent allotted by Providence for the free development of our yearly multiplying millions.'"[24] Mr. O'Sullivan further told his readers: "Until every acre of the North American continent is occupied by citizens of the United States, the foundation of the future empire will not have been laid."[25] Sixty years before he defined it, the Colonists were acting upon this brutal, racist concept.

In 1775, the Continental Congress established the first federal 'Indian' policy. Some highlights of this are as follows:

> That it is represented, and the committee believe with truth, that although the hostile tribes of Indians in the northern and middle departments, are seriously disposed to a pacification, yet they are not in a temper to relinquish their territorial claims, without further struggles.[26]

There is an assumption that the 'territorial claims' of the Indians are to be surrendered. If that involves 'further struggles,' so be it. There is no recognition that the land rightfully belongs to the natives.

> Even if all the northern and western tribes of Indians inhabiting the territories of the United States could be totally expelled, the policy of reducing them to such an extremity is deemed to be questionable; for in such an event it is obvious that they would find a welcome reception from the British government in Canada, which by so great an accession of strength would become formidable in case of any

---

[23] Kevin Kenny, *Peaceable Kingdom Lost: The Paxton Boys and the Destruction of William Penn's Holy Experiment* (New York: Oxford University Press, 2009), 182 (original spelling retained).

[24] Wendy J. Deichmann Edwards, "Forging an Ideology for American Missions- Josiah Strong and Manifest Destiny," in *North American Foreign Missions, 1810-1914: Theology, Theory, and Policy*, edited by Wilbert R. Shenk (Grand Rapids, MI: William B. Eerdmans, 2004), 168.

[25] Carol and Thomas Christensen, *The U.S.-Mexican War* (Bay Books, 1998), 41.

[26] Francis Paul Prucha (editor), *Documents of United States Indian Policy*, 3rd ed. (Lincoln, NE: University of Nebraska Press, 2000), 3.

future rupture, and in peace, by keeping alive the resentment of the Indians for the loss of their country, would secure to its own subjects the entire benefit of the fur trade.[27]

The members of the Continental Congress recognized that the Indians have lost their country, but the idea of total expulsion is only considered in the light of how it might compromise the U.S.'s foreign policy goals, i.e. hostilities with Britain in Canada and, notably, the profitable fur trade.

> That although motives of policy as well as clemency ought to incline Congress to listen to the prayers of the hostile Indians for peace, yet in the opinion of the committee it is just and necessary that lines of property should be ascertained and established between the United States and them, which will be convenient to the respective tribes, and commensurate to the public wants, because the faith of the United States stands pledged to grant portions of the uncultivated lands as a bounty to their army, and in reward of their courage and fidelity, and the public finances do not admit of any considerable expenditure to extinguish the Indian claims upon such lands; because it is become necessary, by the increase of domestic population and emigrations from abroad, to make speedy provision for extending the settlement of the territories of the United States.[28]

The 'uncultivated lands' herein referred to include both lands the Natives used for farming, and wooded land used for hunting. The government had promised lands to members of the army, and stealing that land from the Indians was viewed as completely acceptable.

With the success of the American Revolution, things became worse for the Native Americans, and the downward spiral of their civilization, which began when the first white settlers set foot on the continent, accelerated. Following the end of the war, treaties were created, designating areas of land for the Native Americans, who were treated as a conquered people.

Newspapers of the day were busy in manipulating the public's view of the Natives. In reviewing them today, quoting the work of David Copeland, we see:

> ... how whites viewed Native American groups as sovereign nations and how Native Americans reciprocated. What is also evident is the fact that when the colonies no longer needed Native American assistance or trade, or whenever the numbers of Native Americans

---

[27]Ibid.

[28]Ibid., 4.

within a particular colony decreased to the point they were no longer considered a threat to whites, colonial political actions towards Indians were often harsh. What was needed from Native Americans often determined how the newspaper information was expected to persuade readers.[29]

Colonists' relations with the natives were double-edged: they saw the natives as trading partners, and felt that they would help defend their new and ever-expanding, borders. As Copeland put it, "Colonists used Indians for protection and trade, but most often, whites viewed Native peoples as 'the Sculking Indian Enemy', an often-used phrase to describe Indians in newspapers."[30]

Yet regardless of treaties, more and more hostile settlers streamed into Native territory, taking their land, and introducing an agricultural economy that altered the environment on which the Natives relied. Forests were cut to make farms, destroying the homes of the wild game, the major food source for the Natives. The environment the Natives had lived within for generations untold was quickly disappearing.

Into this mix was added the British government's alliance with most of the Native American tribes. These alliances had been established, or at least strengthened, during the American Revolution. The British wanted to establish a native homeland within western Canada, which would be mutually beneficial: the tribes would be able to continue living as they had for generations, and the area would be easier to defend from a U.S. attack. During this time, British fur traders moved freely through Native territories, and this further helped to strengthen these alliances.

The government and people of the U.S., however, were convinced that British alliances with Native peoples were simply one more evidence of a British plot against them; they were still too close to their old colonial status to see anything but offense in the British associations with the Natives.

---

[29]David A. Copeland. *Debating the Issues in Colonial Newspapers: Primary Documents on Events of the Period* (Greenwod, 2000), 45.
[30]Ibid., 181.

Chapter 2: The War of 1812 (1812–1815)

With ongoing attacks against numerous Native American tribes, the U.S.'s policy of war was becoming fully established. By 1812, a number of factors led the U.S. to declare what, at the time, was referred as the Second War of Independence. As historian David J. Cowen said: "British impressment of US sailors and incursion into American territorial waters were clear violations of the country's nationhood. British forts on American territory in the Northwest and a standing army in Canada were also clear threats."[31]

Prior to war, President Thomas Jefferson issued sanctions, but he greatly miscalculated their impact. As Cowen further stated: "Jefferson believed that Britain needed America more than America needed Britain. In fact, as major trading partners they needed each other equally. Moreover, since Britain was locked in a desperate struggle against Napoleonic authoritarianism, it did not look kindly on the actions of its former colonies. Worst of all, the embargo decimated the American economy".[32] After James Madison became president, war became inevitable.

But how to get the populace to go along? What false flag could be raised to justify the invasion of Canada?

One of the issues that the U.S. press blew out of all proportion was impressment. This was the practice of British sailors boarding U.S. ships and forcing U.S. sailors to serve in their own navy. Some men forced into foreign service in this way spent years with the British. Although proof of citizenship was all that was necessary for their release, obtaining that proof sometimes took several years. Any such incidents were met with rage by U.S. citizens.

However, as is frequently the case in the U.S., things were not always what they appeared to be. British sailors sometimes deserted the Royal Navy and found work on U.S. ships. When British ships encountered U.S. sailing vessels, they were within their rights to board them and search for and remove any British deserters. While the practice of boarding U.S. ships to retrieve deserters was within the law, no assessment of the morality of that practice will be made here.

---

[31]David J. Cowen, "Financing the War of 1812," *Financial History*, Fall 2012.
[32]Ibid.

One such incident that caused much anger in the U.S. concerned the U.S. frigate *Chesapeake*. When Her Majesty's Ship *Leonard* encountered the *Chesapeake* in 1807, Captain Salusbury Pryce Humphreys demanded permission to board it to search for British deserters. This was not an arbitrary demand; Humphreys had in his possession a letter signed by the Vice Admiral of the White, Sir George Cranfield Berkeley, commander-in-chief of the British North American Station. This letter indicated that 'many Seamen' serving on British vessels had deserted when docked in the Cheasapeake Bay, and some of them were believed to have obtained employment on the *Cheasapeake*, which was docked there at the same time.

The British Captain didn't attempt to arbitrarily board the ship. When the *Leopard* first approached the *Chesapeake*, Humphreys called out to the crew, saying he had a message for the captain. Commodore James Barron then signaled that Humphreys could send his crew member over with the message. British Lt. John Meade then sailed in a small boat to the *Chesapeake* and delivered the letter from Berkeley.

Barron refused to recognize Royal Navy authority over his ship, saying that such searches were prevented by the U.S. government. He further stated that he was not aware of any British deserters on the ship from the British ships specifically mentioned in Berkeley's letter. Meade than returned to the *Leopard*.

The *Leopard* moved closer to the *Chesapeake*, and Humphreys again called to Barron. There is some question about this exchange, since witness reports varied. But Humphreys was said to have stated: "Commodore Barron, you must be aware of the necessity I am under of complying with the orders of my commander-in-chief."[33] Barron later reported that his response was "I do not understand what you say".

The *Leopard* then fired, severely damaging the ill-prepared *Chesapeake*, resulting in 21 casualties. The *Chesapeake* is believed to have only returned two or three shots (some reports indicate only one shot was fired from the *Chesapeake*). Crew from the *Leopard* then boarded the *Chesapeake*, and retrieved three British deserters from the ship.

After this incident, Humphreys wrote the following: "No person could regret more than myself that the Admiral should have issued such a circular to the different ships under his command; buy my duty was to obey,

---

[33]Tucker, Spencer C. and Frank T. Reuter, *Injured Honor: The Chesapeake-Leopard Affair, June 22, 1807* (Naval Institute Press, 1996), 8

as a subordinate officer, and as a gentleman, to soften and ameliorate the apparent severity and harshness of the order."[34]

As Tucker and Reuter point out, "Few ships became such a symbol of the War of 1812 as USS *Chesapeake*, a catalyst and victim of the political and military entanglements between Britain and the US."[35]

The fact that the British captain followed generally accepted international protocol wasn't important. A British ship had fired on a U.S. vessel, causing death and destruction. Revenge on the *Leonard* was vowed by subsequent captains of the *Chesapeake*. Tucker and Reuter highlight the determination of these captains with this example: "Stephen Decatur, captain of the *Chesapeake* for the next two years, had hoped he would be the one to avenge the U.S. Navy. He drilled his crew and asserted he would do battle with any British warship on the slightest provocation; in particular, he swore to attack the *Leopard* if he ever encountered her."[36] This might have been seen as an isolated incident, but it was kept in the forefront of the U.S. mind and remained an open wound on the U.S. psyche, helping to garner support for the invasion of Canada.

There are numerous parallels in this. Iraq's alleged possession of 'weapons of mass destruction' (see Iraq: Chapter 24, for example) was seen as threatening the U.S. Additionally, the United States provides more foreign aid to Israel than it does to all other nations combined, and that nation sees anything, including a proposal to have the Fédération Internationale de Football Association (FIFA; the international soccer association) disqualify Israel due to its crimes against humanity, as a threat to its very existence.

So any perceived threat to the U.S. could potentially be exploited to justify war.

The propaganda used in the lead-up and during the War of 1812 repeated themes of the Revolutionary War period in portraying the British as opponents of U.S. liberty.[37] The fact that the U.S. was opposing British and Canadian liberty didn't seem to have any importance to the press.

While letters home from soldiers provided information that was subsequently put in newspaper articles, it was those newspapers that provided most of the information about the war. "After the declaration of war,

---

[34] Ibid., 5.

[35] https://www.thecanadianencyclopedia.ca/en/article/chesapeake-affair-1807/. Accessed on July 13, 2018.

[36] Tucker and Reuter, *Injured Honor*, 189

[37] http://www.americanforeignrelations.com/O-W/Propaganda-Revolution-war-and -propaganda-to-1917.html. Accessed on July 13, 2018.

newspapers remained the prime source of stirring up public opinion."[38]
From June 12 to July 29, civil disobedience in Baltimore was widely reported, as members of the Democratic-Republican Party saw any opposition to war as tantamount to treason. The anti-war newspaper, *Federal
Republic and Commercial Gazette*, published in Baltimore, was the target
of this weeks-long action, and the editor, Alexander Contee Hanson, was
warned by pro-administration newspapers that his position on the war
could incite violence. "Hanson, however, argued that it was his constitu-
tional right to publish his paper as he saw fit and he continued to attack
the policy of President Madison."[39]

This incident with the *Chesapeake*, and the policy of impressments or
enforced slavery, enraged many Americans; whether the anger would have
been the same had it been any other nation that kidnapped U.S. sailors,
or retrieved their own, can only be speculated. The wounds from the
American Revolution, less than thirty years ended, were still fresh, and
the British were still seen as monsters.

The U.S. goal of conquering and annexing Canada was not achieved.
As historian Kerry Able commented, both Canada and the U.S. claimed
victories of sorts: "the Americans because they ultimately did succeed in
forcing British recognition of the nationhood, and the Canadians because
they prevented an American conquest."[40]

---

[38] Martin J. Manning and Clarence R. Wyatt, *Encyclopedia of Media and Propaganda
in Wartime America, Volume 1* (ABC-CLIO, 2010), 130.

[39] Ibid.

[40] Kerry Abel, "Remembering the War of 1812," *Canadian Parliamentary Review* 35,
no. 3 (2012).

Chapter 3: Mexican-American War (1846–1848)

The raising of false flags to gain support for the invasion of Mexico and the annexation of Texas was not difficult to do. For years prior to the actual invasion, circumstances were such that could easily fan the hot flames of jingoism.

Mexico was in a state of severe economic crisis, which would only be worsened by a war with the U.S. Yet due to President Jose Joaquin de Herreraès limited popularity, he received no assistance or support from the Mexican Congress. He was also effectively prevented from making any significant overtures of peace with the U.S., which would have risked the overthrow of his government.

The Mexican province of Texas was sparsely populated, and the Mexican government wanted more people there, hoping to discourage the obvious U.S. designs on the area. Since few Mexicans showed any desire to relocate to Texas, the government provided a number of incentives to Europeans, including land and tax exemptions. One land agent, Stephen Austin,

> ... offered especially large farms at remarkably low prices. In return for just $60 in fees, a married couple received 960 acres plus another one hundred acres for each child and eighty acres for each slave. By comparison, the United States government charged $100 for a farm of just eighty acres, with no bonus for children and slaves. Financially ruined by the depression of 1819 [in the U.S.], many of the settlers from Europe sought to rebuild their fortunes on cheap and fertile land in Texas.[41]

This was successful in drawing people to Texas; however, Europeans emigrating had no loyalty to their new nation. "Shortly before Christmas (1826), the squatters and Cherokees arrested the local Mexican officials and declared the independence of the Republic of Fredonia, which they

---

[41] Alan Taylor, "Remaking Americans- Louisiana, Upper Canada, and Texas," in *Contested Spaces of Early America*, edited by Juliana Barr and Edward Countryman (Philadelphia: University of Pennsylvania Press, 2014), 222

divided into two zones: the southern two-thirds of Texas for 'the White People' and the northern third for 'the Red People'".[42] This revolt was suppressed within months with the assistance of U.S. volunteers.

The U.S. press seized upon this opportunity to rally around these 'freedom fighters.' This resonated with U.S. citizens, still not that distant from their own revolution.

It's important to note that the U.S. assisted in putting down the revolt in Texas, and then used the same revolt and its violent suppression to support Texas in breaking away from Mexico. One hundred and sixty years later, the U.S. did the same thing in Syria, both supporting and opposing ISIS (see chapter 26).

In February 1836, the colorful and extremely controversial Antonio Lopez de Santa Anna, who served as Mexico's president 11 separate times in 22 years, attacked the Alamo. The Alamo was a fortified Franciscan mission, and, as historian Will Fowler commented, Santa Ana realized that, while "the Alamo was not a strategically important objective, he could not ignore it."

> The defenders of the Alamo could cut off his army's retreat and dis-
> rupt their lengthy line of supplies. Although an assault on the fortifi-
> cation would be costly, there seemed to be no other option. Giving
> the Texans one last chance, Santa Anna sent Colonel Juan Nepo-
> muceno Almonte with his offer of allowing the men at the Alamo to
> walk away free as long as they promised never again to take up arms
> against the Mexican nation. A refusal of this generous offer would
> be equivalent to passing their own death sentence. Colonel William
> Barret Travis replied by opening fire on the Mexican forces and, to
> quote Santa Anna, in so doing, sealed the fate of those obstinate
> men.[43]

In the *Military Review* of May/June 2000, journalist Glenn E. Gutting describes the Alamo as a "crumbling, indefensible mission [that] came to be defended rather than destroyed and abandoned as ordained".[44] Defending it contradicted the battle philosophy of General Sam Houston.

Santa Anna's attack was successful and killed 200 soldiers.

Upon hearing of the slaughter, Houston ordered his troops at Goliad to retreat. Santa Anna pursued them, they surrendered, but, instead of

---

[42]Ibid.

[43]Will Fowler, *Santa Anna of Mexico* (Lincoln, NE: University of Nebraska Press, 2007), 166.

[44]Glenn E. Gutting, "The Alamo: An Illustrated History," *Military Review* 80, no. 3 (2000).

being treated humanely, Santa Anna ordered their execution, and 340 Texans were killed.

This brutal action was not to be ignored by the equally brutal U.S. On April 21, 1836, as Santa Anna and his troops camped by the San Jacinto River, Houston's army attacked. "A three-hour massacre followed, making San Jacinto a war atrocity in its own right."[45]Six hundred and thirty Mexicans were killed. Santa Anna was captured, but by agreeing to remove Mexican soldiers from Texas, and advocate for Mexico to recognize Texas as an independent republic, he was freed. Upon his return to Mexico City, he denied ever making such agreements.

Mexico continued having difficulties with Texas. In March 1836, the Texas Convention was convened, in which the delegates voted to become an independent nation, called it the Lone Star Republic, and named an acting president and vice president. Later that same year, the 'Lone Star Republic' petitioned the U.S. for statehood.

The government of Mexico was in too much disarray to do much about this latest development, and continued to view Texas as a province in revolt. U.S. President Andrew Jackson had tried to purchase Texas for years. At this point, he exercised an uncharacteristic restraint, telling Congress: "Beware of a too early movement. ... Prudence ... seems to dictate that we should still stand aloof."[46] He went as far as recognizing the 'Lone Star Republic', but didn't do anything further.

The U.S. popular press, then as now, fanned the flames of jingoism that have always been a precursor to war. Author Paul Foos describes it thusly: "There was a very vocal antiwar press, and they published many accounts of unprovoked depredations upon the Mexican people, but the closed mouths and closed ranks of the volunteers made it difficult to achieve corroboration of these stories."[47] Therefore, reports of atrocities were largely ignored. "Also, Whig political papers had large constituencies in the army, which they were not eager to offend."[48]

Yet even when atrocities were committed, if documented, they "they were usually justified as reprisal for the attacks on American stragglers and small patrols."[49]

---

[45]Christensen, *U.S.-Mexican War*, 26

[46]Ibid., 31

[47]Paul Foos, *A Short, Offhand, Killing Affair: Soldiers and Social Conflict during the Mexican-American War* (University of North Carolina Press, 2003), 116.

[48]Ibid.

[49]Ibid, 123.

The U.S. debated the issue on and off for the next several years. Texas's constitution made slavery legal, which the northern states opposed. The southern states were, of course, in favor of slavery, and were strong proponents of national expansion to the south.

In March of 1845, the U.S. formally offered Texas statehood. Mexico had long said that the annexation of Texas by the United States would be considered an act of war, and immediately severed diplomatic relations with the U.S.

Politically, Mexico was still in turmoil, and the U.S. was more than ready and willing to exploit this vulnerability. Jose Joaquin de Herrera had been named president following the overthrow of Santa Anna. This overthrow, combined with Santa Ana's multiple terms in a two-decade period, indicate the amount of turmoil that Mexico was experiencing at that time. After winning a heavily-contested election in 1845, Herrera was never able to establish a successful government.

By 1846, the start of the Mexican-American War, the U.S. citizenry had overwhelmingly bought into the concept of Manifest Destiny, the forerunner of today's 'exceptionalism'. With Native Americans being routinely slaughtered and/or expelled from their lands to make way for white conquerors, and the failure in Canada a distant memory, new horizons of conquest were required. Having been unsuccessful in northern conquest, the U.S. decided to look to the south, and set its deadly sites on Mexico.

The U.S. had reasons more practical than the demands of 'Providence' to expand. Britain, France and Spain all had an interest in the North American Continent, and the fledgling nation's leaders felt that a larger physical size would help protect it.

Additionally, the issue of slavery was increasingly controversial, and expansion in the south would, it was thought, strengthen the position of the pro-slavery citizens and officials. "It needed no foresight to teach any man, when the foreign territory of Texas was acquired, that it was done expressly and avowedly in order to enlarge the area of slavery and to fortify the political power which rested upon it".[50] While that may have been a simplistic view, it was certainly one of the many factors that caused the annexation of Texas to appear very attractive.

Following the end of the Fredonian revolt, General Manuel de Mier y Teran was sent to examine the U.S.–Mexico border. In their history of the war, Carol and Thomas Christensen wrote: "He warned: 'Texas is contiguous to the most avid nation in the world. The North Americans have

---

[50]Curtis, George Ticknor, *Life of Daniel Webster Vol. 2* (Forgotten Books, 2012), 255.

conquered whatever territory adjoins them. ... In less than half a century, they have become masters of extensive colonies ... from which they have disappeared the former owners, the Indian tribes.' His conclusion: 'Either the Government occupies Texas now or it is lost forever.'"[51]

Mexico was struggling to hold onto its territory in a variety of areas, as its own citizens continued to rebel. The Yucatan became an independent state for a short time; California expelled its Mexican governor; and New Mexico, at that time a very large part of Mexico, had a long list of grievances. Santa Anna had managed to suppress a revolt in Zacatecas, but throughout the country problems continued to plague the government.

In the spring of 1846, just a few months after the U.S. admitted Texas as a state, President James K. Polk, who "held the niceties of diplomacy in contempt",[52] ordered General Zachary Taylor to occupy disputed territory along the Texas–Mexico border. This inevitably resulted in a clash between Mexican and American forces. Polk then made a statement worthy of many of his successors, when he claimed, disingenuously, that Mexico, "after a long-continued series of menaces [has] at last invaded our territory and shed the blood of our fellow-citizens on our own soil".[53] Polk then said that, because of this incident, a state of war existed.

There was no question in the mind of the head of an imperial government that this was 'our own soil.' The fact that the U.S. recognized Texas as an independent republic, when Mexico simply saw it as a province in revolt, did not in any way render it a U.S. possession. But this statement clearly showed Polk's intentions concerning Texas.

Over a century later, President Ronald Reagan referred to Central America as the U.S.'s 'backyard', and that designation became popular with the press. And while it might have been appropriate to refer to Central America as the U.S.'s next door neighbor, one's backyard is one's own possession, and one is free to do with it whatever one sees fit. Everyone has obligations to their neighbors: courtesy, respect for their property, and a willingness and at least an attempt to have cordial relations with them. Yet one can do as one pleases in their backyard: plant a garden, build a garage, let the weeds grow, etc. Both Polk then, and Reagan in the 1980s, saw Central America as merely an extension of the U.S.

Can this be considered a 'false flag'? Polk's proclamation that Mexico had "shed the blood of our fellow-citizens on our own soil" was completely

---

[51] Ibid., 19.

[52] Ibid., 49.

[53] Louis Fisher, "When Wars Begin: Misleading Statements by Presidents" *Presidential Studies Quarterly* 40, no. 1 (2010).

false. Mexico never saw Texas as anything but a province in revolt, it never recognized its self-proclaimed independence, and it certainly never recognized it as part of the U.S.; Mexican government officials had plainly stated that any attempt by the U.S. to annex Mexico would be seen as an act of war.

Although the mighty U.S. had decreed that U.S. blood had been shed on U.S. soil, leaving no room for uncertainty, one can hardly blame the Mexicans for their doubt. To them, the skirmish happened on Mexican, not U.S., soil.

Additionally, it must be remembered that the Fredonian Revolt was suppressed with the assistance of the United States. Then the U.S. used the suppression of the revolt as a reason to go to war, ostensibly to free the struggling Texans from the yoke of Mexican oppression. The revolutionaries in the Fredonian Revolt seemed to be doing that successfully, until opposed by the U.S. This is clearly a false flag: the U.S. put down a foreign revolt, so it could accuse Mexico of oppressing its people, and then come to their 'rescue', and in the process annex a large portion of Mexico.

Chapter 4: Spanish-American War (April 25, 1898–August 12, 1898)

In 1895, Cuba, then a colony of Spain, began its war for independence. The U.S. press carefully followed this effort, and the U.S. citizenry was, in general, entirely sympathetic to the cause. Newspapers in the U.S., most notably the *New York World* and the *New York Journal*, were filled with sensational stories, many of which had little or no truth behind them. James Creelman was a reporter for the *World*, who weekly chronicled alleged atrocities. One example is instructive:

> No man's life, no man's property is safe. American citizens are imprisoned or slain without cause. American property is destroyed on all sides. There is no pretense at protecting it. ... Millions and millions of dollars worth of American sugar cane, buildings and machinery have already been lost. This year alone the war will strike $68,000,000 from the commerce of the U.S. ... Wounded soldiers can be found begging in the streets of Havana ... Cuba will soon be a wilderness of blackened ruins. This year there is little to live upon. Next year there will be nothing. The horrors of a barbarous struggle for the extermination of the native population are witnessed in all parts of the country. Blood on the roadsides, blood in the fields, blood on the doorsteps, blood, blood, blood!

> The old, the young, the weak, the crippled – all are butchered without mercy. There is scarcely a hamlet that has not witnessed the dreadful work. Is there no nation wise enough, brave enough to aid this blood-smitten land? Is there any barbarism known to the mind of man that will justify the intervention of a civilized power?[54]

Like its rival, the *World* also relied on pen sketches to inflame the U.S. public. Both newspapers used editorials to rally the nation to the cause of war against Spain. "Stories of atrocities, injustices and suffering, which were often exaggerated, sowed the seeds of anger and indignation among a great many U.S. Citizens."[55]

---

[54]Marcus M. Wilkerson, *Public Opinion and the Spanish-American War: A Study in War Propaganda* (Baton Rouge: Louisiana State University Press, 1932), 32

[55]Jerry Keenan, *Encyclopedia of the Spanish American and Philippine American Wars* (Santa Barbara: ABC-Clio, 2001), 372.

One example is the work of the *New York Journal*, owned by famed newspaperman William Randolph Hearst. Philip Seib writes:

> Hearst became best known for shamelessly subjecting his newspa-
> pers' reader to one-sided propaganda about issues and people. His
> most famous cause was the Spanish-American War, which some
> Hearst watchers believe could have been avoided had Hearst not
> been in a circulation war with fellow New York press lord Joseph
> Pulitzer, publisher of the *New York World*. One story – possibly
> apocryphal – illustrates Hearst's approach. Before the war, he sent
> famed artist Frederic Remington to Cuba to provide pictures of
> the goings-on there. Remington found little excitement, so he sent
> Hearst a telegram: 'Everything is quiet. There is no trouble here.
> There will be no war. I wish to return.' Hearst's response: 'Please
> remain. You furnish the pictures and I'll furnish the war'.[56]

In 1898, war correspondent Julian Hawthorne was sent to Cuba by Hearst to report on the revolution: "Hawthorne's accounts were given prominent display with one issue carrying two pages of pictures representing emaciated women and children of Cuba, which the *Journal* claimed were photographs but most of which were obviously pen sketches."[57]

The *New York World*, competing with the *Journal* for readership, also engaged in extreme and false propaganda. About their reporting, Wilkerson writes:

> Referring to the ravages of famine and disease on the Island, the
> *World* stated that 200,000 people were starving to death.

> And that from sixty to seventy died daily from hunger. Of the
> 200,000 'dying wretches' perhaps 3,000, the *World* added, were cit-
> izens of the United States engaged in peaceful pursuits. Several
> months later, the *World* said that 'it appears now that nearly seventy-
> five percent of the 400,000 helpless women, children and non-combat-
> ants affected by Weyler's [Captain-General over Cuba, upon whose
> appointment the *Times-Herald* predicted unspeakable atrocities] sav-
> agery are dead.' Reporting that there were 1,500 dead on one plan-
> tation, the newspaper said that 'the creek banks are absolutely filled
> with buried.'[58]

---

[56] Philip Seib, *Campaigns and Conscience: The Ethics of Political Journalism* (Westport, CT: Praeger Publishers, 1994), 1.

[57] Marcus M. Wilkerson, *Public Opinion and the Spanish-American War: A Study in War Propaganda* (Baton Rouge: Louisiana State University Press, 1932), 46.

[58] Ibid., 39.

Although the number of Cubans who died was certainly large, even approximate figures were impossible to estimate. Population statistics for Cuba in 1894, the year before the revolution began, indicate a population of 1,631,696. The official census of 1899, the year after the war, showed a decrease of less than 59,000. Even allowing for some population growth (e.g. births), this shows that the *World's* estimates were greatly exaggerated.[59]

The *Boston Herald* and the *Chicago Tribune* also sought to increase their circulation with 'atrocity' stories from Cuba. "The *San Francisco Examiner*, which was 'playing up' alleged Cuban atrocities, was instrumental in causing the *San Francisco Chronicle* to try to keep pace; and the Associated press, which, during the early part of the revolt, was in competition with the United Press, was also sending out 'thrilling accounts of horrors'" from Cuba.[60]

Spain, in attempting to restrict the access of U.S. news correspondents, either because they didn't want the truth known, or because they felt that some correspondents were providing weaponry to the rebels, expelled many of them. Yet the press continued receiving information, indicating that they were not obtaining first-hand reports. "From what sources they secured 'news' can only be conjectured – from travellers returning from the island, from seamen, from rumors emanating from the Florida coast, and bits of gossip picked up here and there. From whatever source their news came, it is improbable that it was accurate or even approached the truth."[61]

Yet these sources were often referenced when Senators and members of the House of Representatives were introducing or supporting legislation on behalf of Cuba.

This included Republican Senator William Earnest Mason of Illinois, telling Congress that newspapers were the only source they had of information from Cuba; Democratic Senator David Battle Turpie of Indiana, reading newspaper excerpts to encourage action by the U.S. to end the Cuban 'suffering'; and Republican Senator Frank Jenne Cannon of Utah, who, when reading from the *Chicago Tribune*, said it couldn't "be charged with Cuban sympathies". This latter statement was incredible, considering that it was one of the most decidedly pro-Cuban papers that existed at that time.[62]

---

[59] Ibid., 39, 40.
[60] Ibid., 42.
[61] Ibid., 14.
[62] Wilkerson, *Public Opinion*, 54.

In addition to the many stories of, at the very least, dubious accuracy, the newspapers editorialized on the situation. The *World* frequently did so, and one of its most powerful editorials included the following:

- How long are the Spaniards to drench Cuba with the blood and tears of her people?

- How long shall old men and women and children be murdered by the score, the innocent victims of Spanish rage against the patriot armies they can not conquer?

- How long shall Cuban women be the victims of Spanish outrages and lie sobbing and bruised in loathsome prisons?

- How long shall American citizens, arbitrarily arrested while on peaceful and legitimate errands, be immured [confined] in foul Spanish prisons without trial?

- How long shall the United States sit idle and indifferent within sound and hearing of rapine and murder?[63]

Conditions for war were ripe.

Assistant Secretary of the Navy Theodore Roosevelt, later U.S. president, along with Captain Alfred Mahan, a prominent strategist, and U.S. Senator Henry Cabot Lodge, wanted to expand U.S. power. Author Harvey Rosenfeld wrote that they "lusted for expansion and military grandeur. Mahan believed that sea power was the gateway to world power, and Roosevelt and Lodge were willing to follow any plan that would result in increasing the ever-growing U.S. empire."[64]

The actual reasons for the war were varied. National politics certainly played a role. Historian John Offner stated that there were other considerations besides any concern about the Cuban people: "The Republican Party feared an election defeat in 1898. Facing the start of a critical election campaign, Republicans wanted to get out in front of the Cuban issue".[65]

---

[63]Ibid., 40–41.

[64]Harvey Rosenfeld, *Diary of a Dirty Little War: The Spanish-American War of 1898* (Praeger, 2000), 3.

[65]John L. Offner, *An Unwanted War: The Diplomacy of the United States and Spain over Cuba, 1895–1898* (Chapel Hill, NC: University of North Carolina Press, 1992), iii.

Additionally, Japan had defeated China in 1895 and wanted further expansion in the Pacific. With the Philippines rebelling against Spain and the U.S. coveting Hawaii, the U.S wanted a quick resolution to the situation just off its southern border.

And the profit motive could not be discounted. The U.S. had major business investments in Cuba, and the government would not see them jeopardized.[66]

But what could actually be the catalyst for war? Invented atrocities, the lust for empire, and the threat to economic interests were all involved, but the government needed some defining act to push the gullible and war-willing citizenry over the edge. An event in the Havana harbor proved to be that event.

On February 5, 1898, the battleship *Maine* exploded in Havana harbor. It had been sent there as a show of strength and support to the Cubans and to intimidate the Spanish. Two hundred and sixty-six U.S. sailors died in the explosion. The cause was quickly determined. Historian Hyman Rickover documents this. He wrote: "Lieutenant Frank F. Fletcher, on duty at the Bureau of Ordnance, wrote in a personal letter to [Lieutenant Albert] Gleaves: 'The disaster to the *Maine* is the one topic here now. Everybody is gradually settling down to the belief that the disaster was due to the position of the magazine next to the coal bunkers in which there must have been spontaneous combustion.'"[67]

But such an innocent reason for the tragedy didn't sit well with the imperialist war planners, or anyone else in U.S. government who was anxious to go to war. Roosevelt, especially, was desperate to establish the U.S. as a world power and wanted that new power to be demonstrated to Europe.

In order to determine the cause of the explosion, an inquiry was immediately held. In less than a month, this panel confirmed that an underwater mine had detonated, igniting parts of the forward magazines of the ship. The U.S. government, supported then, as now, by a willing press, along with an enraged citizenry, were now fully ready for war. On April 25, 1898, the U.S. declared war on Spain. The battle cry, 'Remember the *Maine*,' helped rally the troops.

Again, as is the situation today, the press was all too willing to take the word of the government and broadcast those words nationwide. The

---

[66] A.B. Feuer, *The Santiago Campaign of 1898: A Soldier's View of the Spanish-American War* (Praeger, 1993), 1.

[67] Hyman George Rickover, *How the Battleship Maine was Destroyed* (University of Michigan Library, 1976), 46.

concept of 'investigative journalism', practiced today by the independent press but hardly at all by the so-called 'mainstream' press, was as alien a concept then as it is now.

Reasonable rebuttals to the finding of the inquiry were not hard to find.

Two highly qualified experts in ordnance were willing to testify, but their offers to do so were rejected. Rickover further wrote:

> Professor Philip Alger, whose abilities had won him an outstanding reputation in ordnance, was available. Professor Charles E. Munroe, president of the American Chemical Society, an authority on explosives, had promptly offered his services. Munroe was familiar with naval procedures, having taken part in an earlier investigation of a paint explosion on the cruiser *Atlanta*. He received an acknowledgment but no request for assistance. At least one newspaper called attention to the absence of technically qualified members on the court.[68]

The reason that Professor Alger's expertise was rejected can be easily surmised. On February 18, immediately after the sinking of the *Maine*, in an interview published in the *Washington Evening Star*, he said this:

> As to the question of the cause of the *Maine's* explosion, we know that no torpedo such as is known to modern warfare, can of itself cause an explosion of the character of that on board the *Maine*. We know of no instances where the explosion of a torpedo or mine under a ship's bottom has exploded the magazine within. It has simply torn a great hole in the side or bottom, through which water entered, and in consequence of which the ship sunk. Magazine explosions, on the contrary, produce effects exactly similar to the effects of the explosion on board the *Maine*. When it comes to seeking the cause of the explosion of the *Maine's* magazine, we should naturally look not for the improbable or unusual causes, but those against which we have had to guard in the past.[69]

It was said that Roosevelt's "own views were hardening toward the conviction that there had been no accident."[70] In his quest to establish worldwide U.S. military superiority, the facts surrounding the *Maine* disaster were unimportant. It was decreed that the ship had been sabotaged, and war was declared.

---

[68]Ibid., 46–47.
[69]Ibid., 64–65.
[70]Ibid., 47.

Seventy-six years later, all available documentation from the earlier investigations was carefully reviewed. The information all indicated that an internal explosion, possibly caused by the ship's design and an alteration in the kind of coal used to fuel it, destroyed the *Maine*. No evidence was found of any penetration of the ship from the outside. The initial investigation, the one that led to war, indicated that the Navy "made little use of its technically-trained officers during its investigation of the tragedy."[71]

Yet the destruction of the battleship *Maine*, docked in Havana harbor where it had no legitimate business being, blown to bits by an internal magazine with Spain having no role in it, was sufficient to launch another war. The government had a variety of reasons for invading Cuba, none of which would have rallied the citizenry to the cause of war: the Republican Party's wish to maintain the White House; the protection of the economic interests of the ruling class; and the desire to establish U.S. military might as a force to be reckoned with. While each of these may have garnered some support for war, it wasn't until the unexpected disaster of the *Maine*'s destruction, and the huge death toll that accompanied it, and the false belief that it had been sabotaged by the Spanish, that there was near-universal support in the U.S. for the war. Another false flag had been raised, and the citizens rallied around it.

It's interesting to speculate on whether or not Roosevelt's interest in war changed after the death of his youngest son in France during World War I. Roosevelt, who blithely sent countless young men to their deaths, was consumed with grief after the death of his son, Quentin:

> After Quentin's death, the once boisterous former president was more subdued, and his physical health declined rapidly. In his final days, Roosevelt often went down to the family's stables to be near the horses that Quentin as a child had so loved to ride. Lost in sorrow, Roosevelt would stand there alone, quietly repeating the pet name he'd given his son when he was a boy, "Oh Quenty-quee, oh Quenty-quee ..."[72]

While propaganda is as old as war, it was during the Spanish-American War that newspapers began to have a great influence on war, and used propaganda as a tool to encourage U.S. war-making. The techniques expanded throughout the next several decades, to the point where the

---

[71] Compare to Bush's selective information in going to war with Iraq; see Chapter 25.

[72] https://www.smithsonianmag.com/smithsonian-institution/letters-unbearable-grief -theodore-roosevelt-death-son-180962743/. Accessed on July 7, 2018.

so-called 'mainstream' media is little more than a tool in the hands of the government to foster its imperial goals.

Chapter 5: Other False Flags From This Period

The United States has always believed in the concept that 'might makes right'. Whether dealing with Native Americans, foreign nations or its own citizens, this has always been its way of resolving problems.

While this chapter will include some additional examples of U.S. aggression from this period of time, and the reasons the U.S. decided each particular victim was the enemy, it will not include all of them. Many of these wars were fought against Native Americans, as the new nation sought more and more land. These include the following:

- Cherokee–American Wars (1776–1795)

- Northwest Indian War (1785–1793)

- First Barbary War (1801–1805)

- German Coast Uprising (1811)

- Tecumseh's War (1811)

- Second Barbary War (1815)

- First Seminole War (1817–1818)

- Winnebago War (1827)

- Black Hawk War (1832)

- Second Seminole War (1835–1842)

- Apache Wars (1851–1900)

While these wars are not included in this section, they, like all wars, caused untold suffering of innocent men, women and children.

Shays' Rebellion (1786–1787)

History books teach the myth that the American Revolution was supported by most of the colonists. The facts contradict this. Historian Harry M. Ward writes that "Most estimates place one-third of Americans as loyalist, one-third on the fence, to be swayed by whomever was winning, and one-third rebel."[73] Soldiers who may have believed it, and who fought for the lofty ideals that we hear today, were seldom, if ever, paid for their 'service'. And after the war, the economy was in tatters, with credit seldom, if ever, being offered, and creditors calling in their debts. Taxes in Massachusetts were higher than they'd ever been under the British.[74]

Daniel Shays was one veteran who, after receiving little pay for helping the new nation to gain independence, found himself ordered to court upon his return home for non-payment of debts. The same government that had used him to gain independence, that hadn't paid him for that work, was now bringing him to court.

Another veteran, identified only as 'Plough Jogger', expressed the difficulty and the complaint succinctly: "I have been greatly abused ... have been obliged to do more than my part in the war; been loaded with class rates, town rates, province rates, Continental rates and all rates ... been pulled and hauled by sheriffs, constables and collectors, and had my cattle sold for less than they were worth."[75]

This behavior on the part of the government was resisted:

> In Worcester and Berkshire counties, men had banded together to repossess from the constable the livestock confiscated from a good neighbor. Everyone knew good men whom creditors had forced into debtors' prison. Everyone was faced with the specter of losing not only his livestock but the land itself, and with his land his standing as a freeman.[76]

The government which had freely used the blood and labor of colonists now took their possessions.

Although current events seem to belie it, there is a point at which men and women will no longer tolerate the abuses of their government. Plough Jogger continued:

---

[73]Harry M. Ward, *The War for Independence and the Transformation of American Society* (New York: Routledge, 1999), 35.

[74]https://www.history.com/topics/early-us/shays-rebellion.

[75]Marion L. Starkey, *A Little Rebellion* (New York: Alfred A. Knopf, 1955), 14.

[76]Ibid.

I have been obliged to pay and nobody will pay me. I have lost a great deal by this man and that man and t'other man, and the great men are going to get all we have, and I think it is time for us to rise and put a stop to it and have no more courts, nor sheriffs, nor collectors, nor lawyers and I know that we are the biggest party, let them say what they will.[77]

This sentiment was reflected in many of the New England farmers of the day; yet, initially, only peaceful means were considered:

Before turning to clubs and muskets, New England farmers pleaded peacefully for relief. Between 1784 and 1787, yeomen in seventy-three rural Massachusets towns – more than 30 percent of all communities in the state – sent petitions to the General Court in Boston.[78]

The same efforts were made in New Hampshire, Vermont and Connecticut.

Eventually, with no redress coming from the government, hundreds of armed farmers began blocking judges from entering courthouses.

The situation escalated in January 1787, when over 1,200 men, some carrying guns, others with clubs and pitchforks, attempted to seize the federal arsenal in Springfield to obtain weapons, led by Daniel Shays, their reluctant leader. ("I their leader? I am not!" he is reported to have said.[79]) They were met and quickly overwhelmed by members of the Massachusetts militia.

Was there a false flag that enabled the government to put down Shays' rebellion? The American Revolution, in which most of the farmers involved in the rebellion fought, began with the rallying cry of 'No taxation without representation'. Yet at this time, residents of Massachusetts were charged higher taxes then they'd paid to the British. This was necessary to ensure healthy profits for business associates of Governor James Bowdoin.[80] The Springfield arsenal was well protected, with General William Shepard in charge, who decided that the raid indicated an attempt by the rebels to overthrow the government.

But was it a threat to the nation? Was a band of men, some armed with guns, but most of them carrying only pitchforks, revolting in a small, New

---

[77]Ibid., 15.

[78]David P. Szatmary, *Shays' Rebellion: The Making of an Agrarian Insurrection* (Ann Arbor, MI: University of Massachusetts Press, 1980), 38.

[79]Starkey, *Little Rebellion*, 68. Original punctuation retained.

[80]https://www.history.com/topics/early-us/shays-rebellion. Accessed on September 13, 2018.

England town, really a danger to the continued existence of the nation? By naming it so, Shepard continued a false flag tradition: exaggerate a situation out of all proportion, and then justify the violence in suppressing it.

The Quasi War (1798–1800)

The Quasi War was waged against France. The U.S. violated a 1778 treaty with France that required the U.S. to assist the French in protecting its colonies in the West Indies, and this violation let to this war.[81]

However, there were other considerations. France had backed the 'colonies' in their revolution, and the newly minted U.S. was to repay the many French loans it had received. When a new government took over in France, the U.S. said its responsibility was to the previous government, so it stopped repaying. The French, in retaliation, began to seize U.S. ships that were trading with Great Britain. This was seen by the U.S. as an outrage, notwithstanding the abrogation of the U.S. responsibility to repay France.

Alexander Hamilton, who had been Secretary of the Treasury, was made a major general as tensions with France escalated. Historian Aaron N. Coleman theorizes that, like many U.S. politicians before and after him, he had his own agenda. Coleman believes that Hamilton "was manipulating the crisis to establish a European-style standing army for the purpose of crushing domestic opposition".[82]

And, like many of his predecessors and followers in government, "Hamilton, according to his critics, also controlled [President] Adams's cabinet as well as former president George Washington, thus forcing the president to place him in de facto command of the military, and thereby fulfilling his all-consuming desire for military glory."[83]

This war was short, and U.S. casualties were less than 100, but the U.S. lost over 2,000 ships, including during the time leading up to the outbreak of hostilities, and during the war. But while such 'esoteric' considerations as treaties and repayment of debt may not have concerned the average U.S. citizen, the seizing of U.S. ships was seen as barbarous. Any justification on the side of the French was simply ignored.

---

[81]Richard K. Kolb, "First Foreign Fight," *VFW Magazine*, June/July 1998, 40.

[82]Aaron N. Coleman, "'A Second Bounaparty?': A Reexamination of Alexander Hamilton during the Franco-American Crisis, 1796–1801," *Journal of the Early Republic* 28, no. 2 (2008).

[83]Ibid.

The Creek Wars (1813–1814)

When the American Revolution ended in 1783, the area around what is now Georgia, populated by the Creek Indians, grew in population. The land on which they lived, extending into what is now Alabama, included towns, fields for growing crops, and areas for hunting.[84] The European settlers, naturally, coveted this territory.

The Creeks were divided into two groups, the Upper Creek towns and the Lower Creek towns, and both had a high degree of autonomy, which resulted in some significant challenges.

Prior to 1790, the Lower Creek Indians entered into treaties with the U.S., surrendering some land to them, but the leaders of the Upper Creek division refused to acknowledge that these agreements were valid. This resulted in Creek attacks on white settlers. Finally, in 1790, both the Upper Creeks and Lower Creeks entered into an agreement with the U.S., making the Ocmulgee River the boundary between Georgia and the nation of the Creeks.

Another treaty, signed in 1805, was supported by William McIntosh, a Lower Creek leader who had ties to the U.S. government. He worked to overcome Creek opposition to this treaty, which extended a road through Creek territory, connecting Georgia and the Mississippi territory. While this road resulted in some new income for some Creeks, it also brought in a flood of new white settlers. The conflicting needs of the colonizers and the Natives are described by historian Sheri M. Shuck-Hall:

> ... growing resentment about westward expansion by white settlers and the concomitant loss of tribal hunting grounds fostered the creation of an Anti-American, nativist political and religious movement. Known as the Redsticks (named after the 'red stick of war'; the Creeks used war clubs painted red), this faction was inspired by Tecumseh and his brother, the Shawnee Prophet, Tenskwatawa. They encouraged American Indian communities from the Ohio Valley to the southern frontier to resist assimilation into Euro-American society and to fight American encroachment onto Indian lands. The Redstick movement culminated in the Creek Civil War from 1813 to 1814—in the midst of the War of 1812—where loyalties split across town and clan lines.[85]

---

[84] https://history.army.mil/html/books/074/74-4/CMH_Pub_74-4.pdf. Accessed on August 7, 2018.

[85] http://www.univ-brest.fr/digitalAssetsUBO/9/9118_UNDERSTANDING_THE_CREEK_WAR.pdf.

A fort in the areas, Fort Mims, was part of one of the largest plantations in the vicinity, consisting of at least ten buildings. Approximately 500 people lived within the complex. An attack on Fort Mims by a group of Redsticks resulted in the deaths of 247 American and Metis Creek men, women and children who were in the fort. The Redstick leader, William Weatherford, had, at one point, "argued that [the Redsticks] should retreat, knowing that they had inflicted great damage but that they too had suffered more casualties than expected. The Redsticks, however, rejected Weatherford's suggestion."[86] Weatherford knew that the Americans would exact revenge.[87]

That retribution quickly followed: "After the battle at Fort Mims, Americans and many Creek Métis vilified the Redsticks as reckless murderers. Americans sought their own retribution; they burned Upper Creek towns and villages with a vengeance. The Redsticks' final stand took place at the Battle of Horseshoe Bend on 27 March 1814, where Andrew Jackson, the Tennessee militia, and allied Cherokees and Creeks cut them down."[88]

This decimated the Creek Nation, as historian Bruce Vandervort notes:

> ... in the bloody First Creek War (1813–14), this formidable people lost nearly two-thirds of their ancestral lands in what are now the states of Georgia and Alabama. Although some diehards would take refuge among their Seminole cousins in the forests and swamps of Florida, the power of the Creek people was definitely broken, and once Andrew Jackson, the man who had beaten them, acceded to the U.S. presidency in 1828, their days in occupation of even a shrunken portion of their homeland were numbered. A Second Creek War, a last-ditch effort to avert dispossession and emigration, was drowned in blood in 1836.[89]

The U.S. called the Creeks "reckless murderers" – forgetting the many atrocities and injustices they had committed against them – and slaughtered them. They took no responsibility for their encroachment on Native lands, which deprived the Natives of the farming and hunting they had relied on for generations. Rather, they named the Creeks as the enemy, when they were simply trying to defend their way of life. The Creeks,

---

[86]Ibid.

[87]Ibid.

[88]Ibid.

[89]Bruce Vandervort, *Indian Wars of Canada, Mexico, and the United States, 1812–1900*, Warfare and History (New York: Routledge, 2005), 107.

along with every other Native tribe on the continent, had been there long before the colonists, and it was only foreign aggression that decimated their numbers.

Ivory Coast Expedition (1842)

The Ivory Coast Expedition is yet another example of the United States' long history of brutality and disproportionate violence. Like many nations, the Ivory Coast was open to exploitation of natural resources by the United States. Liberia was a U.S. colony, ostensibly for freedmen. When two U.S. merchant ships, the *Mary Carver* and *Edward Bartley*, were attacked by the Bereby people of the Ivory Coast, the U.S. Congress approved a 'punitive expedition'. Commodore Matthew C. Perry was put in charge.

This expedition was short but, in typical U.S. style, brutal; on November 29, after landing with seventy-five marines and sailors at the coastal county of Sinoe, Perry met with tribal leaders who accused the Americans of being the aggressors. The U.S. Commodore was not sympathetic; he ordered several native villages burned.

A week later, Perry and his crew landed at Caval, Liberia, and conferred with the African Chief Ben Crack-O, who served as king over all the tribes in the area. At a meeting with Perry, the Chief and several others, Crack-O denied any wrongdoing. Perry accused him of lying, and in the ensuing scuffle, when Crack-O attempted to flee, he was shot and killed.

> Now that hostilities had begun, Perry ordered his men to burn the town, and, after carrying out the objective, the expedition was returning to their ships when ambushed by native warriors in the woods. Another skirmish resulted and the marines and sailors charged towards the Africans and routed them. The three American warships also opened fire and helped silence the enemy, and a few war-canoes were captured as well. When the battle was over, many of the Africans were killed or wounded though the Americans suffered no casualties. Perry then sailed down the coast and the following morning he detected another Bereby settlement. The marines and sailors were again landed and they destroyed seven villages by burning them and inflicted serious losses upon the natives themselves, without suffering any casualties. After this mission the commodore decided that the Bereby people had been punished enough, so he ended the expedition and proceeded on with other duties.[90]

---

[90]https://www.revolvy.com/page/Ivory-Coast-Expedition. Accessed on February 5, 2019.

Section B: Becoming a World Power (1900–1950)

Following Roosevelt's lust for imperial power, future presidents mirrored his desire. By the time the U.S. entered World War I, its power was respected and feared around the world, and by the end of that war, its dominance was unquestioned, although balanced by the Soviet Union.

During the early part of the twentieth century, the U.S. interfered frequently in the Western Hemisphere, in what came to be known as the 'Banana Wars'. In an article by Mark Oliver entitled "The Banana Wars: How the U.S. Plundered Central America On Behalf Of Corporations," he writes the following:

> During the Banana Wars of the early 20th century, the U.S. military toppled regimes and massacred thousands to keep U.S. business booming.
>
> 'I spent 33 years and four months in active military service,' an American veteran named Smedley Butler once wrote, 'and during that period, I spent most of my time as a high-class muscle man for Big Business, for Wall Street and the bankers.'
>
> Butler had fought in the so-called Banana Wars of the early 20th century, when the American military sent their troops south into Central America to keep their business interests there intact.
>
> It was a time when mistreated workers across Central America were getting fed up with working long hours in harsh conditions for less than a living wage. Workers started grumbling. Some went on strike. Some threw together militias and waged full-on rebellions to fight for better conditions.
>
> But for the American government, all this fighting for freedom was bad for business. Companies like the United Fruit Company had a vested interest in keeping their Central American plantations stable and so they called in the American Army to crack down on those who were disrupting the system.
>
> Butler and other soldiers like him were thus sent to Central America to fight the Banana Wars. When a rebellion in the Dominican Republic, for example, damaged an American-owned sugar cane plantation, American troops were sent in, starting in 1916. They took over a small castle called Fort Ozama, killed the men inside and set up a military presence to protect their business interests.
>
> Troops also moved into Haiti to quell the Cacao Rebellion in 1915, partly to protect the interests of the Haitian-American Sugar Company. The U.S. Army stayed behind even after the war was over,

patrolling the streets of Haiti and making sure that no one got out of line.

And in Honduras, where the United Fruit Company and the Standard Fruit Company were worried about their banana sales, the American Army marched in on seven separate occasions throughout the early 20th century. Sometimes the army was called in to crush strikes, other times to stop revolutions—but every time, it was to keep business booming.

Hundreds of American soldiers and thousands of locals died in the Banana Wars. Strikes and revolutions were crushed and put to an end – all while the profits of a handful of companies were maintained.

'I might have given Al Capone a few hints,' Butler said. 'The best he could do was to operate his racket in three districts. I operated on three continents.'[91]

Following the U.S. Civil War, foreign expansion changed from commercial interests, to "establishing American political and military control in the Caribbean and the Pacific."[92] Talk of a canal through some Central American country, linking the Caribbean Sea, and therefore, the Atlantic Ocean, with the Pacific Ocean, had been discussed for decades, and the U.S. had no intention of letting any other nation have control over such a lucrative trade route. Economic power and military control are closely related; U.S. government officials learned this fact early on, and never hesitated to cruelly exploit the people of any nation, if doing so would enhance the U.S.'s power in the world.

Various wars and the occupations of Nicaragua, Haiti and the Dominican Republic that occurred early in the twentieth century will be discussed herein.

---

[91] http://allthatsinteresting.com/banana-wars. Accessed on June 19, 2018.
[92] Hans Schmidt, *The United States Occupation of Haiti, 1915-1934* (New Brunswick, NJ: Rutgers University Press, 1995), 3.

Chapter 6: Cuba (1898–Current)

While the U.S.'s longstanding policies against Cuba – economic embargo and forbidding travel between the two nations – are known to most people, the U.S.'s violent and colonial history with Cuba is not.

Prior to the Spanish-American War, Cuba became the world's leading producer of sugar. Demands for more freedom from an increasingly despotic colonial government resulted in the Ten Years' War, which concluded in 1878. Cubans were promised a greater voice in their own government, and in 1886, slavery was ended. Race relations improved.

When the Spanish–American War (see Chapter 4) ended in the victory of the U.S. over Spain, the U.S. forced Spain to cede all its territories in the Caribbean, including Cuba, to the U.S. The Cubans, according to U.S. propaganda, had been fighting an oppressive regime; indeed, conditions were far from ideal and in 1895 several uprisings marked the start of another bid for independence from Spain. That nation sent over 220,000 soldiers to put down the revolt, and thousands of people died. The mighty U.S., which declared war on Spain by raising the false flag of the attack on the U.S.S. *Maine*, was now going to 'liberate' the Cubans, in its own peculiar manner.

When the U.S. occupied Cuba following the Spanish defeat, there wasn't much opposition to U.S. rule, "in large measure because they [the Cubans] were confident that it would be temporary", according to journalist Max Boot.[93]

However, while the physical occupation was, in fact, brief, the U.S. maintained control over Cuba by the passage of the Platt Amendment in 1901:

> Under its terms, Cuba would be obligated to obtain Uncle Sam's approval before signing any foreign treaty; maintain low foreign debt; ratify all acts of the U.S. military government; and give the American armed forces the right to intervene at any time to protect life, liberty and property. In addition, Cuba would have to provide the U.S. long-term leases on naval bases; it was this provision that would lead to the creation of naval station at Guantanamo Bay in 1903. In

---

[93]Max Boot, *The Savage Wars of Peace* (Basic Books, 2014), 132.

short, the Platt Amendment represented a considerable abridgment of Cuban sovereignty.[94]

Cuba had little choice but to agree to this; the U.S. said it would only leave Cuba upon Cuba's signature. With the signing of the Platt Amendment, the U.S. could 'intervene' in Cuba at any time it wished. It didn't have to wait long.

In 1905, Tomas Estrada Palma was re-elected as president in an election boycotted by the opposition party, and widely viewed as having been rigged. The following year, the Liberal party staged a revolt with about 24,000 men.

Estrada Palma, with no standing army to rely on, asked President Theodore Roosevelt for assistance. The U.S. president was not happy with the situation in Cuba:

> I am so angry with that infernal little Cuban republic that I would like to wipe its people off the face of the earth. All we have wanted from them was that they would behave themselves and be prosperous and happy so that we would not have to interfere. And now, low and behold, they have started an utterly unjustifiable and pointless revolution.[95]

Roosevelt sent naval vessels, but didn't invade. He sent Secretary of War William Howard Taft to negotiate some kind of agreement between the Cuban president and his arch-enemy, the Liberals. Estrada Palma resigned on September 28, 1906, along with his vice president, leaving the country without a government and causing the U.S. to intervene. The following day, 2,000 U.S. Marines landed, and Taft established a U.S.-run provisional government.[96]

In January of 1908, the U.S. military once again departed from Cuba.

As mentioned, the Platt Amendment gave the U.S. the right to intervene in Cuba at any time to protect life, liberty or property. Boot writes:

> On May 20, 1912, the Independent Party of Color, representing Cuba's dispossessed black population, staged a revolt against the Liberal government of Jose Miguel Gomez. The 'Negro revolt' was swiftly crushed everywhere except Oriente province, home to many

---

[94]Ibid., 132.

[95]Lars Schoultz, *That Infernal Little Cuban Republic: The United States and the Cuban Revolution* (Chapel Hill, NC: University of North Carolina Press, 2009), v.

[96]Boot, *Savage Wars*, 137.

U.S.-owned sugar mills. Secretary of State [Philander C.] Knox worried that the revolutionaries would threaten American-owned sugar estates and mines, so on May 31, the U.S. Marines ... landed at Daquiri in Orient.[97]

They withdrew six weeks later.

It would be five years before the U.S. chose to invade again. In the 1916 presidential election, General Mario Garcia Menocal, who had a close identification with U.S. interests in Cuba, was re-elected in another election widely viewed to be fraudulent. During the Liberal revolt the following year, U.S. President Woodrow Wilson supported Menocal's suppression of the revolt and, at Menocal's request, sent 2,600 Marines onto the island the following year. Some stayed until 1922 to protect American property.[98]

For the next three decades, the Cuban government was in nearly constant turmoil. This included:

- 1928: President Gerardo Machado unconstitutionally extends his re-election term to six years, provoking armed insurrections.

- 1933: The United States dispatches Ambassador Sumner Welles to mediate between the Machado government and the opposition. A general strike in August brings the crisis to a climax, with a military coup ousting Machado and installing Carlos Manuel de Céspedes as president. In September, the 'Sergeants' Revolt,' led by Fulgencio Batista, overthrows the Céspedes administration and aids the establishment of a new provisional government headed by Ramón Grau San Martín.

- 1934: In January, Batista overthrows the Grau San Martín government and briefly installs Carlos Hevia and Manuel Márquez Sterling as presidents, and later Carlos Mendieta. In May, with nationalist feelings growing in Cuba, the United States abrogates the Platt Amendment as part of President Franklin D. Roosevelt's 'Good Neighbor' policy toward Latin America.[99]

- 1952: Batista deposes President Carlos Prío Socarrás, cancels the constitution, and suspends elections.

---

[97]Ibid., 140–141.

[98]Ibid., 141.

[99]https://www.ourdocuments.gov/doc.php?flash=false&doc=55. Accessed on January 16, 2019.

- 1953: On July 26, Fidel Castro, leads an unsuccessful revolt against the Batista regime, attacking the Moncada army barracks in Santiago de Cuba.[100]

The U.S. didn't see fit to intervene during this period, because whatever government was in power was willing to bow to its U.S. master. However, the unsuccessful revolt of 1953 can be seen as the end of U.S. influence in Cuba, because of the tremendous influence of its young leader.

In 1953, Fidel Castro was twenty-seven years old, and was already an experienced tactician and guerrilla fighter. Six years earlier, at only 21, he joined Dominican exiles in an attempt to overthrow their cruel, U.S.-supported dictator, General Rafael Trujillo. He participated the following year in revolutionary activities in Bogata, Colombia.

He was a seasoned politician as well. In 1952, he was the Cuban People's Party candidate for a seat in the House of Representatives. That was the year that, prior to the elections, Batista overthrew the government and cancelled elections. The following year, Castro made his first attempt at overthrowing the Batista regime.

Three years after his unsuccessful revolt against the U.S.-puppet government of Batista, with the assistance of Ernesto 'Che' Guevara, Castro began his guerrilla war against Batista. He received further assistance when his brother, Raul, established guerrilla operations in the northern part of the Oriente province.[101]

Batista, at this time, had fallen into disfavor with the U.S., which, in March of 1958, stopped supplying him with arms. There were two possible reasons for this:

1. While the U.S. was busy criticizing the Soviet Union for suppressing democratic movements, the U.S. was doing the same thing in Latin America. One historian noted: "As such, Washington wanted to slowly move away from dictators towards friendly, superficially-democratic puppet regimes."[102]

2. With the country slowly being increasingly controlled by guerrillas, and Batista unwilling to make any concessions, the U.S. tried to

---

[100]https://cri.fiu.edu/us-cuba/chronology-of-us-cuba-relations/. Accessed on January 16, 2019.

[101]https://www.britannica.com/biography/Fidel-Castro. Accessed on October 16, 2018.

[102]https://www.reddit.com/r/AskHistorians/comments/34kztv/why_did_the_us_g overnment_stop_supporting/. Accessed on October 15, 2018.

force his resignation so a new puppet government could be installed. He refused, and the revolution successfully occurred.

Neither of these reasons could match the lofty, oft-proclaimed goals of democracy and self-determination to which the U.S. government pays lip service. But it wasn't difficult to find a reason to stop supporting Batista. According to the terms of the U.S.-Cuba Mutual Defense Assistance Agreement, it was mandated that "U.S. arms and training were only for the defense of the Western Hemisphere, and that Cuba could not devote such assistance to purposes other than those for which it was furnished."[103] Batista, however, was using personnel trained by the U.S. not 'for the defense of the Western Hemisphere', but to fight the anti-government rebels. That would be a sufficient reason to withdraw the assistance.

One must look to the current day, when U.S. foreign aid is ostensibly dependent on other nations' adherence to human rights and international law. Yet Israel, with an atrocious human rights record (see Chapter 29: 'Anti-Communist' Interventions and Dictators Supported by the U.S.), receives $4 billion dollars annually from the U.S. Saudi Arabia, another brutally repressive nation, benefits from massive military purchases from the U.S. In Cuba in the late 1950s, supporting the puppet regime became inconvenient. The Cuban government's violation of the U.S.-Cuba Mutual Defense Assistance Agreement would not have mattered, if the U.S. thought Batista could maintain control of Cuba.

It seems incredible that the U.S. didn't know that the fall of Batista would mean the rise of Castro and a communist government.

At the end of 1959, Batista and his closest associates fled Cuba. Later, in January of 1960, a general strike forced the military government to surrender its power to the 26th of July Movement (named after Castro's failed attack on the Moncada Barracks in Santiago de Cuba on that date in 1953). With a force of only 800 guerrillas, Castro was victorious over the 30,000-man Cuban army.[104] Although the U.S. government recognized the new government of Cuba almost immediately, it was not a marriage made in heaven. In July of 1960, the Cuban government nationalized U.S. businesses, providing no compensation to the previous owners. The U.S. promptly imposed a partial trade embargo. The U.S.-supported Bay of Pigs invasion of 1961, an effort by Cuban exiles to overthrow the government, failed, and caused a deeper rift between the two nations.

---

[103] Lars Schoultz, *That Infernal Little Cuban Republic: The United States and the Cuban Revolution* (Chapel Hill, NC: University of North Carolina Press, 2009), 71.

[104] https://www.times.co.zm/?p=90766. Accessed on September 16, 2019

The so-called Cuban missile crisis of 1962 further damaged relations, with the deployment of Russian nuclear missiles in Cuba. The reasons for Soviet missiles in Cuba included the very real fear of a U.S. invasion of Cuba. That this fear was justified was confirmed by historian Barton J. Bernstein: "The United States had carried out a series of secret CIA marauding attacks on Cuba in the preceding 12 months as part of Operation Mongoose, and had developed secret plans for possible large-scale U.S. military attacks." Additionally, the U.S. had recently placed Jupiter missiles uncomfortably close to Russia, in Turkey. "On October 27, [President John F.] Kennedy made a deal with the Soviets through his brother, [Attorney General] Robert [Kennedy] under which the United States would yield to the Soviet demand for removal of U.S. Jupiter missiles from Turkey."[105] The crisis, which appeared to bring the world to the brink of nuclear war, was resolved.[106]

For the next 54 years, the U.S. would maintain a pointless embargo of Cuba, forbidding U.S. firms from doing business with the country, and preventing any travel between the two nations. U.S. citizens wanting to visit Cuba's pristine beaches would have to travel first to Canada or Mexico, and then fly directly to the island nation. Cuban customs officials were more than happy to leave U.S. passports unstamped, thus preventing one component of solid evidence that some hapless U.S. citizen had dared visit Cuba.

But not all U.S. visitors crept silently to the island nation, and the U.S., in typical 'Big Brother' fashion, is always watching. In 2013, singing stars Jay-Z and Beyoncé travelled to Cuba for three nights to celebrate their wedding anniversary. The U.S. Treasury Department wanted to learn if the visit violated the U.S.'s decades-old trade embargo:

> In a sudden predictable controversy that proves the embers of conflict between Miami and Havana are never far from becoming flames, Treasury officials on Monday said they were working on a response to demands for more information about the trip from two Cuban-American lawmakers from south Florida: Representatives Ileana Ros-Lehtinen and Mario Diaz-Balart, both Republicans, who appear to be using the highly photographed visit to rekindle outrage about Americans going to Cuba for fun.

---

[105] Barton J. Bernstein, "Reconsidering the Perilous Cuban Missile Crisis 50 Years Later," *Arms Control Today*, October 2012.

[106] George C. Herring, *From Colony to Superpower: U.S. Foreign Relations since 1776* (New York: Oxford University Press, 2008), 722.

'Cuba's tourism industry is wholly state-controlled,' Ms. Ros-Leh-tinen and Mr. Diaz-Balart wrote in a letter to the Treasury Department on Friday, 'therefore, U.S. dollars spent on Cuban tourism directly fund the machinery of oppression that brutally represses the Cuban people'.[107]

It must be remembered that the Cuban people are well-versed in over-throwing brutally repressive regimes. Yet for sixty-years they seemingly haven't had any interest in exchanging their government for a U.S. puppet. And the U.S. doesn't hesitate to support brutally repressive regimes (e.g., Israel (every prime minister in its history), Saudi Arabia (current King and Crown Prince), Iran (the Shah), Brazil (General Castelo Branco), Chile (Augusto Pinochet), Romania (Nicolae Ceausescu), South Korea (Syngman Rhee), Uzbekistan (Islam Karimov),[108] to name just a few (please see Chapter 29: 'Anti-Communist' Interventions and Dictators Supported by the U.S., for a more complete listing and discussion of this topic.).

This embargo was created to crush the revolution and force the Cubans back into the U.S. fold by accepting a U.S.-puppet government. One would think that at some point prior to the end of five decades, some U.S. president would have recognized its futility.

Finally, a president did. Between 2014 and 2016, President Barack Obama worked with Cuban President Raul Castro to begin healing the rift between the two nations. The following are just a few of the steps that were taken in those years:

- Travel restrictions were eased.

- Import and export restrictions were relaxed.

- Cuba was removed from the ridiculous and politically-motivated 'U.S. State Sponsors of Terrorism' list.

- Flights between Cuba and the U.S. began regularly in 2016.

- Postal service between the two nations resumed.[109]

---

[107] Damien Cave, "U.S. Investigates Visit to Cuba by Jay-Z and Beyonce," *International Herald Tribune*, April 10, 2013. Accessed on October 20, 2018.

[108] https://allthatsinteresting.com/us-dictator-alliances. Accessed on October 20, 2018.

[109] https://www.essence.com/news/ways-president-obama-improved-us-cuba-relations /. Accessed on October 15, 2018.

This progress was short-lived: with the election of Donald Trump to the U.S. presidency, the hard-line rhetoric typical of conservative U.S. politicians once again became the order of the day. Trump tightened import and export restrictions, along with restrictions on travel. Most hypocritically, he demanded that Cuba end human rights abuses.

Despite over five decades of U.S. embargoes and hopes for a regime change that U.S. officials, but not the Cuban people, want, Cubans have managed well. They are able to trade freely with other countries, and travel to them, and welcome travellers from them. What another two or six years of a Trump presidency may do remains to be seen.

Chapter 7: Philippine War (1899–1902)

When the U.S. defeated Spain in the Caribbean, it demanded possession of Guam, Puerto Rico, Cuba and the Philippines. While the first three are in close proximity to the United States, one might wonder why the U.S. also forced Spain to surrender the Philippines. The answer can be found in the motivation for the later Philippine–American War, which Richard E. Welch calls "a colonial war, fought for the purpose of retaining a Pacific archipelago ceded to the United States by Spain."[110]

President William McKinley was a skilled politician, having been a member of Congress and later, governor of Ohio. He intentionally set out to influence the media, mastering the latest communication technology. Prior to his administration, most of the press coverage surrounded Congress, considered the nation's power center. During the administration of his predecessor, Grover Cleveland, there was one reporter assigned to the Executive Mansion (only later called the White House). His role was mainly to interview visitors to the president as they were leaving. Susan A. Brewer commented on the significant change in the McKinley administration: "McKinley was the first to have his inauguration filmed and to have a secretary who met daily with the press. Reporters were provided with a table and chairs in the outer-reception room where they could chat with important visitors and even the president if he approached them first."[111] His skill in manipulation of the press was new, but one that would be honed and perfected by succeeding presidents. Brewer continues: "The president's staff, which grew from six to eighty, monitored public opinion by studying hundreds of newspapers from around the country daily. To make sure that reporters accurately conveyed the president's views, his staff issued press releases, timing the distribution so that reporters on deadline filed only the administration's version of the story."[112]

In the fall of 1898, as peace talks with Spain began, McKinley embarked on a speaking tour, ostensibly to get the opinion of the citizenry on what

---

[110]Richard E. Welch, Jr., *Response to Imperialism* (University of North Carolina Press, 1987), xiii.

[111]Susan A. Brewer, *Why America Fights: Patriotism and War Propaganda from the Philippines to Iraq* (New York: Oxford University Press, 2009), 15.

[112]Ibid.

to do with the Philippines, but the real goal was to garner support for keeping that nation. According to Brewer, McKinley "linked patriotism with holding the islands" in fifty-seven appearances.[113]

> The president's staff distributed advance copies of formal speeches along with numerous bulletins complete with human-interest anecdotes, which frequently appeared as news stories. Newspaper editors got the message and reported that it looked like the United States would be keeping the Pacific islands.[114]

The version of the story that McKinley wanted portrayed was that the U.S. was invading and occupying the Philippines in order for "Americans to fulfill their manly duty to spread Christian civilization."[115] This, he said, would be done by "benevolent assimilation."[116]

U.S. newspapers then, as now, toed the governmental line. Emilio Aquinaldo, a Philippine general and the nation's first president, was depicted in cartoons in U.S. newspapers as a 'monkey-man' or a cannibal, as all other Filipinos were also depicted. Even the very fact that the Filipinos fought against the conquering U.S. soldiers was seen as an indication of their inferiority.

In 1898, Indiana State Senator Albert J. Beveridge visited the Philippines, and his observations about American soldiers were reported in *The Saturday Evening Post*. They read, in part, as follows:

> Everywhere the pale blue or gray eye, everywhere the fair skin, everywhere the tawny hair and beard. ... Here thoroughbred soldiers from the plantations of the South, from the plains and valleys and farms of the west, look the thoroughbred, physically considered. The fine line is everywhere. The nose is straight, the mouth is sensitive and delicate. ... The whole face and figure is the face and figure of the thoroughbred fighter who has always been the fine-featured, delicate-nostriled, thin-eared and generally clean-cut featured man.[117]

This very description implies superiority over the Filipinos, and adds to the belief in the U.S.'s 'manly' obligation to civilize them.

Reports of atrocities did leak out, as this 'benevolent assimilation' began, but were not given credence. Captain Elliot of the Kansas Regiment

---

[113]Ibid., 26

[114]Ibid.

[115]Ibid.

[116]Veltisezar Bautista, *The Filipino Americans: From 1763 to the Present* (Bookhaus, 2002).

[117]Welch, *Response to Imperialism*, 101.

described the massacre at Caloocan in the spring of 1899: "Caloocan was supposed to contain seventeen thousand inhabitants. The Twentieth Kansas swept through it, and now Caloocan contains not one living native. Of the buildings, the battered walls of the great church and dismal prison alone remain."

This report about the Caloocan massacre was first mentioned in *The Saturday Evening Post*, but following a hurried investigation by the War Department, the *Post* printed a retraction. "H.L. Wells, correspondent for several New York papers, concurrently reported that 'it was a source of great satisfaction to know that earlier reports of the misconduct of our soldiers are disproved'."[118]

More recent studies and commentary shed additional light on the horrors perpetrated by the U.S. government on the people of the Philippines. In October of 2019, Maj. Danny Sjursen (retired) wrote the following:

> Few Americans remember the US invasion, occupation, and pacification – a neat euphemism, that – of the Philippine Islands, but Filipinos will never forget. Perhaps half a million locals died (one-sixth of the total population) at the hands of superior US military technology, induced disease and starvation. The war also reflected and affected the US Army culture of the day. Most of the generals were veterans of the vicious Indian Wars of extermination in the previous decades. Racially pejorative terms for the Filipinos entered the military vernacular. Some, such as "nigger," were reappropriated; others, like *gugu* – thought to be the etymological precursor to the Vietnam-era epithet *gook* – were new.[119]

In 2004, attorney Romeo Capulong of the Public Interest Law Center, wrote this:

> I find the U.S. government accountable for war crimes and crimes against humanity it committed and continues to commit against the Filipino people and peoples of other countries in over more than a century of colonial and neo-colonial rule in the Philippines. To this day, the U.S. government has not apologized for the crimes it committed against the Filipinos and peoples of other countries in the region.[120]

---

[118] Ibid., 34.

[119] https://original.antiwar.com/danny_sjursen/2019/09/30/a-picture-of-a-war-crime-is-worth-a-thousand-words/. Accessed on March 2, 2020.

[120] https://www.bulatlat.com/news/4-33/4-33-crimes.html. Accessed on March 2, 2020.

Doug Bandow, writing for the conservative Cato Institute in August of 2018, commented as follows: "Many conflicts in our history were foolish, counterproductive, and shortsighted. Several were justified by fraud and lies. Yet most retained at least a patina of moral justification, no matter how infirm in practice."[121] Further,

> No such moral veneer can be applied to the Philippine–American War, waged more than a century ago. Indeed, most Americans probably are not even aware of that conflict. They are taught that Teddy Roosevelt and a few other guys, some of whom were on ships, defeated the murderous Spanish Empire and freed Cubans and Filipinos from horrid oppression. What came next is barely mentioned in most civics texts.[122]

Rather than any lofty goals for the Philippine people, the government saw their nation as a future naval base, helping to exploit Chinese markets. Bandow commented further on U.S. atrocities: "Indeed, U.S. forces eventually adopted the brutal Spanish practices used against insurgents in Cuba, which had spurred America's original declaration of war. American officials and officers actually pointed to the virtual extermination of the Native Americans as a possible model."[123]

So why did the U.S. population support the war on the Philippines? As McKinley proclaimed: "And, my fellow-citizens, wherever our flag floats, wherever we raise that standard of liberty, it is always for the sake of humanity and the advancement of civilization. Territory sometimes comes to us when we go to war for a holy cause, and whenever it does, the banner of liberty will float over it and bring, I trust, blessings and benefits to all the people."[124]

These are lofty sentiments that no decent person could argue with. However, in a conversation with Wisconsin Governor Robert LaFollette, McKinley said his actual aim was to "attain U.S. supremacy in world markets".[125] Yet U.S. citizens, then as now, must be protected from the ugly truths of U.S. war-making, so that that deadly activity can continue unabated.

---

[121] https://www.cato.org/publications/commentary/why-do-we-still-have-war-booty-p hilippines. Accessed on March 2, 2020.

[122] Ibid.

[123] Ibid.

[124] Susan A. Brewer, *Why America Fights: Patriotism and War Propaganda from the Philippines to Iraq* (New York: Oxford University Press, 2009), 26.

[125] Ibid., 16.

Chapter 8: Occupation of Nicaragua (1912–1933)

One might think the nation of Nicaragua to be at low risk for United States 'intervention'. It has no strategic value to the U.S., no natural resources coveted by the U.S. and in no way posed a threat to U.S. security. Despite that, the U.S. put it directly in its crosshairs.

Nicaragua struggled for decades in the earlier part of the nineteenth century to establish itself as a viable nation-state. Formerly part of the Kingdom of Guatemala, Nicaragua became part of what was known as the United Provinces of Central America. This organization collapsed in 1838, seventeen years after the demise of the Kingdom of Guatemala. According to historian Luciano Baracco:

> No one had fought for [Nicaraguan] nationhood and, even after 1838, few saw Nicaragua in terms of a nation. For the remainder of the nineteenth century, and indeed well into the twentieth century, the mestizo population of this new state was to be preoccupied by the search for a distinctive identify which would form the basis of a Nicaraguan nation *sui generis* [on its own; separate and independent]. Through a series of dramatic and violent events, the first tentative imagining of nation-ness in relation to Nicaragua can be traced.[126]

This lack of clarity in the status of Nicaragua even among the people who lived there and who governed it was compounded by unclear borders. For example, in 1852, British Minister to the U.S., John F. Crampton, entered into an agreement ceding Greytown – a Nicaraguan port city that was the Caribbean terminus of the transit route and de facto under British control via their Miskito Kingdom protectorate – to Nicaragua, and providing relocation to the Indians. Nicaragua was to pay for obtaining Greytown.

The agreement never passed, because "The Nicaraguan government flatly rejected it, asserting that Nicaragua should not be compelled to pay

---

[126] Luciano Baracco, *Nicaragua: The Imagining of a Nation: From Nineteenth-Century Liberals to Twentieth-Century Sandinistas* (New York: Algora, 2005).

for reacquisition of territory that had always been rightfully Nicaraguan. Since British acceptance of the agreement was conditional upon Nicaraguan consent, Nicaragua's refusal to do so torpedoed the whole scheme."[127]

This nation, Central America's largest, is, like its neighbors, bordered by the Caribbean Sea on the east, and the Pacific Ocean on the west. The idea of a canal connecting these two bodies of water was long discussed, and, as a result, Nicaragua became a focus of foreign imperial powers. The U.S. was first and foremost among them. As early as 1850, the U.S. passed the Clayton-Bulwer Treaty, which approved a canal through Nicaragua. Among its other provisions, this treaty assured that the U.S. and Great Britain, which at the time dominated trade in Central America, agreed to guarantee the neutrality of any canal built there.

Whether or not the U.S. ever intended to adhere to this agreement isn't known, but time proved that it didn't hesitate to violate it. But doing so could not be accomplished without some reason that the public would accept. With the appointment of Solon Borland as the U.S. minister to Nicaragua in 1852, the foundation was set. According to historian John E. Findling, Borland "disliked Nicaraguans, the British and the Clayton-Bulwer Treaty, not necessarily in that order":

> In early 1854, Borland was a passenger on an American-owned steamer cruising on the San Juan River when the captain shot to death a black man in a trivial dispute. When town authorities moved to arrest the captain, Borland protected him, denying that Greytown police had jurisdiction over an American citizen. In a melee that occurred in front of the U.S. consul's residence, where Borland was staying, someone in a crowd threw a bottle which slightly injured the minister.
>
> Deciding that U.S. citizens and property were no longer safe in Greytown, Borland went to the United States and convinced the government that naval protection was needed. Accordingly, the U.S.S. *Cyane*, commanded by Capt. George A. Hollins, was dispatched to serve as a threatening presence in Greytown harbor. The ship arrived in June, and Hollins and the local American consular agent, J.W. Fabens, determined to extract reparations from Greytown officials. After their initial demands were ignored, Hollins issued an ultimatum in July 11, giving the town twenty-four hours to respond to the American demands. When still no answer came, the *Cyane* bombarded the town on July 13, and Hollins then sent a landing party to burn any building that had escaped the naval artillery.

[127] Wilbur Devereux Jones, *The American Problem in British Diplomacy, 1841–1861* (University of Georgia Press, 1974), 104–105.

The town was totally destroyed, but because of Hollins' warning, the townspeople had evacuated and there was no loss of life.[128]

From all available accounts, Borland was in no danger. This was not a revolution, but a 'melee', a small group of people either fighting or in some sort of conflict, but hardly requiring the intervention of a foreign navy.

This was the first major military intervention by the U.S. in Nicaragua. But it was certainly not the last.

The U.S. used a variety of methods to control the Nicaraguan economy. At the dawn of the twentieth century, according to historian Robert E. Hannigan,

> American policy makers had become powerfully attached to the financial protectorate idea as the way by which they might bring the kind of pro-U.S. stability they wanted to Honduras, Nicaragua, and other potential trouble spots in the Caribbean. Concerned that such countries would not 'act responsibly' on their own, American officials saw receiverships as a cheap but effective means of taking charge of their affairs.[129]

Part of this initiative to control the government of Nicaragua was the Knox-Castrillo Treaty, which, according to historian Isaac Joslin Cox,

> ... provided for aid in securing a loan of $15,000,000 from American bankers. The proceeds were to be used in paying claims against the Government, in consolidating the debt and stabilizing the currency, and in building a railroad to the eastern coast. During the continuance of the debt the customs were to be in charge of a collector-general. This official was to be appointed by the Nicaraguan executive on the nomination of the bankers making the loan and his selection was subject to the approval of the State Department.[130]

Note that this agreement was controlled by the U.S.; it set the terms, the banks that were to lend the money were U.S.-based, and the official in charge had to be approved by the State Department.

---

[128] John E. Findling. *Close Neighbors, Distant Friends: United States–Central American Relations* (New York: Greenwood Press, 1987), 21–22.

[129] Robert E. Hannigan, *The New World Power: American Foreign Policy, 1898–1917* (Philadelphia: University of Pennsylvania Press, 2002), 43.

[130] Isaac Joslin Cox, *Nicaragua and the United States, 1909–1927* (Boston: World Peace Foundation, 1927), 712.

President Miguel Davila strongly opposed this treaty, concerned about domestic opposition to it. However, using strong-arm techniques, the U.S. government finally convinced him to sign it. Davila was quickly proven correct in his assessment of domestic opposition to it; he was overthrown just a few months later.

Despite conditions completely favorable to the U.S., the treaty was unacceptable to the U.S. Congress, which never approved it.

In July of 1912, in the convoluted politics of Nicaraguan governance at the time, a revolt began in which President Adolfo Diaz, a former employee of a U.S. mining firm, attempted to depose Luis Mena, who was the most powerful man in the government, from his position as minister of war. Diaz was supported by the Grenadian aristocracy, while Mena had the backing of the army. Mena then proclaimed that he and his followers were in revolt against Diaz. Another, simultaneous revolt in Leon "threatened to cut communications on the railway, which had recently passed under American control".[131] Diaz then "appealed to the United States for aid and to suggest a treaty that would at any time permit the United States to intervene in Nicaragua in order to preserve and maintain a stable government".[132]

Although the last, full intervention by the U.S. had been nearly sixty years earlier, U.S. military presence in the country was nearly constant. The fact that U.S. economic interests were threatened by the ongoing Nicaraguan governmental confusion was the reason for intervention, as it was previously, and would be in the future. The U.S. minister demanded that President Diaz protect U.S. lives and property. In response, the minister of foreign relations claimed that Nicaraguan forces were all required to quell the various rebellions then plaguing the nation. So he wrote the following to the U.S. minister: "In consequence, my Government desires that the Government of the United States guarantee with its forces security for the property of American citizens in Nicaragua and that it extend its protection to all the inhabitants of the Republic".[133]

It is worth recognizing that the request was, first, to protect the property of U.S. citizens, and then, secondly, to protect the inhabitants. And thus began the U.S.'s 21-year occupation of Nicaragua.

By 1926, with Nicaragua still in an uncertain state of stability, and still occupied by the U.S., it was widely rumored that Mexico was 'fomenting

---

[131]Ibid., 717.
[132]Ibid.
[133]Ibid., 718.

Bolshevism' in Nicaragua. Bolshevism was the forerunner of the much-feared communism, a fear that took hold to paranoiac proportions after World War II, culminating with the McCarthy witch hunts of the 1950s. But was Mexico, in fact, doing this?

> During 1926, a large number of American papers carried articles accusing Mexico of 'fomenting Bolshevism' in Nicaragua. The striking similarities of these stories, together with the Washington heading, suggested, but, of course, did not prove, a common origin. The story sent out by the Associated Press began: 'The specter of a Mexican-inspired Bolshevism hegemony intervening between the United States and the Panama Canal has thrust itself into American-Mexican relations, already strained.' The dispatch went on to hint at the anxiety of the Nicaraguan President at the spread of 'Mexican-inspired Bolshevism' in Nicaragua. This is what millions of Americans read.[134]

A journalist from the *St. Louis Post–Dispatch*, Paul Y. Anderson, decided to dig a little deeper to find the source of this frightening story. He learned that the State Department had summoned representatives from the Associated Press, United Press Associations and the International New Service to a meeting, pledging them to absolute secrecy. They were told that the State Department was 'morally certain' that Mexico was spreading Bolshevik propaganda throughout Central America, and "that this picture should be presented to the American people".[135] The representatives from the three news agencies were asked to do their part in disseminating this (mis)information to the general public, a request to which they quickly acquiesced.

U.S. citizens were again misled to support military intervention in a foreign nation, believing first that U.S. lives were in jeopardy, and second that Bolshevism was about to steamroll its repressive doctrines throughout Central America. Neither charge was true, but the military interventions enabled the U.S. to support, protect and maintain its businesses and profits in Nicaragua.

In 1933, the problems in the U.S. resulting from the Great Depression, along with the efforts of Nicaraguan revolutionary leader Augusto C. Sandino, forced the U.S. to finally leave Nicaragua. Of course, that didn't mean the end to U.S. involvement there. For information on more recent U.S. interference in Nicaragua, please see Chapter 18.

---

[134]Frederick E. Lumley, *The Propaganda Menace* (New York: Century, 1933), 41.
[135]Ibid.

Chapter 9: Occupation of Haiti (1915–1934)

By 1910, Haiti was plagued by government instability. Between 1888 and 1915, not a single president of Haiti served out his seven-year term; during that time, one died of natural causes while in office, and ten were either assassinated or overthrown. Between 1911 and 1915, there were seven presidents of Haiti.[136]

A pattern had been established in which a candidate for the presidency would form a *caco,* an army consisting of conscripts and military adventurers, generally organized by local military strongmen. This group would capture the northern port of Cap-Haitien, and the candidate would declare himself a rival to the incumbent president, who often fled the country under these dangerous circumstances, taking part of the national treasury with him. The *caco* would then move on to Port-au-Prince, where the insurgent candidate would be elected president by the Haitian Senate.[137]

The U.S., wanting hegemony throughout Central America, saw Haiti as vulnerable to European influences.

During this period of time, economic exploitation of these nations by foreign countries was common. As historian Hans Schmidt put it:

> Foreign financial interests would float loans at exorbitant rates to an unstable and often corrupt Latin-American government. That Latin-American country would eventually default on its loan payments, and the foreign financial interests would apply to their governments for diplomatic assistance in collecting. If diplomatic pressure and intervention succeeded in forcing a settlement of the debt, the foreign investors would enjoy high-risk rates of return on their loans where there was actually no risk involved at all, thanks to their government's intervention.[138]

The U.S. recognized European financial claims on Central American countries, although the Monroe Doctrine prevented foreign military in-

---

[136]Hans Schmidt, *The United States Occupation of Haiti, 1915–1934* (New Brunswick, NJ: Rutgers University Press, 1995), 42.

[137]Ibid.

[138]Ibid., 45.

tervention in those countries. The Monroe Doctrine, issued by President James Monroe in 1823, was issued because most Latin American nations by that time had achieved, or were close to achieving, their independence from Spain and Portugal, and Monroe decreed that any attempts by European powers to control any other nation in North or South America would be seen as "the manifestation of an unfriendly disposition toward the United States."[139] The U.S. would reserve the right to control those nations itself.

Although this doctrine shifted over the years depending on political conditions in the world, Gilderhus writes that there were three constants: "Policy makers wanted to keep out the Europeans, to safeguard order and stability in areas of special concern, and to ensure open access to markets and resources".[140]

Schmidt writes that in 1904, "the Roosevelt Corollary stated that the United States would intervene as a last resort to ensure that other nations in the Western Hemisphere fulfilled their obligations to international creditors, and did not violate the rights of the United States or invite 'foreign aggression to the detriment of the entire body of American nations.'"[141]

This 'corollary' served as the foundation and justification for numerous 'incursions' by the U.S. into Central America. This was evidenced in Haiti which, despite its chaotic political and governmental situation, had not defaulted on any of its international debts. But the Panama Canal was about to open, and so the U.S. wasn't willing to risk the possibility of any policy in Haiti which might threaten its control of the canal.

In 1912 Secretary of State Philander C. Knox spoke at a banquet in Port-au-Prince, given in his honor. U.S. intentions were made abundantly clear by his words, which included the following:

> At a time when the obligation which my country has assumed as the agent of the interest of all America and of the world in creating a highway for international commerce [the Panama Canal] is about to be realized, we are impressed with the conviction that the fullest success of our world is, to a notable degree, dependent on the peace and stability of our neighbors and on their enjoying the prosperity and material welfare which flow from orderly self-government. A

---

[139] https://web.archive.org/web/20120108131055/http://eca.state.gov/education/engt eaching/pubs/AmLnC/br50.htm. Accessed on January 28, 2020.

[140] Mark T. Gilderhus, "The Monroe Doctrine: Meanings and Implications," *Presidential Studies Quarterly* 36, no. 1 (2006).

[141] https://history.state.gov/milestones/1899-1913/roosevelt-and-monroe-doctrine. Accessed June 22, 2018.

community liable to be torn by internal dissension or checked in its progress by the consequences of nonfulfillment of international obligations is not in a good position to deserve and reap the benefits accruing from enlarged commercial opportunities, such as are certain to come about with the opening of the canal. It may indeed become an obstruction to the general enjoyment of those opportunities.[142]

The U.S. would insist on stability that benefited its interests; the interests of the Haitian people were unimportant.

In 1914 Roger L. Farnham of the National City Bank of New York was advising Secretary of State William Jennings Bryan. In one memorandum, he said that Germany was "seeking 'almost complete control of the financial and commercial affairs of the island'."[143] Farnham also reported to Bryan that Germany and France were conspiring together to take financial control of the island. Despite the fact that this was highly improbably because Germany and France were at war with each other at the time, Bryan was greatly alarmed. Farnham said that if action wasn't taken, U.S. businesses would withdraw from Haiti. This, too, was highly improbable, but caused Bryan further alarm. Indeed, U.S. financial investment wasn't that great: in 1913, U.S. investment totalled only about $4 million, compared to $220 million in Cuba and $800 million in Mexico. Yet Bryan and others saw potential in Haiti, partly due to the perceived availability of cheap labor. According to Farnham: "I think that the Haitian can be taught to become a good and efficient laborer. If let alone by the military chiefs, he is as peaceful as a child, and as harmless. In fact, today they are nothing but grown up children, ignorant of all agricultural methods and they know nothing of machinery. They must be taught."[144]

Farnham wanted the U.S. to control Haitian customs. Bryan agreed, despite the fact that efforts to obtain the necessary receivership had already failed. How it was to be accomplished now was unknown. Yet control of the Caribbean was required, and Haiti was now the country where such control would be firmly established. And European control of Haiti or its neighbors would not suit the U.S. According to Schmidt, "The Wilson administration ultimately came to the conclusion that, because of political instability and domination by foreign capitalists, Haitian guarantees were insufficient and that United States intervention was required to eliminate the threat of European encroachment."[145]

---

[142]Schmidt, *Occupation of Haiti*, 46.

[143]Ibid., 52.

[144]http://thepublicarchive.com/?p=32. Accessed on June 22, 2018.

[145]Schmidt, *Occupation of Haiti*, 56.

While this was the reason for the invasion and subsequent occupation, U.S. citizens were not as concerned about corporate investment in Haiti as were the oligarchs. Never a country to let pass any seemingly-viable reason for a military invasion, the U.S. seized upon Haiti's internal problems as an excuse to invade.

In July 1915, Haitian President Vilbrun Guillaume Sam was overthrown. The U.S. immediately intervened, using 'humanitarian reasons', and stating that U.S. forces were required to prevent anarchy, limit bloodshed and protect U.S. lives and property. This latter reason was, not surprisingly, premature. "In fact, there was no record of any American life having been lost or property destroyed prior to the intervention".[146]

These were the stated reasons, but U.S. warships had been in Haitian waters for at least a year, preparing for the orders to invade. A full year before the invasion, a plan for it included sample letters for advising Haitian officials of U.S. intentions. One stated, "The purpose of the President of the United States is solely for the establishment of law and order."[147] In November of 1914, the Navy developed the 'Plan for Landing and Occupying the City of Port-au-Prince'.

On July 31, 1915, three hundred thirty U.S. marines and sailors landed at Port-au-Prince. On that first day, two were killed. U.S. newspapers reported them as having been killed by Haitian sniper fire; however, the truth was far different. "Subsequent military reports disclosed that there were no indications of enemy fire in the area where the two sailors were killed and that they were accidentally shot in the night by rifle fire from their comrades in the Seaman Battalion".[148]

The U.S. government, ably assisted by a willing press, enjoys perpetuating the myth of its soldiers being welcomed as heroes. They are generally welcomed by an oppressive ruling class that seeks to hold onto its power, and sees it threatened by a popular people's movement. U.S. interventions are seldom, if ever, at the request of the people, but rather at the request of those oppressing the people. This was no less the case in Haiti than it has been anywhere else. As Schmidt writes, "Night curfew patrols were forced to march warily down the middle of the streets of Port-au-Prince in order to avoid being showered with household waste dropped from darkened second-story windows."[149] Although organized military resistance

---

[146]Ibid., 65
[147]Ibid.
[148]Ibid., 67.
[149]Ibid., 68.

to the invasion was minimal, this was possibly because of government disorganization.

Resistance was mainly limited to guerrilla groups comprised of Haitians opposed to the 'intervention' who organized in the hills. That the U.S. government recognized such resistance is indicated by the following correspondence from Secretary of the Navy Josephus Daniels to President Woodrow Wilson:

> U.S. has now actually accomplished a military intervention in affairs of another nation. Hostility exists now in Haiti and has existed for a number of years against such action. Serious hostile contacts have only been avoided by prompt and rapid military action which has given U.S. control before resistance has had time to organize.[150]

The U.S. occupation was not a benign circumstance, as occupations never are. Some of the conditions were as follows:

- Disrupted food supply, resulting in the near-starvation of thousands of Haitians. Rebels tried to pressure the U.S. to leave by cutting off food supplies to major cities. Secretary Daniels was unwilling to provide food to the starving Haitians since they were of African descent, saying that government assistance would cause them to stop working.

- Restoration of the Haitian treasury to the U.S.-controlled Banque Nationale.

- U.S. naval officials overseeing collection of all customs duties.

- U.S. control of all government agencies in the major cities and towns.

The U.S. took it upon itself to write a new constitution for Haiti. Wilson, "the famous stalwart of democratic idealism and the rights of self-determination" who had a passion for constitutionalism, did not take democracy or self-governance into consideration with this document. Instead, as Schmidt puts it,[151] he "sought to crush any hopes of democracy and self-determination in Haiti":

> [The new constitution's] most important provisions were the legalization of alien landownership, indefinite suspension of the elected

---

[150]Ibid.
[151]Ibid., 11.

bicameral Haitian legislature, temporary suspension of the irremov-
ability of judges, and legalization of all acts of the American military occupation. The new Constitution, clearly a device to serve
American ends, was rammed through by means of an illegal, marine-
supervised plebiscite after the Haitian legislature, the only body
legally competent to tamper with the constitution under existing
Haitian law, was summarily disbanded.[152]

During the campaign of 1920, Vice-Presidential candidate Franklin D.
Roosevelt claimed to have authored this document.

The overall treatment of the Haitians by the U.S. occupiers was barbaric:

How American marines, largely made up of and officered by Southerners, opened fire with machine guns from airplanes upon defenseless Haitian villages, killing men, women and children in the open
market places; how natives were slain for 'sport' by a hoodlum ele-
ment among these same Southerners; and how the ancient corvee system of enforced labor was revived and ruthlessly executed, increasing, through retaliation, the banditry in Haiti and Santo Domingo,
was told yesterday by Henry A. Franck, the noted traveler and authority on the West Indies.[153]

Such racism was prominent. According to Schmidt, U.S. wars in Central
America

... involved racism and American disdain for 'savages' and frequently
degenerated into torture, systematic destruction of villages, and military tactics tantamount to genocide. The military logic of guerrilla
warfare, where superior forces equipped with modern weapons were
pitted against elusive, poorly equipped guerrillas who were physi-
cally indistinguishable from non-combatants, dictated vicious hunt-
and-kill tactics which were most conveniently rationalized in terms
of racial and cultural prejudices.[154]

One study conducted in 1969 found that, initially, forty-nine of sixty-
nine prominent journals of the day endorsed the invasion and occupation,
with the other twenty 'strenuously opposed'.[155]

During the 1920 presidential election, the occupation of Haiti was an
issue. This mirrored future elections, wherein candidates of one party or

---

[152]Ibid., 10.
[153]Ibid., 119.
[154]Ibid., 7.
[155]Ibid., 120.

the other denounced the current war or occupation, wherever and whatever it may be. By the time of the election, the tide of public opinion had turned against the occupation, but, as would also be seen in future years, that had little influence on the government.

By 1929, the Haitian people were growing more than a little frustrated by the occupation. The Haitian president, Louis Borno, a complete puppet of the U.S. who did whatever he was told, cancelled elections scheduled for that year, accepting U.S. dictates and the opinion that "The masses of voters are still too ignorant and too much out of touch with the world."[156] This caused a popular uprising that eventually drove the U.S. out of Haiti. "The United States objective was to get out of Haiti as quickly as possible even though this meant an overwhelming victory for anti-American forces in popular elections."[157] While it took another five years for the last U.S. marine to leave, in 1934, the occupation officially ended.

To summarize, "in 1915, the United States invaded and occupied Haiti until 1934, with a brutal Marine occupation resulting in the torture and murder of thousands of Haitians."[158]

---

[156]Ibid., 193.

[157]Ibid., 207.

[158]https://andrewgavinmarshall.com/2012/02/21/punishing-the-population-the-american-occupations-of-haiti-and-the-dominican-republic/. Accessed on November 17, 2018.

Chapter 10: Occupation of the Dominican Republic (1916–1924)

Like Nicaragua and Haiti, the Dominican Republic experienced a prolonged period of instability during the latter end of the nineteenth century and the early part of the twentieth. The U.S., never hesitating to exploit such problems for its own financial gain, saw a prime opportunity in the Dominican Republic, just as it had in Cuba, Panama, Nicaragua, Mexico and Haiti between 1901 and 1916.[159] This was all an attempt to gain regional hegemony in Central America.

Other nations were involved in the Dominican Republic, and the U.S. couldn't allow that. Germany was an unfriendly power that had significant interests in the northeastern part of the country. This would become an issue during World War I, due to "concerns about possible German use of the Dominican Republic as a base for attacks on the United States".[160]

By 1905, political instability in the Dominican Republic was sufficiently widespread to take a significant toll on the economy, such that the nation was unable to pay European and U.S. creditors. One historian commented as follows: "The Dominican Republic, under behind-the-scenes diplomatic pressure, requested that the United States intervene to put the island's financial house in order."[161] (Please see a similar situation in Chapter 20, Grenada).

President Theodore Roosevelt told the U.S. senate that intervention was necessary, otherwise "European nations would absorb all the Dominican revenues and it would be a virtual sacrifice of the American claims and interest in the island".[162] Initially, this was not to be a military intervention, since the U.S. citizenry, despite their never-ending belief in U.S. exceptionalism, was, at this time, growing tired of nearly constant war.

---

[159] Valentina Peguero, *The Militarization of Culture in the Dominican Republic, from the Captains General to General Trujillo*, Studies in War, Society, and the Military (Lincoln, NE: University of Nebraska Press, 2004), 27.

[160] https://2001-2009.state.gov/r/pa/ho/time/wwi/108649.htm. Accessed on July 10, 2018.

[161] https://www.u-s-history.com/pages/h946.html. Accessed on July 10, 2018.

[162] Peguero, *Militarization of Culture*, 28.

Following negotiations with officials from the Dominican Republic, an agreement was approved by the Senate in February of 1907, wherein the U.S. would continue to receive customs duties, as it had since 1905, and any changes to those duties would have to be approved by the U.S.

This intervention was to be 'dollar diplomacy,' which would substitute, in some odd way, dollars for bullets. The U.S. would not invade with an army, but would regulate commerce in the Dominican Republic. Dollar diplomacy was, according to historian Ellen D. Tillman, "to guarantee economic and political stability in the Caribbean region without the need for intrusive, and by 1905, highly controversial, military interventions".[163]

In 1906, the U.S. and the Dominican Republic signed a 50-year treaty. Under the terms of this agreement, the U.S. assumed responsibility for the customs department of the Dominican Republic, in exchange for paying off its international debts.

Yet dollar diplomacy would not be successful. As it had done numerous times previously, and would continue throughout its bloody future, the U.S. ignored its own laws. "Although U.S. policy forbid military interference in the political affairs of the region, the United States intervened anyway, forcing the resignation of Dominican President Francisco Henriquez y Carvaja."[164] In spreading its bizarre brand of democracy, this time to the unsuspecting Dominican Republic, the first measures the U.S. implemented were military control, the disbanding of the armed forces and the police, and strictly censoring the press.[165]

Despite the U.S.'s best efforts to remake the society of the Dominican Republic into a mirror image of the U.S., without the power of that nation but acceding in all ways to it, this proved unsuccessful. In the years between 1912 and 1916, it became apparent to the U.S. military and political leaders controlling the Dominican Republic that 'dollars for bullets' wasn't working. Rather than allow the Dominicans to resolve their own problems, they felt that continued U.S. military and financial control was necessary. On November 29, 1916, U.S. Navy Captain Harry S. Knapp read the formal proclamation, announcing that the U.S. was now occupying the Dominican Republic. This had been the case in fact since 1905, but was now formalized.

Like so many countries in the following decades, the citizens of the Dominican Republic were not interested in whatever it was the U.S. was

---

[163]Ellen D. Tillman, *Dollar Diplomacy by Force: Nation-Building and Resistance in the Dominican Republic* (Chapel Hill, NC: University of North Carolina Press, 2016), 1.

[164]Peguero, *Militarization of Culture*, 27

[165]Tillman, *Dollar Diplomacy*, 1.

shoving down their throats. For example: "In Monte Cristi, where the original landing force was very small, marines reported that the population began to organize a revolution, shooting at them and threatening to kill all inhabitants who had anything to do with the U.S. forces."[166]

This was only the beginning of the opposition. Dominican politicians, members of the clergy and prominent intellectuals all wrote to U.S. senators protesting the occupation. Authors America Lugo and Emiliano Tejera founded the UND (*Union Nacional Dominicana*) as a central organization to protest the occupation. It publicly named anyone who accepted employment that supported the U.S. military as a national traitor.[167]

The U.S. occupiers were determined to inflict upon the Dominicans a more enlightened, 'white' way of life. "Occupying officers at the highest levels, intent on their programs and plans, sometimes tried to replace Dominican culture and social norms with a new, model social order – an approach fed at times by ideas about race and geographical determinism."[168]

The U.S., of course, proclaimed the glories it was providing to the people of the Dominican Republic. The following three quotations tell very different stories. One is by a colonel in the U.S. Marine Corps; the next by Samuel Guy Inman, a prominent clergyman who was a strong advocate of missions to Central America and whose "entire ministry was marked by a concern for the whole person and his or her social context";[169] and the third by Jacinto Lopez, a prominent Dominican editor and author:

> "In Santo Domingo, the achievements of the military government have been highly creditable. ... Critics who assume that the Dominican masses are opposed to American control are misinformed."
> —Colonel G. C. Thorpe, U.S. Marine Corps

> "A foreign military government conducted largely by officials who cannot speak the language of the people and who have no idea of their history or national psychology must necessarily be an unjust government". —Samuel Guy Inman

> "The President of the United States, whoever he may be, disposed of the fortunes and shapes the destinies of the small countries bordering on the Caribbean Sea, according to his own and exclusive personal will; without a consistent and deliberate policy, without

---

[166] Ibid., 73.

[167] Ibid., 149.

[168] Ibid., 3.

[169] http://www.bu.edu/missiology/missionary-biography/i-k/inman-samuel-guy -1877-1965/. Accessed on July 10, 2018.

any knowledge or comprehension of the people of those countries, their problems, their needs, their woes, their aspirations; without any regard for international law; sometimes violating even the very elements of Christian civilization." —Jacinto Lopez[170]

According to Tillman, the U.S. press reported the occupation in a manner that impacted the country's eventual withdrawal: "it eased U.S. public condemnations of marine actions, which lessened U.S. scrutiny of its military's involvement."[171] The Navy was therefore free to remain 'unofficially' involved in the Dominican Republic.

U.S. governance, then as now, always placed the rights of the people secondary to the profit motive. Historian Andrew Gavin Marshall pointed out that "President Woodrow Wilson, the famous stalwart of democratic idealism and the rights of self-determination, sought to crush any hopes of democracy and self-determination in Haiti and the Dominican Republic."[172]

This was the U.S. intervention in the Dominican Republic, done, as all such interventions by the U.S. are done, ostensibly for their own good. But the profit and power motives, combined with the ignorance of the U.S. regarding the people it invades and occupies, and the U.S.'s complete disdain for the self-determination of its victims, belies such 'honorable' motives. When Trujillo overthrew the government, the U.S. advised him that the U.S. would recognize his government if it could be elected in something resembling a democratic process. This was despite the fact that the U.S. government knew that Trujillo would not respect democracy, but would quickly establish a dictatorship. But as long as he acquiesced to U.S. demands, the form of government didn't really matter.

What was the result of this occupation? In Tillman's words: "In the end, as an attempt to control and reform political culture through military force, the U.S. occupation of the Dominican Republic was a clear failure, leaving the country with a more powerful centralized military and surveillance system that long precluded democratic development."[173]

---

[170] Melvin M. Knight, *The Americans in Santo Domingo* (New York: Vanguard Press, 1928), 97.

[171] Tillman, *Dollar Diplomacy*, 201.

[172] https://andrewgavinmarshall.com/2012/02/21/punishing-the-population-the-ame rican-occupations-of-haiti-and-the-dominican-republic/. Accessed on January 23, 2019.

[173] Tillman, *Dollar Diplomacy*, 204. For information on later U.S. interference in the Dominican Republic, please see Chapter 16.

Chapter 11: World War I (1914–1918)

The sinking of the British passenger ship, the *Lusitania*, in 1915, enraged Americans. Germany was already at war with England, and had warned the U.S. that British ships would be targeted, and that U.S. citizens should not board them. The anger of the U.S. towards Germany for the attack was unabated, even when Germany claimed that the ship was carrying munitions to Britain, a claim that was later substantiated.[174] Newspapers darkly warned about the dangers of the U.S. German-American immigrant community, speculating about their possible behavior should the U.S. enter the war. 'Hyphenates' – such as German-Americans – came to be a pejorative term.

Building support for the war started long before the U.S. entered it. At a minimum, fiction and non-fiction in the U.S. presented information about the predicament of those in Europe already embroiled in war. Various events, including the invasion of Belgium and the sinking of the *Lusitania*, provided propaganda material. Among the horror stories reported was one of a Belgian baby whose hands had been deliberately cut off by German soldiers.[175] This brings to mind the Nariyah testimony that led to the Gulf War (see Chapter 22). In his book, *Falsehood in War-Time*, Arthur Ponsonby discusses this particular story at length, declaring, "everyone wanted to believe [it] ... and many [people] went so far so to say they had seen the baby."[176] "However, there has never been a shred of evidence that German soldiers cut off the hands of Belgian boys."[177]

On April 2, 2017, President Woodrow Wilson called a joint session of Congress to request a declaration of war. Only four senators spoke in opposition to the war, including Nebraska senator George W. Norris, "who pointed his finger at bankers, munitions makers, the press, and their propaganda as the reason for America's entry into the war":

---

[174] Frederic Cople Jaher, *Doubters and Dissenters: Cataclysmic Thought in America, 1885–1918,* (Free Press of Glencoe, 1974), 89.

[175] Celia Malone Kingsbury, *For Home and Country: World War I Propaganda on the Home Front* (Lincoln, NE: University of Nebraska Press, 2010), 67.

[176] Ponsonby, *Falsehood in War-Time* (Kessinger Publishing, Llc., 2010), 78.

[177] Stewart Halsey Ross, *Propaganda for War: How the United States was Conditioned to Fight the Great War of 1914–1918* (Progressive Press, 2009), 24.

We have loaned many hundreds of millions of dollars to the allies in this controversy. While such action was legal and countenanced by international law, there is no doubt in my mind but the enormous amount of money loaned to the allies in this country has been instrumental in bringing about a public sentiment in favor of our country taking a course that would make every bond worth a hundred cents on the dollar and making the payment of every debt certain and sure. Through this instrumentality and also through the instrumentality of others who have not only made millions out of the war in the manufacture of munitions, etc., and who would expect to make millions more if our country can be drawn into the catastrophe, a large number of the great newspapers and news agencies of the country have been controlled and enlisted in the greatest propaganda that the world has ever known, to manufacture sentiment in favor of war. It is now demanded that the American citizens shall be used as insurance policies to guarantee the safe delivery of munitions of war to belligerent nations. The enormous profits of munition manufacturers, stockbrokers, and bond dealers must be still further increased by our entrance into the war.[178]

Once the U.S. became involved in the war, the propaganda to support it differed slightly than in previous wars. Writer Celia Malone Kingsbury notes the following:

With most men actively involved in warfare, women and children became a special focus – and a tool – of social manipulation during the war. Cookbooks, popular magazines, romance novels, and government food agencies targeted women in their homes, especially their kitchens, pressuring them to change their domestic habits. Children were also taught to fear the enemy and support the war through propaganda in the form of toys, games, and books.[179]

Woman were targeted through fiction and food; seen as stewards of the kitchen, they were praised for their industry and shamed for any inability in the kitchen.

Herbert Hoover, then the head of the Food and Drug Administration, took a personal interest in this propaganda. Kinsgbury further states that "[the] campaign for scientific cooking became part of Hoover's campaign linking food conservation with military victory. Posters, books and mag-

---

[178]Ibid., 216–217.

[179]https://www.questia.com/library/120074643/for-home-and-country-world-war-i-propaganda-on-the. Accessed on April 2, 2018.

azine articles all ask women, in the name of national security, to conserve food".[180]

Consider how effective this must have been. A woman at home, while her husband, brother, son or father, is risking his life for what they were told was 'the war to end all wars', felt a great need to do something for the war effort. The U.S. government, anxious to exploit this normal desire for its own benefit, began producing propaganda for this exact purpose. For example, "The Food Administration was writing articles and sending them out to magazines and newspapers with the expectation that the materials would be published as they were."[181] Historian William Clayton Mullendore comments "that the press 'gave evidence of their appreciation of this opportunity for service by making a special effort to give publicity to news of the Food Administration' is another masterpiece of Orwellian newspeak. Even in light of 'shrinking' food supplies, the idea of a 'free' press publishing government-authored articles is bound to raise red flags and illustrates how coordinated war propaganda was."[182]

Big corporations, always ready to make a profit off the suffering of others, whether owned by U.S. citizens or citizens of far-off nations, were busy during World War I. For example, an Ivory soap advertisement showed "not an upper middle-class woman but a soldier pulling a bar of Ivory from his kit. The copy tells readers, 'That boy of yours will think of home every time he washes if you put a cake of Ivory in his comfort kit'."[183]

As mentioned, children were not exempt: they were to be the soldiers in the U.S.'s future wars, so grooming them to support war was of vital importance. While the toy 'GI Joe' wouldn't be available for another fifty years, and the violent war video games of today were unknown, there were other methods of indoctrinating impressionable, vulnerable young minds.

Like their parents, children needed to believe in and support the war. During World War I, they wore uniforms of soldiers and Red Cross nurses; toy weapons were commonplace. There were multiple reasons for this. Ponsonby, in *Falsehood in War-Time*, suggests that encouraging children to support the war was for the purpose of "inflam[ing] popular passion sufficiently to secure recruits for the continuance of the struggle".[184] But in order to assure continued support for the war, "propaganda in the United States, Great Britain and France urged children to fall in line, so

---

[180]Kingsbury, *Home and Country*, 35.
[181]Ibid., 39.
[182]Ibid.
[183]Ibid., 76.
[184]Ponsonby, *Falsehood in War-Time*, 14.

to speak, to save their pennies, inform on slackers, eat oatmeal rather than wheat, and above all to hate everything German."[185]

Another reason for indoctrinating children was that the government recognized this as an effective method of reaching their parents. Children could be exposed to whatever propaganda the school agreed to serve, and that information, or mis-information, would be brought home and discussed at the dinner table. "No door-to-door solicitor could persuade like the guilt-inspiring pleas of a child to her or his parents. No law or officer could be as effective."[186]

One anecdote is instructive:

> In New York City, recorded in 1918 minutes of the Board of Education, one scamp supposedly went on a hunger strike after her father refused to by a bond. "So I did not eat my supper, though my father and my mother begged me to eat; and I went [to] bed. In the morning my father said, 'Nettie eat your breakfast.' But I said, 'No; I am an American. You will not buy a bond; I cannot eat.' Then my father said to my mother, 'Go, buy a bond'."[187]

That the propaganda for war was intentional cannot be denied. On April 13, 1917, just one week after the U.S. entered the war,

> ... three members of the cabinet – Secretary of State Robert Lansing, Secretary of War Newton D. Baker, and Secretary of the Navy Josephus Daniels – addressed a letter to the president, on Lansing's stationery, calling for him to create, 'without waiting for further legislation,' what they called a Committee on Public Information [CPI], adding, 'because of the importance of the task, ... we trust that you will see fit to do so.' It was the opinion of the signers that 'the two functions – censorship and publicity – be joined in honesty and profit'.[188]

According to Stewart Halsey Ross, the CPI's "euphemistic title was calculated to convey the very essence of a republic; nowhere appeared the distasteful term 'propaganda'".[189] Yet its effects were far-reaching: "The

---

[185]Kingsbury, *Home and Country*, 169.

[186]Ross F. Collins, *Children, War and Propaganda* (Peter Lange, Inc., 2011), 78.

[187]Stephan F. Brumberg, "New York City Schools March Off to War. The Nature and Extent of Participating of the City Schools in the Great War, April 1917–June 1918," *Urban Education* 24, no. 4 (1990), 459, citied in Collins, *Children, War and Propaganda*, 78, footnote 65.

[188]Ross, *Propaganda for War*, 226.

[189]Ibid., 23.

Committee on Public Information not only helped unify American public opinion, its incessant drumbeat for conformity fed an exploding national intolerance of political dissent."[190]

For a nation that prides itself on free speech and freedom of the press, the establishment of the CPI should never have happened. The myths of free speech and freedom of the press were shattered during World War I: "For the first time in United States history, a government organization not only 'conditioned' all important news originating in Washington, but totally controlled it."[191]

The CPI worked hard; some of its activities are as follows:

- Prepared press releases and new stories by the bushelful;

- Enlisted scholars to write propaganda pamphlets;

- Printed and distributed those pamphlets by the tens of millions.

- Organized and coordinated a nationwide network of tens of thousands of speakers;

- Prepared and placed advertisements in hundreds of newspapers and magazines;

- Produced film documentaries

- Rigidly controlled the content of Hollywood-made motion pictures, and

- Had ghost writers produce newspapers stories, magazine article and books for government figures to put their names on.[192]

In January of 1937, Cedric Larson, who was a staff member at the Library of Congress, discovered the CPI's records in the basement of a building of the War Department. Along with James Mock, he published a comprehensive study of U.S. propaganda during World War I.[193]

While the propaganda itself was disturbing, Larson and Mock were equally concerned with some of its more subtle results. Because of the nationalism the propaganda engendered, government censorship increased

---

[190] Ibid.

[191] Ibid., 226.

[192] Ibid., 226.

[193] Gerd Horten, *Radio Goes to War: The Cultural Politics of Propaganda during World War II* (Berkeley, CA: University of California Press, 2002).

to an alarming degree. They commented: "America went under censorship during the [First] World War without realizing it."[194]

Yet when former purveyors of propaganda began recanting their stories of atrocities after the war, coupled with lofty moral appeals, the citizenry became, for a short time, skeptical. They heard too many confessions of fake atrocities, and too many boasts of success in creating enthusiasm and support for the war. "The propaganda [both British and American] was not only responsible in a large degree for the American entrance into the war, but it was also responsible for the temper and irrationality of the peace treaty and the vindictiveness of the post-war years."[195]

So when the false flag of the sinking of the 'innocent' *Lusitania* was raised, along with the very real (but unimportant to the U.S. government) suffering of people in various countries in Europe, hatred of and hostility toward the German people was a natural consequence, strongly encouraged by U.S. authorities. While Germans were hated, American servicemen were revered.

This reverence the general population holds for soldiers and their 'service' is another target and goal of official propaganda. We see parallels today. As these words are being written, U.S. hostility towards Iran is increasing. As early as 2008, when Hillary Clinton first ran for president, she said that the U.S. would 'totally obliterate' Iran if it attacked Israel. She didn't say she would destroy the government; no, her hostility was, like that of U.S. citizens during World War I towards Germany, directed towards all Iranians. A February 10, 2018, Gallup poll indicated that 17% of the population had a 'mostly favorable' or 'very favorable' opinion of Iran, while 70% had a 'mostly' or 'very' unfavorable opinion.[196] Why this is – considering Iran hasn't invaded another country since 1798, while the U.S. has been at war for well over 200 years of its existence – is an excellent example of pro-war and false-flag propaganda.

There were two 'false flags' that enabled the U.S. to enter World War I with the enthusiastic support of the citizenry:

1) The German sinking of the *Lusitania*, a passenger ship that just happened to carrying munitions to Britain, and

2) The 'evils' of the German people, and everything associated with their country.

---

[194]Cedric Larson and James R. Mock, *Words That Won the War: The Story of the Committee on Public Information* (New York, 1968), 4, 19, 215.

[195]Ibid.

[196]http://news.gallup.com/poll/116236/iran.aspx. Accessed on April 4, 2018.

As demonstrated above, U.S. citizens – children and adults – were encouraged to hate the Germans, and do everything in their power to defeat them. This pattern is seen repeatedly throughout history, mirrored today in hostility to all things Iranian, as the U.S. ratchets up its war-mongering rhetoric towards that country.

Chapter 12: World War II (1939–1945)

The horrors of World War II are beyond the scope of this work and will not be detailed here; others have covered that topic extensively elsewhere.[197] Rather, the purpose of this chapter is to demonstrate how the U.S. government manipulated its citizenry to support this war, using the vast array of propaganda techniques at its disposal.

During the Great Depression, the language of war permeated the rhetoric of the National Recovery Administration (NRA). President Franklin D. Roosevelt said he would request "broad Executive power to wage a war against the emergency, as great as the power that would be given to me if we were in fact invaded by a foreign foe."[198] Governor Alfred Landon, R-KS, responded by proclaiming, "I now enlist for the duration of the war".[199] The logo of the NRA, a blue eagle, "was displayed in shop windows, on letterheads and invoices, and on clothing labels to indicate that companies were participating in NRA polices and fulfilling their patriotic duty."[200] Historian Gerd Horten wrote the following:

> By 1935, most observers agreed with E. Pendleton Herring's assessment of the New Deal publicity two years after its initiation: 'No longer is official propaganda confined largely to war. ... Never before has the Federal Government [during peacetime] undertaken on so vast a scale and with such deliberate intent the task of building a favorable public opinion toward its policies.'[201]

Military parades were organized throughout the nation, further solidifying the idea of war in the minds of the people.

As pointed out in the previous chapter, the government has fostered a near-reverence for soldiers for generations. Historian Ross F. Collins notes that "[t]he *ésprit* of the hero, the discipline of the men in battle, the precision of obedience, the loyalty of teamwork, the honor of courage,

---

[197]Please see *The Second World War* by Martin Gilbert; *Germany's War* and *The Origins, Atrocities and Aftermath of World War II*, by John Wear.
[198]Horten, *Radio Goes to War*, 14.
[199]Ibid.
[200]Ibid.
[201]Ibid., 18.

the courage of patriotism – humble service for a cause greater than a man: all these echo through the literature of war as a noble pursuit through centuries and continents. The truth is rather less ennobling."[202] In March of 1945, reporter Marguerite Higgins visited the European 'theater', and what she saw was far from what she expected:

> Cities ruined and stinking. Dead bodies everywhere, some mangled or torn apart, the American and German equally awful. 'More shocking were the wounded, many her own age or younger. Some were blinded, others cruelly disfigured.' The faces of the Allied soldiers which she had expected to register a degree, at least, of satisfaction over their victories were only 'weary' and 'bitter'.[203]

Yet the myth continues to this day. In February of 2015, former Marine Adam Kokesh interviewed people who had just seen the movie *American Sniper*, the story of a mass murderer working for the U.S. military. Kokesh, who fought in Iraq before recognizing the evil and illegality of that particular war, tried to explain, as he spoke with these movie patrons, how it was the Iraqi 'insurgents' who were defending their homeland from U.S. invaders. He talked about how wrong he was in what he had done in Iraq. Yet, without exception, the people he spoke with glorified his time in Iraq, even when he specifically told them there was no honor, and only disgrace, in what he had done.[204] Remember this aspect of 'The Big Lie': "Even though the facts which prove this to be so [that what they were told was untrue] may be brought clearly to their minds, they will still doubt and waver and will continue to think that there may be some other explanation. For the grossly impudent lie always leaves traces behind it, even after it has been nailed down."[205]

Today, the 'war on drugs', a trillion-dollar boondoggle, and the 'war on terror', waged by the nation that perpetrates the most terror in the world, had their foundations in the 'war' Roosevelt declared against the economic downturn of his day. The concept of any 'war', be it one fought with guns on the battlefield or against minor drug-traffickers in the U.S.'s inner cities, inexplicably always has appeal to the citizenry.

With the ground prepared among the public, some action was still needed to justify an actual entry into the war. Enter Pearl Harbor.

---

[202]Collins, *Children, War and Propaganda*, 27.

[203]Paul Fussell, *Wartime: Understanding and Behavior in the Second World War* (New York: Oxford University Press, 1990), 12.

[204]https://www.youtube.com/watch?v=XDUPQuv6VFE. Accessed on April 17, 2018.

[205]Ron Fridell, *Dictatorship* (New York: Marshall Cavendish Benchmark, 2007), 58.

The U.S. and the rest of the world were told that, in their quest for world power, Japan decided to bomb Pearl Harbor. However, as is always the case with the U.S. and war, the facts were far from the statements of government officials. Like the Germans, the Japanese were all to be hated, even to the point of incarcerating U.S.-born Japanese-Americans in concentration camps for years. Japanese people in cartoons and literature were depicted as evil, conniving and, often, stupid. This view was fostered by the Roosevelt administration.

However, Dr. E. Stanley Jones, a well-known missionary with extensive experience in the Orient and who had served as an unofficial mediator with the Japanese, said this:

> The idea that all the Japanese officials and people were united in their approval of aggression and their plans for further conquests in the Orient, even to the point of war with the United States, is commonly held. It has been carefully nurtured by propaganda. The American citizen is supposed to believe that a united Japan undertook world-wide conquest, with no inhibitions and no internal opposition. But the idea is disastrously false. From the time of the attack upon China, the Japanese nation went through a deep struggle of mind and soul ...[206]

The attack on China that Jones referred to was the July 1, 1938, bombing of Nanking, Canton and other defenseless cities, after which the U.S. government imposed a 'moral embargo' on sales of aircraft to Japan. Incidentally, while the U.S. feigned outrage at the bombing of Chinese cities with no discernible military importance, it was just a few years later that the U.S. did the same thing, only hundreds of times worse, when it dropped nuclear bombs on the Japanese cities of Hiroshima and Nagasaki.

The U.S. took other steps indicating hostility to Japan, in addition to the embargo of sales of aircraft, prior to the attack on Pearl Harbor. These included the abrogation of the Japanese-American commercial treaty of 1911, announced on July 26, 1939, to take effect on January 26, 1940. Ambassador Joseph C. Grew commented on this action: "I have pointed out that once started on a policy of sanctions we must see them through and that such a policy may conceivably lead to eventual war."[207] Steps

---

[206] George Morgenstern, *Pearl Harbor: The Story of the Secret War* (New York: Devin-Adair, 1947), 100.

[207] George Morgenstern, "The Actual Road to Pearl Harbor," in *Perpetual War for Perpetual Peace: A Critical Examination of the Foreign Policy of Franklin Delano Roosevelt and Its Aftermath*, edited by Harry Elmer Barnes (Caldwell, ID: Caxton Printers, 1953), 322.

the U.S. government subsequently took indicated that, regardless of the risk of war, the policies would be continued.

Although it was nearly six months after war was declared that the Office of War Information was established, it took only three days for the Office of Censorship to come into existence. Franklin Roosevelt declared: "All Americans abhor censorship, just as they abhor war. But the experience of this and of all other nations has demonstrated that some degree of censorship is essential in wartime, and we are at war."[208] Authors Collins and Washburn commented: "The press did not complain. As in World War I, nearly every media outlet in the country squarely stood behind, or in fact became a partner with, the government in promoting its wartime requirements."[209]

This included hiding the harsh reality of war. With much of the country having a loved one – father, son, brother, uncle, etc. – in uniform in some far-off corner of the world, seeing other soldiers 'mangled or torn apart', as American journalist Marguerite Higgins, said, would not do much for morale at home. And at this point, that morale was seen as crucial to victory: "no one wants to hear how one of them might have really died: not in a noble charge against a fearsome enemy, but flat as a flagstone, run over by one of your own tanks in another debacle of the supposedly precision-inspired planning of the U.S. Army."[210]

Yet if seeing such things would horrify innocent children (and their armchair warrior parents), children still needed to be part of the 'total' war effort. This included participating in air-raid drills in schools. These drills "became more controversial as the shock of Pearl Harbor receded and the reality of scaring children for no reason became more concerning; some authorities believed these drills to be good training, but others thought it was a waste of time at the least, at most, detrimental."[211] In some communities, children were issued a dog-tag-like information tag in case they were killed, or suffered injury in some highly unlikely attack.

One commonality with propaganda in both World War I and World War II was that "children were encouraged to confront general anxiety about the war by making it part of their games. This also was addressed expressly in the *Life* magazine how-to for parents. Photographs empha-

---

[208]Ross F. Collins and Patrick S. Washburn, *The Greenwood Library of American War Reporting, Volume 5: World War I and World War II* (Westport, CT., Greenwood Press, 2005), 250, cited in Collins, *Children, War and Propaganda*, 32).

[209]Ibid., 321.

[210]Fussel, *Wartime*.

[211]Collins, *Children, War and Propaganda*, 36.

sized the importance of making the war a game as a way to make it less fearful, and more acceptable".[212] The fact that *Life* was one of the many publications censored by the U.S. government during World War II, coupled with its presenting of war as play, indicates its willingness to follow government-issued directions for war reporting and information.

During World War II, children were asked to do 'volunteer' work which, had they been offered payment for it, would have violated child-labor laws. Historian Ross Collins writes: "Critics muttered darkly about a return to a world in which exploited children shined shoes, hawked newspapers, delivered parcels and generally worked like small dogs doing what adults did not want to do."[213] Roosevelt supported such efforts, saying that it gave children a "sense of involvement".[214]

While the German army was fighting the U.S. and its allies, U.S. businesses were busy supplying both sides of the war, thus ensuring maximum profits, regardless of the outcome. For example, Ford and General Motors built vehicles "that were the backbone of the German transportation system."[215] The chairman of Standard Oil of California "told *Life Magazine* in 1940, 'If the Germans ever catch [any of my ships] carrying oil to the Allies they will have my hearty permission to fire a torpedo into her.'"[216] These and many other activities of U.S. businesses in support of Axis powers were happening while U.S. soldiers were dying fighting the Germans.

Film portrayals tend to show World War II as an heroic undertaking. Commenting on public opinion about the war, Glen Jeansonne and David Lurssen write: "Americans generally regard World War II as a time when parties, races, and classes set aside their differences, united in common cause against encirclement by foes bent on destroying the nation's way of life."[217] Movies made during and since World War II mostly follow this theme.

Although these sanitized stories are what helped encourage support for the war – and help contemporary audiences to see it as a great, noble and unifying adventure – the truth is not quite so pretty. Seldom is it men-

---

[212] Ibid., 37.

[213] Ibid., 53.

[214] Ibid., 53.

[215] http://www.rationalrevolution.net/war/american_supporters_of_the_europ.htm. Accessed on May 4, 2018.

[216] Collins, *Children, War and Propaganda,* 77.

[217] Glen Jeansonne and David Luhrssen, *War on the Silver Screen: Shaping America's Perception of History* (Lincoln, NE: Potomac Books, 2014), 28–29.

tioned that "The Roosevelt administration seized forty plants and, briefly, the national railroad system to prevent strikes from disrupting the war economy. Race riots requiring military intervention broke out in Detroit and in Harlem, while in Southern California, off-duty sailors and soldiers clashed with Chicano youth in the 'Zoot Suit Riots'. Tens of thousands of U.S. citizens of Japanese heritage were interned in 'war relocation centers' in response to public anxiety over the loyalty of Japanese-Americans and fears of sabotage on the West Coast."[218] One popular wartime move, *Since You Went Away* (1944), portrayed housing shortages as a grand adventure. For those experiencing those shortages, it was probably an 'adventure' they could have happily lived without. But for the millions of viewers who watched the movie, it helped to minimize any recognition of the suffering the war caused, and therefore encouraged support for the war.

The exploitation of children helped to rear a generation that saw war as play, was shielded from the harsh realities of death and destruction that are part of any war, and helped maintain the U.S. as the world's foremost warrior nation. If their fathers, brothers or uncles died while in the military, a 'Gold Star' was proudly displayed in a window in their home, further enhancing the myth of a glorious death for country.

The U.S. trained its children well, enabling the country to continue its global conquests into the next millennium.

---

[218]Ibid., 29.

Section C: Global Killing Fields (1951–Present)

After World War II, the United States became the undisputed most powerful country in the world. Since that time, it has invaded and/or destabilized at least 35 countries, and killed at least 20,000,000 people. Its capacity for colonization – done today under the guise of installing its twisted version of democracy upon victim nations, who then must endure some U.S. puppet as their leader – and for killing, goes beyond what earlier imperialists would ever have dreamed possible. This section focuses on the time period of 1950 to 2019.

Chapter 13: Korean War (Jun 25, 1950–Jul 27, 1953)

Following World War II, the nation of Korea was divided into a communist north, supported by Russia and China, and a non-communist south, supported by the United States. Anti-communist fervor was rampant, and the infamous McCarthy era, wherein Wisconsin Republican Senator Joe McCarthy ruined lives and careers by accusing people of being communist, or communist 'sympathizers', was only a few years away.

The U.S., which worked to prevent any communist 'takeovers' in Europe under the Marshall Plan, was equally concerned about Asia. When Russia invaded Korea towards the end of World War II, the U.S. was concerned about it getting a foothold in that part of the world. This resulted in the division of the country into North Korea and South Korea.

Yet the Korean people were never all that thrilled with this arrangement, and border clashes were frequent. In June of 1950, North Korea invaded the South; the United Nations favored the South, with the U.S. as its principal supporter. China and Russia provided assistance to the North.

It wasn't difficult for the U.S. government to convince the populace, who feared there was a dreaded communist hiding under every bed, of the need to intervene.

The Korean War was the first 'limited' war of the now-globally-powerful United States. It was President Harry S. Truman who called it a 'police action'. During a press briefing, Truman was asked: "Mr. President, everybody is asking in this country, are we or are we not at war."[219] Truman responded directly and emphatically, saying, "We are not at war."[220] Another journalist, seeking a more substantial response, "prompted Truman with a trick that periodically worked at his press conferences: he put words in the president's mouth. Would it be correct, he asked, to refer to U.S. involvement in Korea as a police action under the UN? Truman's response: 'Yes, that is exactly what it amounts to.'"[221]

---

[219] Notes on Cabinet Meeting, July 8, 1950, box 1, Connelly Papers, HSTL, cited in Casey, *Selling the Korean War*, 372.
[220] Ibid.
[221] Ibid.

This didn't fully dispel the confusion about just what to call U.S. military involvement in Korea. The U.S. government and the media covering the war had difficulties on how to refer to it, possibly because 'war' was so much more dramatic than 'police action'. The latter could refer to the local police responding to a minor traffic accident down the block; who really cares about such an event? Some clarification was required.

Government officials saw the internal conflict not as a civil war, but as a salvo in the Cold War, with the ever-feared communist aggression rearing its ugly head. As indicated in the Connelly papers, there was much consternation "when [General Douglas] MacArthur's headquarters released a communiqué announcing that the United States was 'actively intervening in the Korean civil war'. In an effort to limit the damage, an exasperated State Department soon sent out clear instructions to every official stressing that 'labels can be terrifically important.' 'Wherever practicable,' PA [Public Affairs] advised, the terms 'North Korean invaders' or 'International Communist invaders' should be employed, rather than more neutral phrases like 'North Korean forces' and the 'Korean War.'"[222]

Truman made the announcement of war on June 27, 1950. The purpose, he said, was to assist the 'democratic' nation of South Korea to fend of the attack by the communist North. That the government of the South was not democratic, but a puppet regime installed by the U.S., wasn't mentioned. U.S. involvement, he stated, would help stem the spread of dreaded communism, the much-feared bugaboo that was now the U.S.'s chief enemy.[223]

Historian Steven Casey observed the U.S. need to control the war narrative: "In the first two weeks of the Korean War, [Secretary of State] Dean Acheson often fretted about the problem of how to dominate the domestic debate."[224] Because it was certain that the 'domestic debate' must be dominated by the powers that be; truth, often said to be the first casualty of war, did not live long once this particular war began.

So while U.S. soldiers were dying, to say nothing of North Korean men, women and children who would soon be slaughtered, U.S. officials were agonizing over how best to sell the war. Calling the North Koreans 'invaders' and linking them to communism, the government slowly took hold of the narrative.

---

[222]Ibid., 41–42.

[223]https://www.history.com/this-day-in-history/truman-orders-u-s-forces-to-korea-2. Accessed on May 12, 2018.

[224]Steven Casey, *Selling the Korean War: Propaganda, Politics, and Public Opinion in the United States, 1950-1953* (New York: Oxford University Press, 2008), 41.

U.S. leadership felt this was necessary for a variety of reasons. The U.S. citizenry seemed to vacillate between supporting disarmament, and wanting the U.S. to strike first before Russia struck the U.S. Remember, the Korean War was seen not as a civil war by the U.S., but as a proxy war between the U.S. and Russia.

Two events caused this dichotomy. Russia tested an A-bomb in September 1949, and in January 1950 Truman decided that the U.S. would build a 'super' H-bomb. Author Steven Casey reported the following: "In February and March, a number of senior Democrats had reacted to these disturbing developments by calling for disarmament. Although their intention had been to counter Soviet propaganda, the State Department had fretted that a complacent public, which had a 'false sense of security', might take such ideas [as disarmament] seriously."[225] Such notions must be countered: "Public Affairs had therefore started to contemplate a 'psychological scare campaign' to 'whip up sentiment', while Acheson had made a series of speeches widely viewed in the media as the 'toughest' of the Cold War and a firm riposte to all those who advocated a disarmament conference with the Soviet Union."[226]

The problem with using scare tactics was that some portions of the population were already in panic mode, fearing a disastrous conflict with the Soviets that would result in World War III, and wanting the U.S. to make the first strike, rather than waiting like sitting ducks for Russia to strike the U.S. These people were pushing for a larger war than the U.S. was willing to engage in in Korea. In a poll from the spring of 1950, 40% of respondents named war as their main concern. This was the highest percentage of people identifying war as their chief worry than at any time since the end of World War II. A relatively small number, 22%, expected the U.S. to be at war with the Soviets within one year, while 57% expected such a war within the next five years. Government officials feared that the public would push for a 'preventive' strike, rather than waiting to be bombed by the Soviets.[227]

During much of the war, "communist brutality against POWs had been a common refrain of administration propaganda. No less than a third of all reports issued by the UNC [United Nations Command] between July 1950 and October 1951 had contained some mention of savage communist acts."[228]

---

[225] Ibid., 32.

[226] Ibid.

[227] Ibid.

[228] Ibid., 280.

At different points during the war, the idea of creating a propaganda agency – as had been done in both World War I and World War II – was discussed but ultimately discarded. Truman believed "that a propaganda agency was a creature of total war".[229] Unless another all-out war was declared, such an agency, Truman thought, would not be appropriate.

Yet somehow government officials needed to be on the same page; too many conflicting reports of a war – or 'police action' – that was not going well were making major news. Philip Jessup from the State Department warned that "[t]he worst thing that could happen at this point was loose statements by government officials".[230]

Truman, like presidents before him and, to an even greater extent, those that came afterwards, issued a 'gag order', prohibiting all government officials from making any public statements about 'controversial' foreign policy issues. Additionally, all speeches needed to be cleared by his office in advance.[231]

The press was highly regulated, so many newspapers simply ran accounts by 'unnamed' sources, simply restating what U.S. officers told them.

Censorship was imposed in a number of ways. China entered the war in November of 1950, two months after the Inchon Harbor invasion, which was part of General Douglas MacArthur's 'Home by Christmas' campaign. The Inchon Harbor invasion had been a great victory for the U.S., but the glory didn't last long once China became involved. At that point, as historian Nancy Bernhard writes, "army-press tensions once again escalated. Criticism of the president and senior military staff mounted as the United Nations forces retreated to the Pusan perimeter on the southern tip of the Korean peninsula during the first two weeks of December".[232]

At this point, the 'need' for censorship increased: "Secretary of Defense George Marshall invited representatives of the three largest news services, The American Society of Newspaper Editors, and the BAC to the Pentagon to discuss 'the best means to handle news coverage of the combat zone to eliminate stories of value to the enemy'."[233] At a meeting on December 18, 1950, this group determined, dangerously, that "the security of information from the combat area is the responsibility of the

---

[229]Ibid., 217.

[230]Ibid.

[231]Ibid., 218–219.

[232]Nancy Bernhard, *U.S. Television News and Cold War Propaganda* (New York: Cambridge University Press, 1999), 107.

[233]Ibid.

military, not correspondents in the field, their editors, or their companies' executives."[234] Bernhard continues:

> Whether or not reporters found their jobs easier, the effect of formal censorship on war news was not to increase security but to give the military more control over content. The censors deleted not only military information that might compromise the war effort; they also excised 'comments indicating a low morale or poor efficiency on the part of United Nations troops,' the word 'retreat', and any information that would 'injure the morale of our forces' or 'embarrass the United States, its allies or neutral countries.' In a cold war, their reasoning went, security means eliminating not only classified information, but embarrassing information; in such a propaganda war, good morale is itself a victory as well as a means to victory.
>
> The threat of censorship, like the other threats that broadcasters faced during the war, was resolved by consultation rather than edict. But censorship, unlike financial hardship or government takeover, was enacted rather than averted.[235]

Discussion to end the conflict began as early as June of 1951, but dragged on since even the agenda couldn't be agreed upon. During this time, the Press Information Office (PIO) hesitated to release information, not wanting to build unrealistic public expectations. It also feared weakening the U.S. bargaining position. This didn't sit well with the press pool, who criticized the lack of information; some members of the press began obtaining information from the communist side, which enraged the PIO, which then accused some journalists of fraternizing with the enemy. This caused further hostility on the part of the press towards military public relations.[236]

One account quoted by Casey states "that the U.S. military peddled 'a mixture of lies, half-truths, and serious distortions'", and that when members of the news media protested this, "censorship at the peace talks became total."[237]

What was it that the United States population wasn't told?

According to Blaine Harden, author and former *Washington Post* reporter, more than half a million tons of bombs were dropped by the U.S. on North Korea. Napalm and chemical weapons were used. "'Although

---

[234]Ibid.

[235]Ibid., 109.

[236]Ibid., 273.

[237]Casey, *Selling the Korean War*, 280.

the ferocity of the bombing was recognised as racist and unjustified elsewhere in the world,' says Harden, for many Americans it was just another conflict in a distant and poorly understood country, he concludes. Not for nothing is it called the forgotten war."[238]

The head of the strategic air command during the Korean War was General Curtis LeMay. He estimated that the U.S. killed 20 per cent of the population. "We went over there and fought the war and eventually burned down every town in North Korea."[239]

This explains, to a great extent, the hostility that North Korea has for the U.S. today.

The false flag of a communist threat was raised to get a frightened population to support the 'conflict' in Korea. Censorship of the facts served to help the citizenry believe that the war was going well, despite the truth. And most Americans were unaware of the savage, unspeakable carnage that was being committed in their names.

---

[238]https://www.irishtimes.com/news/world/asia-pacific/unknown-to-most-americans
    -the-us-totally-destroyed-north-korea-once-before-1.3227633. Accessed on May 12,
    2018.
[239]Ibid.

Chapter 14: Lebanon (1958)

The U.S.'s first invasion of Lebanon, like all its invasions and 'interventions', was based on lies. In 1958, Lebanese President Camille Chamoun requested that the U.S. assist in putting down what he saw as a growing communist threat. Prime Minister Rashid Karami had not hidden his pro-Soviet leanings, even participating in the fortieth anniversary celebrations marking the Bolshevik Revolution. "President Chamoun, like virtually everyone at the time, believed that America was the premier force in the world offering opposition to communism, and so he appealed to us for help."[240]

In Iraq, King Faisal had recently been assassinated, and fear of a communist 'takeover' there was rampant. As a result of this instability in the Middle East, and Chamoun's request, the U.S. sent Marines to Lebanon. However, as is so often the case, the U.S. merely used the military as a smokescreen for its real goals. As John F. McManus, one of the Marines deployed to Lebanon at the time, said: "We were sent into action, yet none of the Marines and Army personnel who joined in that deployment had a clue about why we were in Lebanon."[241]

"At the height of the Cold War," Scott Lasensky and Kerem Levitas observe, "the United States consistently supported autocratic, albeit loyal regimes at the expense of potentially more moderate emerging leaders."[242] Lebanon was just one of the many countries so victimized by the U.S. The goal was always to prevent any possibility that the Soviets might exploit some political instability and install a pro-Soviet leader. It wasn't that the U.S. believed that the figures leading democratic rebellions were necessarily communist; simply that "American officials could not shake the fear that the nationalists would somehow advance the Soviet cause by breaking with the West".[243]

---

[240] John F. McManus, "Lebanon: A Case of U.S. Subversion," *The New American*, August 21, 2006, 44.

[241] Ibid.

[242] Scott Lasensky and Kerem Levitas, "Modern History and Politics: Crisis and Crossfire: The United States and the Middle East since 1945," *The Middle East Journal* 60, no. 3 (2006).

[243] Ibid.

The fact that the U.S. wasn't concerned about the will of the people, but merely wanted to assure that its own interests were met, is clear:

> Eisenhower dispatched the U.S. Marines to the country, ostensibly to maintain law and order but actually to prevent an array of leftist and Arab nationalist forces from threatening the rule of a very unpopular president. Although the Marines did not engage in battle and were quickly withdrawn, their presence sent a clear signal about U.S. support for the right-wing leadership in the country, led by the Maronite Christian establishment.[244]

Lebanon presented no threat to the U.S. in any way; there was no risk to U.S. security, and even the U.S.'s sacred economic interests were not in danger. But with the memory of the McCarthy witch hunts still fresh in the minds of government officials, and the U.S. citizenry seeing a communist hiding under every bed, those officials were happy to exploit those fears to maintain their power and influence in the Middle East.[245]

---

[244] As'ad AbuKhalil, "Lebanon: Key Battleground for Middle East Policy," *Foreign Policy in Focus*, February 2000.

[245] For information on the U.S.'s later interference in Lebanon, please see Chapter 19, Lebanon (1983–1984).

Chapter 15: The Vietnam War (Major U.S. involvement: 1964–1975)

The War in Vietnam took a toll in the U.S. that was unparalleled, but not in terms of the number of deaths. No, the biggest effect was in public attitudes, and an astonishing decrease in trust in the government. Never before had any war been met with so much opposition,[246] initially from university students, but eventually from housewives, unions, religious leaders, the media and finally, politicians. How the U.S. first became involved in Vietnam stems from the rabid fear of communism that the government had stoked completely out of proportion for generations, and which reached its peak during the disgraceful Congressional hearings chaired by Wisconsin Republican Senator Joseph McCarthy.

Vietnam had long been a colony of France, which France attempted to maintain with little success. The fact that the Vietnam situation was seen as part of the Cold War complicated matters.

In 1954, the Geneva Conference was held. The Chinese and Soviet allies of Vietnam feared that the U.S. would intervene militarily in Vietnam if, as Ho Chi Minh wanted, the country were to unify under a communist government. The Geneva Accords that resulted from this conference therefore established Vietnam as a nation divided north and south, with the communist DRV (Democratic Republic of Vietnam) government, led by Ho Chi Minh ruling the North, and Ngo Dinh Diem leading the U.S.-puppet government in the south. The U.S. had no strategic or significant commercial interest in Vietnam. But the frightening specter of communism, a specter long exaggerated and maintained by the U.S. government, had to be opposed wherever it appeared. No U.S. government official wanted to appear 'soft' on communism; such a charge assured electoral defeat. As a result, the U.S needed to prevent an ostensibly free South Vietnam (although run by a U.S. puppet) from reunifying with the communist North.

President Truman, once accused by Senator McCarthy of being 'soft' on communism, had first raised the alarm. His successor, President Dwight D.

---

[246]Donald R. Hickey, in his book, *The War of 1812: A Forgotten Conflict*, said that that war "generated more intense opposition than any other war in the nation's history, including the war in Vietnam," but that claim is open to question.

Eisenhower, monitored the situation, and sent thousands of 'advisers' to Vietnam, in violation of international law. His successor, President John F. Kennedy, sent four hundred Green Berets to teach counter-insurgency to the Vietnamese. As historian Howard Zinn stated:

> Under the Geneva Accords, the United States was permitted to have 685 military advisers in southern Vietnam. Eisenhower secretly sent several thousand. Under Kennedy, the figure rose to sixteen thousand, and some of them began to take part in combat operations. [South Vietnam's President Ngo Dinh] Diem was losing. Most of the South Vietnam countryside was now controlled by local villagers organized by the NLF [National Liberation Front, the Communist army in South Vietnam].[247]

When Kennedy became president, South Vietnam was under the control of Ngo Dinh Diem, first president of the Republic of Vietnam. The U.S. had been a strong supporter of the Diem government, but following the Vietnamese government's brutal response to a May 8, 1963, anti-government demonstration, when crowds were seeking government permission to commemorate Buddha's birthday, that changed.

On that day, government troops fired on unarmed, peaceful demonstrators, killing seven. The following day, 10,000 people demonstrated against the government, demanding that Buddhists be accorded the same rights as the devoutly Catholic Diem provided to Catholic citizens of South Vietnam. The crisis spread throughout the country and on June 11, a Buddhist monk named Quang Duc publicly burned himself to death in protest. This was the first in a series of self-immolations that focused world attention on Vietnam.

It's interesting to observe, once again, the influence of the press. As this is being written, Israeli soldiers are firing upon unarmed, peaceful Palestinian demonstrators commemorating Land Day, yet there is little press attention given to this situation. The press today, even more than in the years of the Vietnam War, is a tool of the government and special interest groups.

When U.S. diplomatic pressure to force Diem to provide some relief to those suffering under the oppressive policies of his government failed, a new course of action was formulated: "An August 24, 1963, cable from the State Department authorized the new ambassador, Henry Cabot Lodge, to indicate to Vietnamese military officers that the United States would

---

[247]Howard Zinn, *A People's History of the United States* (Harper Collins, 2003), 474.

support a successor regime emerging from a military coup against Diem. From that point, 'We [were] launched on a course of action from which there [was] no longer any respectable turning back, the overthrow of the Diem regime,' argued Lodge."[248] On November 1, 1963, Diem and his brother Nhu (who also served as his chief political advisor) were assassinated. While the U.S. had planned and supported the overthrow of this government, it had no idea of what would replace it.

After Diem's assassination, General Dương Văn Minh became president. He lasted three months, and was then overthrown by General Nguyễn Khánh. Although Phan Khắc Sửu was named head of state, power actually remained with Khánh and a junta of generals, who seldom were able to agree with each other.

With the chaos that began with the U.S.-backed overthrow of Diem, the U.S. gradually began increasing its presence in Vietnam. Following the assassination of President Kennedy, which occurred just three weeks after Diem's assassination, President Lyndon B. Johnson, also wanting to appear strong against communism, needed a reason to escalate the war. A new false flag had to be created, to entice the U.S. citizenry into yet another deadly military foray. Fortunately for the president, an opportunity soon presented itself.

Off the coast of China and northern Vietnam is the Gulf of Tonkin, which was the staging area for the U.S. Seventh Fleet in the early 1960s. On the evening of August 4, 1964, the U.S. destroyers *Maddox* and *C. Turner Joy* were in the Gulf, when the *Maddox*'s instruments indicated that the ship was under attack or had been attacked. Both ships began firing into the darkness, with support from U.S. warplanes. However, they "later decided they had been shooting at ghost images on their radar. ... The preponderance of the available evidence indicates there was no attack."[249]

But this non-event gave Congress the perfect ploy to escalate the war. It was presented to the world as an act of aggression against the U.S., and Congress quickly passed the Gulf of Tonkin resolution.

As historian of diplomacy Donald E. Schmidt wrote, when the Navy notified Washington that some naval vessels in the Gulf of Tonkin were being attacked,

---

[248]Ibid., 102.

[249]John Whiteclay Chambers, *The Oxford Companion to American Military History.* (New York: Oxford University Press, 1999). Chen Jian, *China's Road to the Korean War: The Making of the Sino-American Confrontation*, 151.

... the White House was ready and sprang immediately into action. Operation Pierce Arrow was the American response: sixty-four sorties from nearby aircraft carriers pounded North Vietnam that evening. Near midnight, when the retaliatory attack was concluded, President Johnson appeared on American television to announce that 'gunboats and certain supporting facilities in North Vietnam' had been attacked by American aircraft. A few days later a somber and better-informed Lyndon Johnson privately expressed disgust at the August 4 phantom attack: 'Hell, those dumb, stupid sailors were just shooting at flying fish.' But the deed had been done: the U.S. had attacked and killed North Vietnamese over a nonexistent attack on the Gulf of Tonkin. With that, the war began to escalate.[250]

The knowledge that no attack occurred didn't deter the war-planners in Washington. According to Gareth Porter, General Maxwell Taylor "called for exploiting 'any opportunities presented by the communists (such as Gulf of Tonkin attacks)' to help 'hold South Vietnam together' as well as to produce 'mounting pressures on the will of Hanoi.'"[251]

By the end of the following year, the number of U.S. soldiers invading Vietnam increased from 23,000 to 184,300. Eleven years later, with over 55,000 U.S. soldiers dead, hundreds of thousands wounded, and, by conservative estimates, 2,000,000 Vietnamese dead, the U.S. fled Vietnam in defeat.

In 2010, transcripts released by the Senate Foreign Relations Committee clearly demonstrate that several Senators and President Johnson knew that the event never happened, but wanted to conceal that fact from the citizenry. During an investigation by the Senate Foreign Relations Committee into the situation, the political 'need' to conceal the truth was evident. Senator Mike Mansfield, Democrat of Montana, stated, "You will give people who are not interested in facts a chance to exploit them and to magnify them out of all proportion."[252]

Senator Frank Church, Democrat of Idaho, stated:

... all I am cautioning us is this: let's be very careful before we take this into the open. We both understand that this is by far the most serious inquiry we have ever launched upon; and secondly, that we have the evidence that can substantiate the charge, and otherwise

---

[250]Donald E. Schmidt, *The Folly of War: American Foreign Policy, 1898-2005* (New York: Algora, 2005), 265.

[251]Gareth Porter, *Perils of Dominance: Imbalance of Power and the Road to War in Vietnam* (Berkeley, CA: University of California Press, 2005), 201.

[252]https://waylon1776.wordpress.com/tag/walter-cronkite/

we will discredit ourselves totally, and you can be sure that the big forces in this country that have most of the influence and run most of the newspapers and are oriented toward the presidency will lose no opportunity to thoroughly discredit this committee unless we have evidence.[253]

Once again, the power of '...the big forces in this country that...run most of the newspapers' is demonstrated. The much-vaunted freedom of the press in the U.S. is meaningless, when the largest news outlets are owned by corporate giants with their own, often deadly, agendas.

The U.S. government had reasons to invade Vietnam, but none of them were legitimate. This was known to policy-makers at the time, and was revealed to the U.S. citizenry decades after the fact. A deeply insecure president, combined with an irrational fear of communism, caused untold suffering in Vietnam, Cambodia and Thailand,[254] and protest and violence in the streets of the United States unlike anything that had been seen since the Great Depression. The Civil Rights marches may have been met with an equal amount of police violence, but in sheer numbers, those actively opposing the Vietnam War were greater.

---

[253]Ibid.

[254]The latter two countries were also bombed by the U.S. during the war; see Chapter 29.

Chapter 16: Dominican Republic (1965–1966)

U.S. involvement in the Dominican Republic dated back for decades (see Chapter 10: Dominican Republic). In 1930, Rafael Leonidas Trujillo Molino came to power following an election in which the official count of votes in his favor exceeded the total number of voters in the country. This was unimportant to the U.S., as historian Raymond Pulley reveals:

> In March 1930, the State Department informed its representative in Santo Domingo, Charles B. Curtis, that it expected 'to recognize Trujillo or any other person coming into office as a result of the coming elections and will maintain the most friendly relations with him ...' Even though the farcical nature of the election was known to the United States, Trujillo was accorded official recognition from America on the day of his inauguration, August 16.[255]

Although America is forever declaring itself a bastion of democracy, its leaders seem to believe that as long as a nation simply has elections – regardless of their legitimacy – it counts as a democracy.

If the stolen election wasn't sufficient to raise red flags for any other nation that believed in human rights and law, Trujillo quickly showed what kind of leader he was to be. As Pulley put it: "Through civil intimidation and political assassination, he quickly constructed one of the most cynical and brutal dictatorships of the twentieth century."[256] That this was known to U.S. government officials cannot be questioned. By 1936, various periodicals were openly criticizing him in the U.S., despite the very favorable articles in U.S. publications that Trujillo planted. Three critical reports are as follows:

- In February 1936, *Foreign Policy Reports* wrote this: Trujillo's "own force of character, his tactics of ruthless repression, combined with

---

[255]R. Pulley, "The United States and the Trujillo Dictatorship, 1933-1940: The High Price of Caribbean Stability," *Caribbean Studies* 5, no. 3 (1965), 22-31. Retrieved from http://www.jstor.org/stable/25611893.

[256]Ibid.

absolute control of all government patronage and appointments have made his influence supreme."[257]

- In June 1936, the *Review of Reviews* called Trujillo a "dusky despot" and commented that his "political opponents have a way of conveniently disappearing".

- In July 1936, *The Literary Digest* said, "he is a despot whose iron hand has wiped out opposition, clamped down on all freedom of press and speech and he has enriched himself by monopolizing the country's key industries".[258]

Despite this, there is no evidence that the Roosevelt administration ever protested Trujillo's barbaric practices. Perhaps this is because business with the tiny nation was so lucrative. According to Louis M. Vidal, Latin American representative of Trajewski-Pesant Steel Company at the time: "We have a staunch friend in the Dominican Republic, which makes 76% of all its foreign purchases in the United States."[259] What's a little oppression, torture and mass murder when there are such profits to be reaped?

When Trujillo visited the U.S. in July 1939, he was greeted by Roosevelt and his wife, accompanied on his tour of the nation's capital by American military officials and diplomats, and given the red-carpet treatment.

By 1940, the prominent journalist Alfred H. Sinks wrote this: "Here in ten years' time Rafeal Leonidas Trujillo has built the most thoroughgoing of all current dictatorships. It is an absolute monocracy with no democratic frills. The dark-hued Dominicans have considerably less liberty than Mussolini's or Hitler's subjects; their civil rights are approximately those enjoyed by inmates of a penitentiary under a particularly headstrong and unscrupulous warden".[260]

Why would the U.S., that self-proclaimed beacon of peace and freedom, support such a regime? The so-called 'Good Neighbor Policy' that Roosevelt initiated rejected protecting U.S. interests in Central America by means of armed intervention. In Trujillo, as with other dictators in the region, he had an ally who kept his country stable, encouraged trade with the U.S. and basically did as the U.S. demanded. "In other words," according to Pulley, "the Marines and intervention were replaced by a

---

[257]Ibid.
[258]Ibid.
[259]Ibid.
[260]Ibid.

home-grown dictator who based his power upon a Marine-trained constabulary force as a means of creating stability."

As is the case with most U.S.-supported dictators, this couldn't last forever, although he remained in power long enough to commit unspeakable atrocities. But in May 1961, Trujillo was assassinated by political rivals, leaving the nation in turmoil. Following a year and a half of chaos, Juan Bosch was elected, only to be overthrown in less than a year. He was succeeded by businessman Donald Reid Cabral, who was installed by conservative elements within the military. Eighteen months later, in April of 1965, he, too, was overthrown, setting the stage for a civil war between the so-called 'Constitutionalists', who worked for the return of Juan Bosch as president, and those who opposed him, known as the 'Loyalists'.

During this period, whenever the U.S. saw the possibility of its economic power or political influence threatened in any part of the world, the monster of communism was always raised. In this case it was no different, as military historian Lawrence Yates demonstrated:

> Officials at the American embassy in Santo Domingo had voiced strong concerns about 'extremist participation in [the] coup.' The revolt against Reid, they believed, represented not just an internal Dominican power struggle, but part of a Soviet and Cuban blueprint to promote instability and revolution in the Western Hemisphere.[261]

By April 26, 1,700 U.S. troops were positioned off the coast of the nation. The following day, they began evacuating U.S. citizens from the nation's capital.

Some context is necessary to understand the U.S. citizenry's acceptance of this action, and two points are important to consider. First, the U.S. government, represented by both major parties, has never fully recovered from the 'Red Scare' of the McCarthy era. During the early 1950s, Minnesota Senator Joseph McCarthy began accusing government officials and employees, along with writers, actors, producers and many others, of being communists. That designation inspired fear and hatred among the populace, coming so soon after World War II. Raising it during a civil war in the Dominican Republic was only natural, since the citizenry seemed to accept, if not welcome, any war or military intrusion that was meant to stop communism. Second, the world was becoming aware of Vietnam, where

---

[261]Lawrence A. Yates, "Intervention in the Dominican Republic 1965–1966," in *The Savage Wars of Peace: Toward a New Paradigm of Peace Operations*, edited by John T. Fishel (Boulder, CO: Westview Press, 1998), 136.

the U.S. was 'intervening', ostensibly to prevent a communist takeover of that nation.

The U.S. incursion into the Dominican Republic of 1965–1966 was one of its less deadly misadventures, considered a success by the U.S. government because a pro-U.S. government was installed. As Yates writes:

> The goal of U.S. policy during the intervention was to produce long-term stability in a non-communist Dominican Republic. By that standard, the intervention was a success, at least from Washington's perspective, even though no one then or today would claim that progress in the political arena was matched by similar breakthroughs in alleviating the country's social and economic problems.[262]

Once again, the U.S. sought for a political resolution with no regard for the needs of the people of the Dominican Republic.

---

[262]Ibid., 151.

Chapter 17: Angola (Sporadic U.S. involvement: 1975–2002)

The civil war in Angola began shortly after that nation gained its independence from Portugal in 1975. Prior to that, Angola was the richest of Portugal's colonies, with coffee, diamonds and iron ore its chief exports. Of the population of about 6.4 million people in 1974, there were 320,000 whites.

With its new independence, according to Robert Schmults, "Angola quickly became one of the hottest spots on the Cold War map. Fighting flared with varying intensity for the next 16 years between the U.S.-backed National Union for the Total Independence of Angola, UNITA, and the Soviet-supported government of the Popular Movement for the Liberation of Angola, the MPLA."[263] With UNITA support from South Africa, and MPLA support from Cuba, this became a proxy war between the U.S. and the Soviet Union.

After the collapse of the Portuguese dictatorship in 1974, a third rebel group – the Front for the Liberation of Angola (FNLA) – was led by Holden Roberto, in addition to the MPLA, led by Antonio Agostinho Neto, and UNITA, led by Jonas Savimbi.[264] An agreement reached between the outgoing Portuguese government and the three rebel groups for a transitional government that would rule Angola until official independence, to occur on November 11, 1975, was never fulfilled. In the spring of that year, civil war erupted. The U.S. supported both the FNLA and UNITA. According to professor of foreign policy Piero Gleijeses:

> Although U.S. officials knew that an MPLA victory would not threaten American strategic or economic interests, [Secretary of State Henry] Kissinger cast the struggle in stark Cold War terms: the freedom-loving FNLA and UNITA would defeat the Soviet-backed MPLA. He believed that success in Angola would provide a cheap boost to

[263] Robert C. Schmults, "Bloodshed and Blame in Angola," *Insight on the News*, March 1, 1993

[264] Inge Tvedten, *Angola: Struggle for Peace and Reconstruction* (Boulder, CO: Westview Press, 1997), 29.

U.S. prestige and to his own reputation, pummeled by the fall of South Vietnam a few months earlier.[265]

Soviet aid was limited, but the MPLA was winning the war; the CIA said it was because the MPLA was "more effective, better educated, better trained, and better motivated".[266]

Seeing possible victory by the MPLA, the U.S. urged South Africa to intervene, which it did. The South African government opposed the MPLA because of the group's strong opposition to apartheid. On November 4, just a week prior to what would have been Angola's independence day, Cuba, in response to MPLA requests, sent troops and halted the South African attack.

At this point, U.S. lying and propaganda went into overdrive. Not wanting to be seen as interfering in Angola's internal affairs, and certainly not wanting to be associated with such an ignominious defeat, Washington "claimed, loudly, that it had nothing to do with the South Africans, and it condemned their intervention in Angola."[267] With this betrayal by the U.S., in addition to now being seen around the world as aggressors and facing increasing numbers of Cuban soldiers, the last of the South African troops departed Angola on March 27, 1976.[268]

The U.S. then raised the time-tested and time-honored cry of the communist 'threat', declaring that Cuban soldiers were mercenaries sent by Moscow. But even this fantasy could not last. As Gleijeses points out:

> Even Kissinger was forced to reconsider. 'At the time we thought he [Castro] was operating as a Soviet surrogate,' he writes in his memoirs. 'We could not imagine that he would act so provocatively so far from home unless he was pressured by Moscow to repay the Soviet Union for its military and economic support. Evidence now available suggests that the opposite was the case.'[269]

U.S. intervention and involvement in Angola isn't well-publicized, or much discussed, today. Africa scholar Elaine Windrich writes:

> Although much of that war remains shrouded in secrecy, at least one aspect is open to investigation, and that is the media's coverage of

---

[265]Piero Gleijeses, *Visions of Freedom: Havana, Washington, Pretoria and the Struggle for Southern Africa, 1976-1991* (Chapel Hill, NC: University of North Carolina Press, 2013), 28.

[266]Ibid., 28-29.

[267]Ibid., 29

[268]Ibid., 29.

[269]Ibid., 20, citing Kissinger, *Years,* 816.

it. What the American public knows about Savimbi and his war to overthrow a government recognized by the entire international community (with the exception of the United States and South Africa) is what they read in their newspapers, hear on their radios and see on their televisions. But this 'information' has all too often been derived from official sources, either spokesmen for the Reagan/Bush administrations or agents of the Pretoria regime, both of which have a vested interest in promoting Savimbi's cause.[270]

One of the many propaganda tools the U.S. uses is the elevation of some brutal thug or 'rebel' leader to the status of freedom fighter. In Angola, that person was Jonas Savimbi, the leader of UNITA. "The image of Jonas Savimbi as a 'freedom fighter' deserving of U.S. support," writes Windrich, "was largely a product of the publicity efforts of the Pretoria regime and American right-wing pressure groups that had unique access to the Reagan/Bush White House."[271] On December 13, 1985, Richard Cohen of the *Washington Post* wrote that "Savimbi is a pariah in black Africa – the continent's Number 1 Uncle Tom."[272]

The South African government worked tirelessly to promote Savimbi's image in the United States. South Africa's goal was, quite simply, the destabilization of the MPLA-led Angolan government, which was assisting guerrillas of the South West African People's Organization (SWAPO), who were fighting for Nambian independence.[273]

The U.S. was a willing partner in elevating Savimbi to the level of freedom fighter. It had backed UNITA and the FNLA in the civil war, and had been defeated, mainly because of assistance provided to Angola by Castro. This had to be put off until Reagan's election, according to Windrich, "because the revelation of American involvement in a secret war on the side of an apartheid regime prompted the U.S. Congress to enact legislation (known as the Clark Amendment) to prohibit any further covert military operations in Angola".[274] However, according to Schmults, during the Reagan administration, "UNITA and its leader, Jonas Savimbi, won prominence as a success story for the Reagan Doctrine of arming anti-Soviet insurgencies around the world".[275]

---

[270] Elaine Windrich, *The Cold War Guerrilla: Jonas Savimbi, the U. S. Media, and the Angolan War* (New York: Greenwood Press, 1992), ix.

[271] Ibid., 1.

[272] Ibid.

[273] Ibid.

[274] Ibid., 1–2.

[275] Schmults, "Bloodshed."

The U.S. and its ever-compliant media overlooked Savimbi's brutality. Windrich writes that during a visit to the U.S., where he was feted by the top echelons of government, including President George Bush,

> ... a report appeared in the *New York Times* indicating that UNITA forces had been escalating their attacks on civilian targets in government-controlled areas. Ironically, the date of the attack that was reported was September 17, the day on which the State Department had issued its statement of unqualified support for Savimbi's position at the Kinshasa summit he refused to attend. Nevertheless, the report provoked no adverse comment about his intentions, despite the evidence it provided of his blatant disregard for the cease-fire that he had so recently reaffirmed in Pretoria. One reason for this failure to make an impact was that while the report was about a specific incident of UNITA brutality against civilians – with survivors speaking of fleeing villagers shot in the back or hacked to death; children, the elderly and the blind massacred; and houses, shops, farm equipment and a medical clinic destroyed – [*New York Times* reporter] Kenneth Noble apparently felt that he had to generalize such violence in order to 'balance' his dispatch. The obvious effect of this approach was to let UNITA off the hook by equating its atrocities with similar (but unspecified and undocumented) abuses by MPLA forces. 'Both sides have been accused of periodically sweeping through remote towns,' he wrote, 'sometimes killing and kidnapping as they rampage'.[276]

The U.S. used the false flag of a possible communist 'takeover' to intervene in Angola, despite the fact that the MPLA was winning elections and had the backing of at least a plurality of Angolans. U.S. government officials praised a brutal, murderous rebel leader, and provided him with funding, all the while portraying him as an anti-communist hero of the people.

U.S. spokespeople didn't hesitate to lie about U.S. involvement, as indicated in documents declassified in 2002. According to the *New York Times*:

> Historians and former diplomats who have studied the documents say they show conclusively that the United States intervened in Angola weeks before the arrival of any Cubans, not afterward as Washington claimed. Moreover, though a connection between Washington and South Africa, which was then ruled by a white government

---

[276]Windrich, *Cold War*, 135.

under the apartheid policy, was strongly denied at the time, the documents appear to demonstrate their broad collaboration.[277]

The Angolan civil war lasted 27 years; how much shorter it would have been had the Angolan people been left alone by the U.S. to manage their own affairs can only be guessed. During that time, at least 500,000 people died as a result of the conflict. Problems resulting from the war persist, as a 2017 article in the *New York Times* explained: "Fifteen years after the end of one of Africa's longest wars, Angola remains one of the world's most heavily mined countries. Swaths of Angola are still littered with land mines, some produced decades ago in countries that no longer exist."[278]

The U.S. intervened in Angola partly to erase the sting of the defeat in Vietnam, partly to prevent a communist government from taking hold, and partly to diminish Soviet influence on the African continent. Never were the genuine concerns of the Angolan people considered.

---

[277] https://www.nytimes.com/2002/03/31/world/from-old-files-a-new-story-of-us-role-in-angolan-war.html
[278] https://www.nytimes.com/2017/04/26/world/africa/angola-land-mines.html.

Chapter 18: Nicaragua (1978–1986)

Following World War II, the U.S. populace was terrified of the idea that communists – the 'Red Menace' – might somehow overtake the government and force the American people into the kinds of horrors experienced in the Soviet Union during the heights of the Revolution or the Great Terror. The government shared and fostered this belief and used its power to thwart any people's movement anywhere on the planet that seemed to lean too far to the left of the U.S.'s tastes. Nicaragua in the 1970s and 1980s was one such country.

The Somoza family had been in power since the 1930s, and with U.S. assistance had become increasingly powerful. As is generally the case when a right-wing government is backed by the U.S., the people of the country were deprived of the wealth and luxury that the rulers enjoyed.

During the 1970s, Anastasio Somoza was the 'president' of Nicaragua, although in actuality he was its dictator. As opposition to his regime grew, he took matters into his hands to continue it: with his four-year term ending in 1971, he amended the constitution to extend it for a year. As opposition increased he negotiated an agreement with opposition members in his own party and external to it, installing a three-member junta that would rule the nation until 1974.[279]

An example from his time as president/dictator is instructive.

In 1972, an earthquake devastated Managua, the nation's capital, killing at least 10,000 people. As political scientist Brian Meeks put it, "Somoza used state power and privilege to buy damaged and destroyed plants and businesses at bargain-basement prices."[280] In order to maintain the loyalty of his National Guard, he offered Guard's members "a stake in the numerous possibilities for fraud and profit offered by the earthquake," writes Nicaraguan intellectual and former vice president Sergio Ramirez. "Guard officers and men were involved in selling 'free' aid and supplies at

---

[279] http://countrystudies.us/nicaragua/11.htm. Accessed on November 30, 2018.

[280] Brian Meeks, *Caribbean Revolutions and Revolutionary Theory: An Assessment of Cuba, Nicaragua and Grenada* (Barbados: University of the West Indies Press, 2001), 98.

exorbitant prices on the black market and exercised increasing brutality against the displaced persons."[281]

Conditions in Nicaragua continued to be difficult for the average person not benefiting from the advantages of a connection to the Somoza family, and this began to plant the seeds of revolution. The brutality of the government left the population in constant fear. One example from Meeks:

> After the December 1974 raid on the house of Somoza *confidante* Chema Castillo which led to, among other things, a U.S. $2 million ransom, and the release of political prisoners, Somoza imposed a 33-month state of siege. The brutality unleashed in this period, more than any other action, served to secure popular resentment against the regime. Napalm and defoliants were used to track down and eliminate the FSLN [Frente Sandinista de Liberación Nacional, or Sandinista National Liberation Front] militants, peasant huts were burnt and an estimated 3,000 people killed during the period of the state of siege.[282]

Further increasing the anger of the people were the actions of the Guard, who, "isolated from the people and directly responsible only to their leader, did not hesitate ... to commit openly genocidal acts".[283] Such atrocities were common.

But Somoza did as the U.S. directed, and his extreme right wing government was acceptable to the U.S., human-rights abuses notwithstanding. When the revolution began in 1978, the U.S. government felt the need to intervene, lest the will of the people become the law of the land. Thus began one of the U.S.'s many secret and illegal covert actions, one of the few that was exposed as it was ongoing.

The U.S. opposed the revolution from the beginning, supporting the 'Contras'. Historian Roger Peace writes:

> Soon after the revolution, scattered groups of former National Guardsmen of the deposed Somoza government began to form guerrilla units under the guidance of Argentine advisors. The Central Intelligence Agency (CIA) began working with these contra-revolucionarios, or Contras, in early 1981 and assumed full control the following year. Operating out of bases in Honduras, Costa Rica,

---

[281] George Black, *Triumph of the People: The Sandinista Revolution in Nicaragua*, 1981, 5. Black's quotation is from Sergio Ramirez, *El Pensamiento Vivo de Sandino* (San Jose: EDUCA, 1980), vii.

[282] Meeks, *Caribbean Revolutions*, 100.

[283] Ibid.

and within Nicaragua, the Contras destroyed economic assets, attacked rural villages, kidnapped young men and killed thousands of civilians deemed pro-Sandinista.

The CIA, in addition to training, arming, and directing the Contras, conducted military actions on its own, including aerial raids against military bases and oil storage tanks, and the mining of Nicaraguan harbors in early 1984. The Reagan administration also blocked international loans to Nicaragua, imposed an economic embargo against Nicaragua in May 1985, subsidized internal opposition groups besides the Contras, sidestepped peace initiatives promoted by Latin American leaders, ignored a World Court decision in 1986 that ruled U.S. actions against Nicaragua illegal, and created a special agency, the Office of Public Diplomacy, to win U.S. public and Congressional support for its policies. This agency was shut down by Congress in 1987 after the General Accounting Office found it had engaged 'in prohibited, covert propaganda activities designed to influence the media and the public to support the Administration's Latin American policies'.[284]

In order to finance these policies and keep them from government oversight, the Reagan Administration violated U.S. law by selling weapons to Iran and funnelling the proceeds towards its illegal activities in Nicaragua. The exposure of these arms sales resulted in the Iran-Contra Affair, which was the subject of Congressional hearings and ended the career of some top administration officials.

What wasn't known then, but discovered much later, was how the CIA used drug addicts' need for more drugs in the U.S. to finance its activities in Nicaragua:

> *San Jose Mercury News* reporter Gary Webb has detailed a disgraceful alliance of drug dealers, Los Angeles youth gangs and the CIA operatives who backed the Nicaraguan Contras. For almost a decade, beginning in the early 1980s, a drug ring based in the San Francisco Bay Area sold thousands of pounds of cut-rate cocaine to Los Angeles street gangs and used the money to buy arms for the Contras, the so-called freedom fighters that Lt. Col. Oliver North all but canonized during the Reagan administration.[285]

North's career was one of the victims of his own schemes.

---

[284] Roger Peace, "The Anti-Contra-War Campaign: Organizational Dynamics of a Decentralized Movement," *International Journal of Peace Studies* 13, no. 1 (2008).

[285] "On CIA, Once More: 'Abolish the Damned Thing'" (Editorial), *National Catholic Reporter*, September 6, 1996, 2.

Eventually, in 1990, in elections judged to be fairly legitimate, the United Nicaraguan Opposition, a party much more pleasing to the U.S., came to power.

But at what price? During the eight years of the Contra war against the people of Nicaragua, at least 30,000 Nicaraguans died; thousands more were maimed and wounded. An estimated 350,000 were displaced, and the economic loss was over $9 billion.[286]

---

[286]Peace, "Anti-Contra-War Campaign".

Chapter 19: Lebanon (1983–1984)

The U.S. invasion of Lebanon resulted from the June 1982 Israeli invasion. The goal of Israel's incursion into Lebanon was to eliminate PLO (Palestine Liberation Organization) members from that country. But there was no reason for Israel to attack Lebanon. Israeli claims of eliminating Palestinian 'terrorist' attacks were disingenuous; "there had been no Palestinian-inflicted Israeli deaths in the Galilee for nearly a year".[287] The entire exercise was designed to strengthen Israel's illegal hold over the Galilee area. As John H. Kelly put it at a RAND conference in 1995, "Amidst a great international furor, the scene was set for a Western military intervention."[288]

Following the Israeli invasion, the U.S., under President Ronald Reagan, blocked United Nations efforts to stop the fighting. At the same time, the U.S. increased "military assistance to Israeli forces even as civilian casualties escalated into the tens of thousands," according to foreign policy expert As'ad AbuKhalil. "Under Israeli guns, the Lebanese parliament elected Bachir Gemayal, leader of the fascist Phalangist militia, as the new president. He was assassinated soon afterward and was succeeded by his brother Amin."[289]

Although the U.S. government, under Reagan, neither encouraged nor discouraged this invasion, the extreme brutality of Israeli actions eventually caused them to oppose it. Initially only to 'protect' Israel's borders, Israeli forces quickly moved into Beirut. As author Ralph A. Hallenbeck said:

> The tactic was incredibly lethal, devastating to the Lebanese towns and civilian population, but militarily successful. Within four days the Israeli Army had reached Beirut, having had 107 Israeli soldiers

---

[287] http://www.isreview.org/issues/50/Lebanon1982.shtml. Accessed on Oct. 28, 2018.

[288] John H. Kelly, "Lebanon: 1982-1984," in *U.S. and Russian Policymaking With Respect to the Use of Force*, edited by Jeremy R. Azrael and Emil A. Payin (RAND Corporation, 1996), https://www.rand.org/pubs/conf_proceedings/CF129/CF-129-chapter6.html.

[289] As'ad AbuKhalil, "Lebanon: Key Battleground for Middle East Policy," *Foreign Policy in Focus*, February 2000.

killed, while purportedly killing more than 2,000 Palestinian guerrillas. On the other hand, it was estimated that approximately 15,000 Lebanese and Palestinian noncombatants also had been killed, and another 30,000 wounded by Israeli firepower.[290]

This level of carnage brought international outrage, and, as Hallenbeck also said: "Indeed, as the tolls of death and destruction rose, it became ever harder for U.S. leaders to ignore accusations of U.S. complicity as Israel's primary armorer and ally."[291]

As negotiation to end the conflict continued with little effect, a 'multinational force', ostensibly to stabilize the region, was suggested. President Ronald Reagan announced that he had "agreed in principle to contribute a small contingent of U.S. personnel subject to certain [unspecified] conditions."[292] He emphasized that his goal in doing so was in conformity with the goals of the multinational force: to bring stability to the Middle East. This goal was not met.

In order to attempt to regain some semblance of order, "U.S. troops moved into Beirut to help in the evacuation of Palestinian forces, but the Americans exited prior to an Israeli-facilitated Phalangist massacre of thousands of Palestinian refugees".[293] In one of the most shocking war crimes committed by Israel and condoned by the U.S., thousands of Palestinian refugees were herded into an enclosure, disarmed and slaughtered by Israelis at the Sabra and Shatila refugee camps. Between 2,000 and 3,000 Palestinian men, women and children were killed. Israel targeted these camps after 8,300 Palestinian fighters had been granted free passage out of Lebanon. Once they were gone, Israeli forces entered the refugee camps and slaughtered the remaining residents, mostly women and children. Hadas Thier writes that after the exit of PLO fighters, around 3,000 Palestinian civilians were killed in three days. He quotes the following reports:

> At the massacre's end 'lamenting relatives and Red Cross workers ... covered their faces against the odor of death as they unearthed several hundred corpses and parts of bodies that had been bulldozed

---

[290]Ralph A. Hallenbeck, *Military Force as an Instrument of U.S. Foreign Policy: Intervention in Lebanon, August 1982-February 1984* (New York: Praeger Publishers, 1991), 6.

[291]Ibid., 9.

[292]Ibid., citing *Weekly Compilation of Presidential Documents*, July 12, 1982, 876.

[293]Ibid.

into hasty graves.'[294] Two Israeli reporters gave the following description:

"In addition to the wholesale slaughter of families, the Phalangists
indulged in such sadistic horrors as hanging live grenades around
their victims' necks. In one particularly vicious act of barbarity, an
infant was trampled to death by a man wearing spiked shoes. The
entire Phalangist action in Sabra and Shatila seemed to be directed
against civilians....

We have had many accounts of women raped, pregnant women, their
fetuses cut out afterward, women with hands chopped off, earrings
pulled."[295]

Israel's own investigation into the war, the Winograd commission, was
harshly critical of the government. In commenting on the investigation's
findings in 2007, Stephen Zunes said that the report "is indicative of how,
despite years of military occupations and war crimes against its neighbors
by successive governments, as well as the systemic discrimination against
the country's Arab minority, Israeli democracy is strong enough to allow
for a rigorous investigation of their leaders' decision to launch an unnecessary and self-defeating war".[296] (Such sporadic "democratic" practices
have long since disappeared by this writing.)

The war, according to Thier, "resulted in thirty to forty thousand Palestinian and Lebanese deaths, with a hundred thousand seriously wounded,
and half a million made homeless."[297]

When sending U.S. soldiers to Lebanon, President Reagan told the press
on September 28: "And the Marines are going in there into a situation
with a definite understanding as to what we're supposed to do."[298] The
soldiers, however, reported that they had no idea why they were there.

They sent us to Beirut

To be targets who could not shoot.

Friends will die into an early grave,

---

[294] David Shipler, "The massacre brings on a crisis of faith for Israelis; mourning, anger,
and moral outrage," *New York Times*, September 26, 1982, quoted from http://ww
w.isreview.org/issues/50/Lebanon1982.shtml. Accessed on Oct. 28, 2018.

[295] Ze'ev Schiff and Ehud Ya'ari, *Israel's Lebanon War*, edited and translated by Ina
Friedman (New York: Simon and Schuster, 1984), 118–19. http://www.isreview.o
rg/issues/50/Lebanon1982.shtml.

[296] Stephen Zunes, "U.S. Role in Lebanon Debacle," *Foreign Policy in Focus*, May 18,
2007.

[297] http://www.isreview.org/issues/50/Lebanon1982.shtml.

[298] Ibid., citing Department of State *Bulletin*, July 1982, 55-56.

Was there any reason for what they gave?[299]

This short poem, written by an unknown soldier on the door of an underground bunker, was well known by many of the U.S. soldiers there.

A year after the invasion, several Marines were interviewed about their experiences in Lebanon for the *New York Times*: "The Marines spent a total of 533 days in Beirut, suffered 240 deaths and more than 130 wounded and accomplished virtually nothing. It wasn't a group of radical students at Berkeley who were passing that harsh verdict, nor revisionist historians come to look at the record anew. It was the Marines themselves."[300]

The result of the war was the exact opposite of what the U.S. wanted: hostility toward Israel and the United States increased greatly in Lebanon.

Two questions arise, as they always do when the U.S. 'intervenes' in any other nation: 1) What was the stated reason for the intervention?, and 2) what was the real reason?

Following the savage Israeli invasion, the world was shocked by the carnage, and the U.S. sent soldiers ostensibly to protect the innocent. They were given instructions not to engage in combat, but could 'defend' themselves if required. This was the official reason.

As for the reality, the U.S. simply attempted to maintain or install a government that would do U.S. bidding, using as a template the 'successful' model of the 1958 invasion. The will of the people of Lebanon was never a consideration.

Richard Armitage, later Deputy Secretary of State, commented on what the attack, so strongly pushed for by the U.S., achieved: "The only thing that the bombing has achieved ... is to unite the population against the Israelis".[301]

Once again, the U.S. sacrificed the lives of thousands of innocent people to further its own geopolitical goals. And once again, even those disgraceful goals were not achieved.

---

[299]https://www.nytimes.com/1984/04/08/magazine/america-s-failure-in-lebanon.htm l. Accessed on October 29,2018.
[300]Ibid.
[301]Zunes, "U.S. Role in Lebanon".

Chapter 20: Grenada (October–November 1983)

One might well wonder what caused the mighty United States to invade Grenada in 1983. The country is the size of Philadelphia, with a population roughly that of Dayton, Ohio.[302] But unusual is the country, regardless of size, demographics or geographical position, in which the U.S. doesn't have its imperialistic finger. Grenada was no exception.

Conservative politicians, now in power in Washington, D.C., were anxious to show U.S. strength following the defeat nine years earlier in Vietnam, as the liberals had done just years before in Angola. With no real opportunity to do so presenting itself, it was time to raise yet another false flag.

Grenada was ruled for years by Prime Minister Sir Eric Gairy, a brutal and corrupt leader. Under his rule, "Grenadians witnessed decades of corruption and bribery," writes Anne Marie Davis. "Furthermore, Gairy terrorized the people through the use of his 'Mongoose Gang' and 'Night Ambush Squad' to suppress any internal dissent."[303]

Oppression of any opposition to Gairy's rule was strong. These included:

- Banning any published material that was critical of the Gairy government; this resulted from the Newspaper Act of 1975;

- The Essential Services Act of 1978, which prohibited workers from striking; and

- The Public Order Act of 1978, which made it illegal for opposition parties to use loud speakers without police protection.[304]

---

[302] http://historybuff.com/that-time-united-states-valiantly-stopped-threat-from-grenada-1-2VwZqngyd4G6 (accessed on September 1, 2017).

[303] Anne Marie Davis, "United States Foreign Policy Objectives and Grenada's Territorial Integrity," *The Journal of Negro History* 79, no. 1 (1994), http://www.questia.com/read/1G1-17311110/united-states-foreign-policy-objectives-and-grenada-s.

[304] Ibid.

Gairy's government and his dreaded secret police suppressed internal dissent, and were supported by Chile's Augusto Pinochet, the brutal dictator put in power and completely supported by the U.S.

Despite the U.S.'s frequent proclamations that it supports the human rights struggles of people around the world, it never objected to Gairy's repression and brutality, perhaps because Gairy supported U.S. foreign policy objectives in the Caribbean.

In 1979, when Gairy was out of the country, his government was overthrown and he was replaced by Maurice Bishop. The U.S., under the watchful, anti-communist eye of President Ronald Reagan, observed this development carefully. Bishop had definite communist sympathies, and Reagan saw the possibility of Russia getting a stronger foothold in the Caribbean. Cuba was working with the Bishop government to improve health care, and new schools, hospitals and roads, all desperately needed, were being constructed with Soviet aid.

But all was not well within Bishop's circle, and in 1983 he was overthrown by members of his own government. The new leadership was even more 'communist-leaning' than Bishop. This, in the view of the U.S., simply could not be allowed. Yet there seemed no legitimate reason to invade.

With a population of just around 100,000, and no military strength to speak of, Grenada couldn't be seen as a threat to the U.S.'s 'national security.' Neither could atrocities against the Grenadian people be believably invented; the government had been building roads, hospitals and schools, and was more than likely to continue to do so under the new government.

But the creative minds of the U.S. public relations department apparently worked overtime, and finally came up with something. There were, studying in Grenada, about 800 U.S. medical students, and Reagan claimed that they needed protection in the volatile atmosphere of the revolution. But even this wasn't so simple, as Stephen Zunes points out:

> Grenadian and Cuban officials had met only days earlier with administrators of the American medical school and guaranteed the students' safety. Urgent requests by the State Department's Milan Bish to medical school officials that they publicly request U.S. military intervention to protect the students were refused. Five hundred parents of the medical students cabled President Reagan to insist he not take any 'precipitous action'. Staff members from the U.S. embassy in Barbados visited Grenada and saw no need to evacuate the students.[305]

---

[305]https://www.globalpolicy.org/component/content/article/155/25966.html.

It wasn't only Grenadian and Cuban officials, medical school officials, embassy staff members and parents who didn't feel that the students' safety was in jeopardy: "The medical school's chancellor, Charles Modica, polled students and found that 90% did not want to be evacuated."[306] Following the invasion, he "angrily denounced the invasion as totally unnecessary and a far greater risk to the students' safety than Grenada's domestic crisis."[307]

Immediately prior to the invasion, the U.S. received a formal request from the Organisation of Eastern Caribbean States to protect the students. This request was supposed to have legitimized the invasion. However, as reported by the *New York Times* on October 29:

> The formal request that the U.S. and other friendly countries provide military help was made by the Organization of Eastern Caribbean States last Sunday at the request of the United States, which wanted to show proof that it had been requested to act under terms of that group's treaty. The wording of the formal request, however, was drafted in Washington and conveyed to the Caribbean leaders by special American emissaries. Both Cuba and Grenada, when they saw that American ships were headed for Grenada, sent urgent messages promising that American students were safe and urging that an invasion not occur.... There is no indication that the Administration made a determined effort to evacuate the Americans peacefully. ... Officials have acknowledged that there was no inclination to try to negotiate with the Grenadian authorities. ... 'We got there just in time,' the President said. ... A major point in the dispute is whether in fact the Americans on the island were in such danger as to warrant an invasion. No official has produced firm evidence that the Americans were being mistreated or that they would not be able to leave if they wanted.[308]

As mentioned above, government officials, starting with the president, wanted some show of military force.

> The real reason for the operation was Reagan's belief that the U.S. needed a victory—any victory, anywhere. After the United Nations passed a resolution condemning the invasion as a 'flagrant violation of international law,' he brushed it off by saying that the resolution 'didn't upset my breakfast at all.' Several members of Congress

---

[306] Ibid.

[307] Ibid.

[308] Paul F.J. Aranas, *Smokescreen: The US, NATO and the Illegitimate Use of Force* (New York: Algora, 2012), 46.

visited Grenada to bask in the glory, among them Rep. Dick Cheney of Wyoming, who said the invasion proved that the United States was once again 'steady and reliable.'

'Our days of weakness are over!' Reagan exulted in a speech to the Congressional Medal of Honor Society in New York. 'Our military forces are back on their feet and standing tall.'[309]

Two days after the invasion, a resolution denouncing it and demanding a withdrawal of all foreign forces was introduced to the United Nations Security Council. Eleven nations supported it, three abstained and the U.S. vetoed it.

Despite its assertion that U.S. medical students needed to be protected, the U.S. continued to find additional justification for the invasion. The Reagan administration proclaimed that it had evidence Grenada posed a serious threat to the national security of the U.S. According to scholar of international relations Paul Aranas, this included "previously unknown" documents "that showed Grenada had signed arms deals with the Soviet Union, Cuba, and North Korea":

> These deals referred to arms shipments of thousands of rifles, machine guns, and grenades. The U.S. media published the most 'incriminating' documents that it could find on the relationship between Grenada and Washington's adversaries. Former U.S. ambassador Sally Shelton referred to these documents as a 'public relations bonanza for the U.S. government'.[310]

Yet not all journalists bought in to this particular fairy tale. They questioned how serious a threat Grenada could be, "...citing that some of those weapons found by the U.S. military dated back to the nineteenth century; however, these handful of voices were drowned out by the mass media's proclamations that the United States had been victorious in stopping a Cuban and Soviet take-over of Grenada."[311]

These various justifications – protecting medical students, preventing a communist takeover of Grenada – "were trumpeted by an obedient mass media, with hardly a dissenting voice to be heard".[312]

As a result of this invasion, 19 U.S. soldiers were killed, along with 45 Grenadian and 24 Cuban soldiers. The invasion was condemned almost

---

[309]http://america.aljazeera.com/articles/2013/10/25/invasion-grenadaronaldreagan.html.

[310]Aranas, *Smokescreen*, 44.

[311]Ibid., 44–45.

[312]Ibid., 45.

universally. The U.N. General Assembly passed a motion condemning it by a vote of 109 in favor, ten against (Antigua and Barbuda, Barbados, Dominica, El Salvador, Israel, Jamaica, Saint Lucia, Saint Vincent, the Grenadines, and the United States) and 27 abstaining.

Once again, there was no reason for the invasion, but the U.S. had an ulterior motive. After the defeat in Vietnam, it had to show that it was 'standing tall' again. The fact that this resulted in the deaths of 98 people, was condemned by the international community and helped to increase hostility toward the U.S. was unimportant. The powers that run the U.S. wanted a victory, and so another false flag was sent to wave in the jingoistic breeze.

Chapter 21: Panama (1989–1990)

During the administrations of Reagan and Bush Sr., there was much talk of the nations of Latin America being 'democracies in jeopardy', because of drug trafficking and left-wing social movements. However, the U.S. defines nations as 'democratic' depending solely on those nations' adherence to U.S. dictates. Actual democratic processes are irrelevant. As Christina Jacqueline Johns and P. Ward Johnson write in their study of the media and the Panama invasion:

> Democracy means something more than the holding of regular elections, despite what the Reagan and Bush administrations categorically refused to acknowledge. The Reagan administration, in fact, conducted a concerted campaign to define democracy and human rights as almost exclusively the holding of regular elections. But it's easy to see the emptiness of show elections, characterized by massive fraud, in repressive countries considered by the Reagan and Bush administrations as budding democracies – countries such as El Salvador, Guatemala, and Honduras.[313]

Further, the U.S. has actually opposed democratic movements when they seem to be too far to the left, or if their leaders don't jump when the U.S. speaks; governments have been overthrown, with countless people killed due to U.S. efforts to thwart democracy. One Latin American example will suffice from Johns and Johnson (citing Noam Chomsky): "early efforts by the Sandinista government in Nicaragua [See Chapter 18] to provide resources to the impoverished minority of Nicaraguans, which would have allowed them to have genuine political participation, led Washington to initiate 'economic and ideological warfare, and outright terrorism'."[314]

The United States' association with Panama in the latter half of the twentieth century is complicated, corrupt and ugly. From 1983 to 1989 when he was overthrown, Gen. Manuel Noriega ran the country, having worked for years as a well-paid informant for the CIA: "[H]e worked with multiple U.S. intelligence agencies who agreed to ignore allegations that

---

[313]Christina Jacqueline Johns and P. Ward Johnson, *State Crime, the Media, and the Invasion of Panama* (Westport, CT: Praeger Publishers, 1994), 2.
[314]Ibid.

he was a drug trafficker in exchange for a staunch anti-communist ally in Central America during the height of the Cold War."[315] Noriega was paid handsomely for his help, "about $10,000 per month at one point".[316] He remained on the U.S. payroll from the late 1960s until February of 1989.[317]

Noriega knew a good thing when he saw it, and 'good' had nothing to do with the improvement of conditions for the people of the country he eventually came to rule. As the *Guardian* reported:

> Noriega made himself valuable to the US during the Contra wars when he allowed the US to set up listening posts in Panama and by helping the US campaign against the leftist Sandinista regime in Nicaragua. Noriega allowed Panama to be used as a conduit for US money and weapons for the Contras as then US president Ronald Reagan sought to undermine the Sandinistas.[318]

He met Bush on several occasions. He had worked, at least indirectly, with Lieutenant Colonel Oliver North, National Security Advisor John Poindexter, CIA chief William Casey and other top people in the Reagan administration "who, allegedly, connived in the supply of arms to Nicaragua's Contra rebels paid for with Medellín cartel drug cash."[319]

As Noriega eventually learned, nothing good lasts forever. By the end of the Reagan era, even Noriega's good friend, then vice-president and future president George Bush, had grown disillusioned. Yet it wasn't his cruelty and absolute power in Panama, or his drug-trafficking, that so offended the mighty United States. As mentioned above, Noriega had provided a 'listening post' for the U.S., spying on Guatemala, El Salvador and Honduras. He had too much embarrassing information on top U.S. officials to be the wild card in Latin America. Therefore, his overthrow was required.

In this case, the false flag was easy to raise. While the U.S. supported Noriega and his related atrocities, even financing them, the government always knew he was a notorious drug-dealer. That alone could be the

---

[315] https://abcnews.go.com/International/panamanian-dictator-manuel-noriegas-complex-us-ties-lessons/story?id=47722429. Accessed on August 27, 2018.

[316] Ibid.

[317] https://www.theguardian.com/world/2010/apr/27/manuel-noriega-us-friend-foe. Accessed on August 27, 2018.

[318] Ibid.

[319] https://www.theguardian.com/commentisfree/cifamerica/2010/apr/28/noriega-panama-france-america. Accessed on August 17, 2018.

reason for his overthrow. Prior to the decision to invade Panama, the Senate Committee on Foreign Relations concluded this:

> The saga of Panama's General Manuel Antonio Noriega represents one of the most serious foreign policy failures for the United States. Throughout the 1970s and 1980s, Noriega was able to manipulate U.S. policy towards his country, while skillfully accumulating near-absolute power in Panama.

> It is clear that each U.S. government agency which had a relationship with Noriega turned a blind eye to his corruption and drug dealing, even as he was emerging as a key player on behalf of the Medellin Cartel. (Committee on Foreign Relations 1988: 2-3).[320]

What Noriega's actual association with the Medellin Cartel was is not fully known. When tried in the U.S. on drug charges, it was "on 10 narrowly defined drug-related counts".[321] One would think that if he were as major a player in the Medellin Cartel as U.S. government spokespeople proclaimed, the charges could have been less 'narrowly defined.' But it was certainly in the U.S.'s interest to paint him as a notorious drug dealer.

Once again, the U.S. government successfully manipulated its citizenry to support yet another imperial invasion.

> What accounted for the success? First, through the propaganda technique of selection, the U.S. government carefully chose those 'facts' that supported its predetermined objective of removing General Manuel Noriega from power. Concomitantly, it concealed the information that would have undermined the veracity of its story: (1) the fact that Noriega was its Frankenstein monster; (2) its poor record on democracy in Panama; (3) the fact that there was no serious threat to American lives or interests; (4) the enormous human and material carnage occasioned by the invasion; and (5) the various violations of international law. Further, the traditional sources of public influence—the Democratic Party, major opposition party to the Republicans, and the American press—failed to provide competing perspectives. In fact, they joined the government's propaganda bandwagon. The result was that the American public be-

---

[320] John Hagan, *Who Are the Criminals?: The Politics of Crime Policy from the Age of Roosevelt to the Age of Reagan* (Princeton, NJ: Princeton University Press, 2010), 146-147.

[321] https://www.theguardian.com/commentisfree/cifamerica/2010/apr/28/noriega-panama-france-america. Accessed on January 23, 2019.

came convinced that the Bush administration's 'official story' was the truth.[322]

We will look at this in some detail.

The 'war on drugs', a trillion-dollar boondoggle that still wastes taxpayer money, was in full swing by the late 1980s. U.S. citizens were concerned as they saw drug abuse taking its toll in their homes and communities. The government used this concern and depicted Noriega as a Colombian drug cartel–connected narco-terrorist. As political scientist George Klay Kieh Jr. writes:

> [T]he American government, *vis* the various public opinion polls, was cognizant of the fact that the American people considered the drug trade to be the central threat to U.S. national security. The United States government reasoned that General Noriega, if perceived as a major drug lord, would be discredited in American public opinion; hence, the U.S. government would win domestic public support for the general's ouster.[323]

Following this, a grand jury in Miami indicted Noriega on various drug-related charges. The U.S. government then pressured the Panamanian president to dismiss Noriega from his role as Chief of the Panamanian Defense Forces (PDF). This had an unexpected impact: as a result, the Panamanian National Assembly dismissed President DelValle and placed Noriega back as head of the PDF.

Following this failure, the U.S. government told Noriega it would drop the drug charges if he gave up his position and left Panama; he refused. A second attempt by the Deputy Assistant Secretary of State, William Walker, had the same result. The U.S. then recalled its ambassador to Panama. Finally, the Reagan administration decided to use economic sanctions against Panama.

Months later, when President George Bush invaded Panama, the government's propaganda machine when into overdrive. It presented to the citizenry these reasons for the invasion, all of which resonated with U.S. citizens:

---

[322] https://www.tandfonline.com/doi/pdf/10.1080/10584609.1990.9962888. Accessed on August 27, 2018. Available at: https://www.researchgate.net/profile/George_Kieh/publication/232843572_Propaganda_and_United_States_foreign_policy_The_case_of_panama/links/596ce6afa6fdcc44f7d2f1f6/Propaganda-and-United-States-foreign-policy-The-case-of-panama.pdf

[323] Ibid.

- *The apprehension of General Noriega, allegedly a major player in the drug epidemic that was plaguing the U.S.*

The drug 'epidemic' had been discussed and promulgated for years; nearly everyone in the country knew someone who'd been arrested or was in some way troubled due to substance abuse.

- *The promotion of democracy in Panama.*

As already mentioned, U.S. public relations organizations proclaim the U.S. as a model democracy; spreading that 'democracy' to other nations, whether they want it or not, is a tried and true reason for U.S. invasions.

- *Protection of U.S. lives.*

Most citizens would consider it treason to suggest that the protection of U.S. lives is an inadequate reason for any invasion. It should be noted that "[o]n December 16, 1989, in an altercation involving Noriega's troops and U.S. military men, a U.S. marine was shot and killed in Panama City."[324] It should also be noted that the U.S. military had no business there in the first place. The invasion began four days later.

- *To protect the rights of the U.S. under the Panama Canal Treaty.*[325]

To say that these reasons only told half the story would be incorrect; they were barely considerations, if they were considered at all.

> ... the Bush administration deliberately withheld from the American public the real motives and underpinnings of the invasion and the general campaign to remove Noriega from power. This was done in several ways. First, the American people were never told about the long-time patron-client relationship between their government and General Noriega.
>
> [Noriega] was trained at the notorious U.S.-run School of the Americas for dictators and at various American military academies. In the 1960s, he was hired by the Central Intelligence Agency (CIA) as an informant. Based on his performance, the U.S. government helped to facilitate his rise to power.

---

[324]https://www.newyorker.com/news/daily-comment/manuel-noriega-a-thug-of-a-different-era, Accessed on August 28, 2018.
[325]Ibid.

Specifically, he performed the following functions: (1) provided the
United States with intelligence information on Cuba and Nicaragua;
(2) facilitated the holding of U.S.-sponsored military exercises in
the region, and (3) was pivotal to the U.S. government's proxy war
against Nicaragua [he provided training sites for the contras and
conduits for funneling money via dummy corporations that were established by then Lt. Col. Oliver North and his associates]. The
United States paid Noriega about $200,000 per annum for his ser-
vices, during the greater portion of the Reagan presidency.[326]

Noriega was arrested, sent to the U.S., and tried and convicted of many
drug-related charges. But it's significant that he was tried in the U.S. and
not Panama, although Panama demanded his return for trial there; the
U.S. government ignored that demand.

At his trial, none of Noriega's above-referenced, long-term employment
with the U.S. government was allowed as evidence. Also, according to the
Guardian:

Noriega claimed to have proof of senior US politicians' connivance
in drug trafficking for political purposes. But none was allowed in
evidence. In Panama, Noriega would have been free to tell all he
knew. And for many powerful men in Washington, some of whom
are still alive, that prospect was potentially dangerous. The outcome
of the Noriega case in Miami, like the 1989 invasion, was never in
doubt from day one. It was a show trial, a warning to others. It
was pure vengeance. It was a cover-up of decades of illicit regional
meddling. But it was also a demonstration of raw American power,
of which the world was soon to have more frightening examples.[327]

Journalist Edward S. Herman summarized U.S. military policy in the
1980s and early 1990s:

The Grenada and Panama invasions during the 1980s and the Gulf
War in 1991 were military successes, but disastrous media failures.
In part, the failures were a result of military restriction on access, but
the media did not react to these official constraints by more aggressive investigative and reporting efforts in areas open to them, nor
did they struggle very energetically to get the restraints removed. In
the cases of Grenada and Panama, once the great military triumphs
over two of the tiniest countries in the world were completed, and

---

[326] Kieh, tandfonline.com.
[327] https://www.theguardian.com/commentisfree/cifamerica/2010/apr/28/noriega-pan
ama-france-america. Accessed on August 28, 2018.

officials turned their attention elsewhere – the mainstream media dutifully did the same.[328]

Once again, the U.S. supported a cruel, oppressive dictator when it suited its imperial purposes to do so. And when that dictator ceased to be useful, he needed to be overthrown. The U.S. citizenry is mainly ignorant of the true motives in either supporting or opposing any particular world leader. But when Noriega fell into disfavor, his involvement in the international drug trade, fully condoned by the U.S. when he was useful to it, was raised as a false flag to justify the invasion of Panama. This is the repeating pattern in U.S. foreign policy.

---

[328] Edward S. Herman, "The Media's Role in U.S. Foreign Policy," *Journal of International Affairs* 47, no. 1 (1993).

Chapter 22: The Gulf War (Aug. 2, 1990 to Feb. 28, 1991)

The reasons for U.S. military aggression in the Middle East can always be traced to one of two sources, and often to both: Israel and oil. The Gulf War was fought mainly for oil. The U.S. has long had a 'complicated' relationship with Iraq; had they been a married couple, any counselor would have suggested divorce years earlier. But such a course of action would have deprived the U.S. of access to oil, so severing ties was not meant to be.

A look at the U.S.'s history in Iraq is telling. As early as 1958, the U.S. supported the regime of Abdel Karim Kassem, seeing him as a counter to Gamal Abdel Nasser of Egypt. However, by 1961, Kassem was attempting to build up armaments sufficient to rival Israel, and was talking of challenging U.S. dominance in the Middle East. The U.S. began efforts to undermine his government, including arming Kurdish rebels. In 1963, Kassem was overthrown and quickly executed.

For his replacement, the CIA looked into the anti-communist Arab Socialist Ba'ath Party, and worked closely with a 25-year-old party member named Saddam Hussein. The U.S. armed this new regime.

During the 1980s, the U.S. government, under President Ronald Reagan, supported Iraq in its war against Iran, even though it needed to remove Iraq from its list of 'state sponsors of terror' in order to do so (it had been so designated in 1979). This was done in 1982, opening the way for the Hughes Aircraft company to ship 60 Defender helicopters to Iraq later that year. In 1983, the Reagan administration allowed several of Iraq's neighboring countries to transfer U.S. weapons to Iraq, including Howitzers, Huey helicopters, and bombs. Early the next year, the U.S. confirmed the shipment of heavy trucks, armored ambulances and communications equipment to Iraq. Perhaps most shocking, between 1986 and 1989, the U.S. licensed 70 biological exports to Iraq, including at least 21 batches of lethal strains of anthrax. During that time the U.S. also approved shipments of chemicals to Iraq that are used in the manufacture of mustard gas.

It is worth noting here how a country receives the designation of 'state sponsor of terrorism.' According to the website of the U.S. Department of State, puzzlingly subtitled 'Diplomacy in Action,' this is how such a designation is determined: "Countries determined by the Secretary of State to have repeatedly provided support for acts of international terrorism are designated pursuant to three laws: section 6(j) of the Export Administration Act, section 40 of the Arms Export Control Act, and section 620A of the Foreign Assistance Act."[329] While the U.S. issues that designation quite subjectively, and doesn't care to see that the U.S. itself would be so designated by any independent observation, the fact is that no change in Iraq's policies enabled it to escape the 'state sponsor of terrorism' list, only its war with a nation that the U.S. fears even more.

To say that U.S. government policy is short-sighted is a major understatement. Author Grant Elder writes:

> A report on ABC Nightline news in June 1992 perhaps sums it all up very well: 'It is becoming increasingly clear that George Bush Sr., operating largely behind the scenes throughout the 1980's, initiated and supported much of the financing, intelligence, and military help that built Saddam's Iraq into [an aggressive power].'[330]

Iraq's war against Iran left it deeply in debt, mainly to Saudi Arabia and Kuwait, both of which refused to cancel the debt. By 1990, two years after the Iraq–Iran war, Iraq was unable to meet its international debts, and other nations stopped issuing credit to Iraq for any additional weaponry. By the middle of that year, inflation in Iraq was at 40%, and cash reserves could only cover the next three months of imports.

Iraqi leader Saddam Hussein also felt that Iraq was isolated in the Arab world, and sought a means to end that isolation. Kuwait, an oil-rich country on its border, may have been seen as the answer to many questions, as described by national security experts Anthony Cordesman and Abraham Wagner:

> Combining Kuwait's oil reserves with those of Iraq meant Iraq could become an oil power second only to Saudi Arabia and would give Iraq a decisive edge in 'oil power' over Iran. Seizing Kuwait also meant sending a signal to the Arab world and Iran that Iraq could safely ignore the U.S., other Western states and other Gulf powers

---

[329] https://www.state.gov/j/ct/list/c14151.htm. Referenced on April 2, 2018.
[330] Grant Elder, *Wiki vs NWO (New World Order): Moving to Collaboration from Domination* (Friesen Press, 2014), 163.

and take decisive unilateral action. It meant exposing the U.S. as a 'paper tiger' and greatly increasing Iraq's strategic leverage over the other southern Gulf and Arab states.[331]

Prior to the Iraqi invasion of Kuwait, Saddam Hussein met with U.S. ambassador to Iraq April Glaspie. International relations expert Miron Rezun writes: "Saddam's man in Washington was probably telling him that the United States had not sent troops when Turkey invaded Cyprus, it did not interfere when China invaded Tibet, nor did it intrude in force when the Soviet Union invaded Afghanistan. So there was no reason to worry; Saddam could stand tough with [U.S. President George] Bush's ambassador."[332]

As relations between Iraq and the U.S. deteriorated, Ambassador Glaspie met with Hussein to reassure him of continued, or at least potential, U.S. support: "She emphasised that President Bush had rejected the idea of trade sanctions against Iraq" and further told him that "I have a direct instruction from the President to seek better relations with Iraq."[333]

After trying to explain the importance of Iraq to the U.S., Ms. Glaspie said this: "I admire your extraordinary efforts to rebuild your country. I know you need funds. We understand that, and our opinion is that you should have the opportunity to rebuild your country. But we have no opinion on Arab-Arab conflicts like your border disagreement with Kuwait."[334] On August 2, 1990, Iraq invaded Kuwait, and within days, annexed it, with Hussein announcing Kuwait as Iraq's nineteenth province.

The importance of Kuwait to the United States cannot be doubted. In 1947, imports of crude oil to the U.S. were about 0.4 million barrels. According to economics Professor Vo Xuan Han, "in 1950, U.S. imports from the Middle East jumped to 41.6 million barrels, which was almost one-quarter of total U.S. crude imports. At the same time, U.S. Middle East imports came almost totally from Kuwait, the biggest supplier".[335]

This importance continued to grow, and President Jimmy Carter, in his State of the Union Address on January 23, 1980, affirmed that the U.S. was willing to go to war with Russia to protect the Gulf's vast oil sup-

---

[331] Anthony H. Cordesman and Abraham R. Wagner, *The Gulf War* (Westview Press, 1996), 37.

[332] Miron Rezun, *Saddam Hussein's Gulf Wars: Ambivalent Stakes in the Middle East* (Praeger, 1992), 61.

[333] Geoff Simons, *Iraq: From Sumner to Saddam* (Palgrave Macmillan, 1996), 349

[334] Ibid.

[335] Vo Xuan Han, *Oil, The Persian Gulf States, and the United States* (Palgrave Macmillan, 1994), 18.

ply. The Carter Doctrine indicated "that Soviet Action in Afghanistan was a prelude to further expansion southward into the Persian Gulf, and therefore a threat to the security of Western oil sources in the Arabian Peninsula."[336] It seems interesting that the U.S. would be willing to sacrifice American lives to protect the security of 'oil sources,' but at least, perhaps, Carter was being more honest than presidents that followed him. This doctrine, along with the Iraqi invasion of Kuwait and the U.S.'s involvement in that war, indicate the importance that the U.S. and other industrialized countries give to the idea of global 'oil security.'

While the U.S. needed, and continues to need, more oil than the rest of the world in order to operate, an invasion of Kuwait by Iraq was not something the citizenry was particularly incensed about. In order to gain support for the war, Congress and President Bush relied heavily on what is commonly referred to as the Nayirah testimony. On October 10, 1990, a 15-year-old girl referred to only as "Nayirah," who claimed to have been a hospital volunteer, tearfully testified of seeing babies dumped by Iraqi soldiers from hospital incubators. She stated:

> I volunteered at the al-Addan hospital with twelve other women who wanted to help as well. I was the youngest volunteer. The other women were from twenty to thirty years old. While I was there, I saw the Iraqi soldiers come into the hospital with guns. They took the babies out of the incubators, took the incubators and left the children to die on the cold floor. It was horrifying.[337]

This, in the eyes of Congress and the president, highlighted the monstrosity of Iraq, and was widely used to gain support for the war. Five months after the Iraqi invasion of Kuwait, and three months after the 'Nayirah' testimony, the U.S. entered the war.

However, like nearly all of the information the government feeds to the citizenry to start its wars, this testimony was all lies. "Nayirah" was actually the daughter of the Kuwaiti ambassador to the U.S. She later admitted that she had once visited the hospital in question, but only for a few minutes. She did see an infant removed from an incubator, but only very briefly. A group called Citizens for a Free Kuwait had hired one of the world's foremost public relations firms, Hill and Knowlton (H&K), to create the illusion of legitimacy for an invasion. And it should be

---

[336]Herbert D. Rosenbaum and Alexej Ugrinsky, *Jimmy Carter: Foreign Policy and Post-Presidential Years* (Praeger, 1993), 20.

[337]Michael Kunczik, *Images of Nations and International Public Relations* (Mahwah, NJ: Lawrence Erlbaum Associates, 1997), 280.

noted that Citizens for a Free Kuwait "was financed almost entirely by the Kuwaiti government".[338] H&K coached 'Nayirah' on what to say and how to say it when she appeared before Congress.

In Michael Kunczik's estimation, "of all the accusations made against Saddam Hussein, none had more impact on the American public than the one about Iraqi soldiers removing 312 babies from incubators and letting them die."[339] These and other atrocity stories were requested by the head of H&K, Robert Keith Gray, in a memo to Citizens for a Free Kuwait.[340] Further reports show that George Hymel of H&K and his staff provided the witnesses, wrote scripts of 'testimony', and coached the witnesses for maximum effectiveness.

Like many lies, this one continued to grow, and the "reported number of incubator deaths eventually jumped from the fifteen stated in Nariyah's written testimony to 312 – far more than the total number of incubators in the tiny Arab nation".[341]

Congress members were apparently unaware that this seemingly unfortunate, vulnerable little girl, who had seen such horrors, was actually the sheltered daughter of the Kuwaiti ambassador to the U.S. They also seemed to be ignorant of the size of Kuwait's medical capabilities; otherwise they may have questioned the large number of alleged incubator deaths. However, it is more likely that they simply wanted to jump on the bandwagon of war, thus appearing 'strong' on the sacred cow of 'national security.' Facts have no place when hubris is on display.

The public relations firm of Hill and Knowlton was thorough. According to Ted Rowse for *The Washington Monthly*:

> H&K sent its own camera crew to film this hearing that it had helped cast and direct. It then produced a film that was quickly sent out as a video release used widely by a gullible media. Too late some alert reporter unmasked the story as a hoax and revealed that Nayirah was the Kuwaiti ambassador's daughter living in Washington. Once more the press served as patsies for the public-relations staged event.[342]

---

[338] Ted Rowse, "Kuwaitgate," *The Washington Monthly*, September 1992, http://www. questia.com/read/1G1-12529902/kuwaitgate.

[339] Michael Kunczik, *Images of Nations and International Public Relations* (Mahwah, NJ: Lawrence Erlbaum Associates, 1997), 279.

[340] Ibid.

[341] Rowse, "Kuwaitgate."

[342] Ibid.

Whether or not 'the press served as patsies,' or were willing co-conspirators in another war for oil, is questionable.

The video, produced, directed, cast and scripted by H&K, was aired by approximately 700 television stations. That evening, October 10, 1990, about 53 million people across the U.S. watched 'Nayirah' as she lied tearfully and convincingly to them. Once more, a false flag had been unfurled, and the U.S., once again, under the guise of protecting the downtrodden and vulnerable, was at war to protect oil reserves and corporate profits.

What impact did this perjured testimony have on the war? According to public relations specialist Susanne Roschwalb, it "seriously distorted the American debate about whether to support military action. Seven senators cited the story in speeches to back the January 12 resolution authorizing war."[343]

These lies were given additional credence by the careless, but highly regarded, Amnesty International. On December 12, 1990, that organization reported this: "In addition, over 300 premature babies were reported to have died after Iraqi soldiers removed them from incubators, which were then looted."[344]

President Bush also used this false evidence in convincing the citizenry of the need for war. Five days after the infamous 'Nayirah' testimony, he said this: "I met with the Emir of Kuwait. And I heard horrible tales: newborn babies thrown out of incubators and the incubators then shipped off to Baghdad."[345] He repeated this theme when he rallied the troops to this 'noble' cause: "It turns your stomach when you listen to the tales of those that have escaped the brutality of Saddam the invader. Mass hangings. Babies pulled from incubators and scattered like firewood across the floor."[346]

During later questioning, Frank Mankiewicz, vice-president of H&K, was asked whether he believed the 'Nayirah' testimony helped mobilize support for the war. He responded that he was opposed to the war, and

---

[343] S. A. Roschwalb, "The Hill & Knowlton cases: A brief on the controversy". *Public Relations Review* 20 (1994).

[344] http://articles.latimes.com/1991-01-17/local/me-68_1_amnesty-international.

[345] Kenneth Osgood and Andrew K. Frank, eds., *Selling War in a Media Age: The Presidency and Public Opinion in the American Century* (Gainesville, FL: University Press of Florida, 2010), iii, 232.

[346] Kathleen Hall Jamieson and Paul Waldman, *The Press Effect: Politicians, Journalists, and the Stories That Shape the Political World* (New York: Oxford University Press, 2004), 16.

any such decision was Bush's. But he did say that the Kuwaiti project was a great success for his company.[347]

By the time the U.S. invaded Iraq, three months after the perjured Nayirah testimony, Hill and Knowlton had received nearly $11,000,000 from 'Citizens for a Free Kuwait'. With that funding, it arranged a press conference with a Kuwaiti 'freedom fighter', "organized 'National Pray Day' services for Kuwaiti and American servicemen, and 'Free Kuwait' rallies at 21 college campuses".[348]

The question can reasonably be asked: Did Hill and Knowlton, an international public relations firm, lead the U.S. into war? "The answer is probably no," writes another public relations expert, James Grunig. As author Susan Trento, who wrote a book on H&K's influence on the war, put it: "H&K's efforts succeeded in the United Nations, the Congress and the media, because in each case, there was a receptive audience. The diplomats and congressmen and senators wanted something to point to to support their positions. The media wanted interesting, visual stories."[349]

While the infamous Nayirah testimony was by far the most influential lie to gain support for the war, it wasn't the only one. Prior to the U.S. invasion, President George H.W. Bush said that if not stopped in Kuwait, Iraq would move on to invade Saudi Arabia:

> Citing top-secret satellite images, Pentagon officials estimated in mid-September that up to 250,000 Iraqi troops and 1,500 tanks stood on the border, threatening the key US oil supplier.
>
> But when the *St. Petersburg Times* in Florida acquired two commercial Soviet satellite images of the same area, taken at the same time, no Iraqi troops were visible near the Saudi border – just empty desert.[350]

Estimates of dead from the war range from about 100,000 Iraqis (U.S. government numbers), to over 200,000 (most other sources). And while the horrific brutality that the dishonest 'Nayirah' related never took place, the U.S. was guilty of the most heinous war crimes. As the war was drawing to a close, using far-superior U.S. weaponry, soldiers showed no

---

[347]Michael Kunczik, *Images of Nations and International Public Relations* (Mahwah, NJ: Lawrence Erlbaum Associates, 1997), 282.

[348]James E. Grunig, "Public Relations and International Affairs: Effects, Ethics and Responsibility," *Journal of International Affairs* 47, no. 1 (1993).

[349]Ibid.

[350]"In War, Some Facts Less Factual; Some US Assertions from the Last War on Iraq Still Appear Dubious," *The Christian Science Monitor*, September 6, 2002.

mercy: "Even when the Army went 'over the top' into the Iraqi trenches, the slaughter was wholesale. An armored bulldozer buried alive the Iraqi defenders, unless they came out with their hands up."[351] To quote Col. Lon Maggart: "People somehow have the notion that burying guys alive is nastier than blowing them up with hand grenades or sticking them in gut with bayonets. Well it's not." It has been estimated that thousands of Iraqi soldiers, young men defending their nation, were buried alive by the U.S. military.

How much was the United States really interested in the welfare of the Kuwaiti people? And how much was it appalled by the behaviors of Saddam Hussein? As mentioned above, "the Western powers tolerate dictators when it suits their interests. In fact, they tolerated, financed and armed Saddam Hussein himself when they needed someone to prevent Iran under Khomeini coming to dominate the Gulf area and threaten their oil supplies."[352]

Once more, a false flag was raised to justify a war, this one for oil. Propaganda, in the form of well-publicized perjury committed by the daughter of the Kuwaiti ambassador to the U.S., helped gain support for the war. And the savagery of the U.S. military was again on prominent display.

---

[351]"Probing a Slaughter: A U.S. Assault on Iraqi Troops Was 'A Grouse Shoot' but Was It an Excessive Use of Force?" *Newsweek*, May 29, 2000.

[352]https://www.worldsocialism.org/spgb/socialist-standard/1990/1990s/no-1035-november-1990/economic-causes-gulf-war/. Accessed on January 23, 2019.

Chapter 23: Afghanistan War (2001–Present)

In 2001, Afghanistan posed no threat to the U.S., had no natural resources coveted by the U.S, and at first glance would seem to have had no great importance to the world's most violent nation. But that didn't stop the U.S. from invading it. Why was that?

Afghanistan, towards the last quarter of the twentieth century, knew nothing but war. The Soviets invaded in 1979 and fought there for a decade.

The U.S., under President Ronald Reagan, feared Soviet influence in Afghanistan, and couldn't countenance a Soviet puppet government. Reagan and his cohorts wanted a *U.S.* puppet government to run the country. So by the middle of the 1980, the U.S. was supporting Afghanistan with $650 million, although this was still 'covert'. Historian Chester Pach said that "Congress, at times, took the initiative in boosting funding, mainly because of the efforts of Representative Charles Wilson (D-TX), who wanted to avenge U.S. losses during the Vietnam War".[353]

In March of 1985, Reagan signed a policy statement, establishing the goal of assisting in the defeat of the Soviets in Afghanistan. "The CIA not only dramatically increased the flow of arms to the mujahideen," writes Pach, "but also provided Stinger surface-to-air missiles."[354]

Soviet President Mikhail Gorbachev was growing disillusioned with the Soviet misadventure in Afghanistan by this time. In 1986, he commented that he wanted to end the Soviet's military involvement within the next two years so they wouldn't be fighting "for another 20–30 years."[355] He was evidently more farsighted than any U.S. president since then.

The Soviet departure left a power vacuum. Historian Thomas Barfield succinctly expressed the situation in Afghanistan after the Soviet war: "In

---

[353]Chester Pach, "The Reagan Doctrine: Principle, Pragmatism, and Policy," *Presidential Studies Quarterly* 36, no. 1 (2006).

[354]Ibid.

[355]Transcript, meeting of the CPSU CC Politburo, 13 November 1986, Cold War International History Project. Retrieved August 28, 2005, from http://www.wilsoncenter.org/index.cfm?topic_id=1409&fuseaction=library.document&id=342

the subsequent civil war that erupted in the 1990s, Afghanistan became a failed state, ignored by the world."[356]

As a result of the civil war, the Taliban – Muslim jihadists – came to power. This was gradual: following the civil war, the Sunni Muslim state of Pakistan recognized the Taliban, apparently in the hope that it would bring stability to its northern border. Saudi Arabia soon also began supporting the Taliban.

By the end of 1995, the Taliban ruled 12 of Afghanistan's 31 provinces. By the end of the following year, there was no longer any significant opposition in Afghanistan to the Taliban. This was troubling to much of the world, since its rule was sure to be one of repression and violence. Journalist Pierre Azzi stated that "[t]he Taliban's ideological basis for government is based on a strict and harsh interpretation of the Koran. It differs greatly from all mainstream Muslim regimes".[357]

The Soviets had finally left, but not with the result Reagan had hoped for: "none of the major factions that constituted the mujahideen embraced liberal democracy. They shared a common adversary with their U.S. patrons, but not common values."[358]

The U.S.'s role in the Taliban's rise is not often discussed, but cannot be avoided. In an interview on October 6, 2009, with CBS News Anchor Katie Couric, Secretary of State Hillary Clinton said this:

> And the United States, to some extent, has to acknowledge being among the creators of the problem we are now dealing with. It seemed like a great idea, back in the '80s to— embolden— and train and equip— Taliban, mujahidin, jihadists against the Soviet Union, which had invaded Afghanistan. And with our help, and with the Pakistani support— this group— including, at that time, Bin Laden, defeated the Soviet Union. Drove them out of Afghanistan, eventually. Saw the fall of the government that they had installed. And the rest we know. They eventually took over. But when we accomplished our primary mission of seeing the Soviet Union thrown out of Afghanistan, we withdrew. And we left the problems of a well-equipped, fundamentalist, ideological and religious group that had been battle hardened to the Afghans and the Pakistanis.[359]

---

[356]Thomas Barfield, *Afghanistan: A Cultural and Political History* (Princeton, NJ: Princeton University Press, 2010), 1

[357]Pierre Azzi, "Harsh Rule: Recognizing the Taliban," *Harvard International Review*, Spring 1999.

[358]Chester Pach, "The Reagan Doctrine: Principle, Pragmatism, and Policy," *Presidential Studies Quarterly* 36, no. 1 (2006).

[359]http://www.cbsnews.com/8301-18563_162-5367884.html. Accessed on January 21,

Barfield writes: "At the beginning of the twenty-fist century, [Afghanistan] burst back onto the world scene when radical Muslim jihadists planned the 9/11 attack against the United States from there."[360]

Following those attacks, the U.S. citizenry was ripe to be manipulated into supporting yet another war. The U.S. demanded that Afghanistan surrender those suspected of planning the 9/11 attacks, including Osama bin Laden. According to U.S. spokespeople and the ever-compliant media, the government of Afghanistan refused. Proclaiming that it wouldn't tolerate another government supporting anti-U.S terrorists, the U.S. then invaded Afghanistan.

However, the easy explanation given to the U.S. citizenry wasn't exactly the truth. The Taliban were willing to send the suspects, including bin Laden, to the U.S., if the U.S. provided some proof of their involvement in the attacks. Then, when the U.S. refused to do so, the Taliban offered to send bin Laden to any other nation but the U.S., from which he could have been quickly extradited to the U.S. This still wasn't good enough, so the U.S. simply invaded.

It wasn't difficult to bring U.S. citizens around: their 'sacred' nation, the God-appointed world leader, that beacon of peace and freedom, had actually been attacked. With sufficient motivation, U.S. citizens are always ready to rally around a war, and the invasion of Afghanistan was no exception.

They were told that Osama bin Laden was hiding somewhere in this mostly Muslim country, and the associations between Islam and terrorism were always at least hinted at, if not blatantly stated. Muslim places of worship don't resemble most churches in the U.S.; Muslim women don't parade their bodies publicly as is done in the 'enlightened' U.S. No, different equals dangerous among the ignorant, and that ignorance is skillfully used by the government and its fawning press.

There was no question that the Taliban was and is a repressive regime, as U.S. spokespeople and the press repeatedly proclaimed. And it was well known that bin Laden was in Afghanistan.

But was a war – one which has now lasted for nineteen years, and is the longest war in the bloody history of U.S. war-making – really necessary? One could easily argue that Afghans would be much better off with the Taliban as their government, and the U.S. withdrawing completely. If the goal was, in fact, to bring bin Laden to whatever passes in the U.S.

2013.

[360]Barfield, *Afghanistan*, 1.

for justice, surely intelligence agencies could have located him. But would simply locating him and bringing him to justice have sufficed? One doubts it; after all, he has now been dead for seven years, and U.S. troops continue to fight the Taliban.

But if capturing bin Laden, and introducing what turned out to be a bizarre form of "democracy" to Afghanistan along the way, wasn't the motivation for the war, what was? As Gore Vidal wrote soon after the invasion:

> Since the Iran-Iraq wars of the '80s and early '90s, Islam has been demonized as a Satanic terrorist cult that encourages suicide attacks – contrary, it should be noted, to the Islamic religion. Osama [bin Laden] has been portrayed accurately, it would seem, as an Islamic zealot. In order to bring this evil-doer to justice (dead or alive) Afghanistan, the object of the exercise, was made safe not only for democracy, but for Union Oil of California, whose proposed pipeline, from Turkmenistan to Afghanistan to Pakistan and the Indian Ocean port of Karachi, had been abandoned under the Taliban's chaotic regime. Currently, the pipeline is a go-project thanks to the junta's installation of a Unocal employee as American envoy to the newly born democracy whose president is also a former Unocal employee.[361]

And what of Osama bin Laden? How did some obscure individual gain so much notoriety? How did he become sufficiently influential to be blamed, and possibly responsible for, the September 11 attacks on the U.S.? Expanding on what Hillary Clinton is quoted as saying above, Grover Furr writes:

> The first contact with Bin Laden was in 1979, when the new graduate from the Univ[ersity] of Jedah got in touch with the U.S. embassy in Ankara, Turkey. With the help of the CIA and the U.S. Armed Forces intelligence services he began to organize in the early 1980s and network to raise money and to recruit fighters for the Afghan mujahidins that were fighting the Soviets. He did this from the city of Peshawar in Pakistan, bordering Afghanistan.[362]

From an article in the *Times of India* (March 6, 2001):

---

[361]Gore Vidal, *Dreaming War: Blood for Oil and the Cheney-Bush Junta* (Thunder's Mouth Press, 2002), 20.

[362]https://msuweb.montclair.edu/~{}furrg/pol/wtc/oblnus091401.html. Accessed on November 2, 2018.

The Central Intelligence Agency worked in tandem with Pakistan to create the 'monster' that is today Afghanistan's ruling Taliban, a leading US expert on South Asia said.

'I warned them that we were creating a monster,' Selig Harrison from the Woodrow Wilson International Centre for Scholars said at the conference here last week on "Terrorism and Regional Security: Managing the Challenges in Asia."

Harrison said: "The CIA made a historic mistake in encouraging Islamic groups from all over the world to come to Afghanistan." The US provided $3 billion for building up these Islamic groups, and it accepted Pakistan's demand that they should decide how this money should be spent, Harrison said.[363]

And according to Steve Coll writing for the *Washington Post*: "In all, the United States funneled more than $2 billion in guns and money to the mujaheddin during the 1980s, according to U.S. officials. It was the largest covert action program since World War II."[364]

The idea of invading Afghanistan wasn't new; it didn't result simply from the 9/11 attacks. Those attacks merely provided the means for the U.S. to invade, for Congress to approve the invasion, and the U.S. public to support it. As early as 1997, Zbigniew Brzezinski, National Security Advisor to President Jimmy Carter, explained the need for U.S. interference in Afghanistan. "It follows that America's primary interest is to help ensure that no single power comes to control this geopolitical space and that the global community has unhindered financial and economic access to it."[365] As Gore Vidal summarized this view: "Brzezinski then, reflexively, goes into the standard American rationalization for empire; We want nothing, ever, for ourselves, only to keep bad people from getting good things with which to hurt good people."[366] Note the importance of 'financial and economic' considerations.

The war in Afghanistan is sometimes referred to as 'the forgotten war.' In an article in October 2016, former U.S. member of Congress Ron Paul asked: "How many Americans know that we still have nearly 10,000 troops in Afghanistan? Do Americans know that the Taliban was never de-

---

[363] Ibid.

[364] Ibid.

[365] Zbigniew Brzezinski, *The Grand Chessboard: American Primacy and its Geostrategic Imperatives* (Basis Books, 1998), 148.

[366] Vidal, *Dreaming War*, 21.

feated, but now holds more ground in Afghanistan than at any point since 2001?"[367]

One would think that ending the war, or any war, would be a goal of the government waging it. Yet that is far from the case. War is big business, and those companies making huge profits are very generous to U.S. politicians who do their bidding. The following table shows just some of the biggest money-makers, and their political donations.[368]

This list shows only the top five (5) money-makers, and their political contributions and lobbying expenses. The list of companies making billions of dollars from U.S. wars is extensive.

While the oil component was certainly a major factor in the U.S. invasion of Afghanistan, and in its continuing occupation of, and violence against, that country, it isn't the only one. Afghanistan is a major supplier of the world's opium and, despite its 'War on Drugs', the U.S. government would be loathe to see that dry up. The vast sums that the opium trade brings in can be very useful to unscrupulous governments. As commentator Ryan Dawson said: "For a largescale professional example of this just take a look at [the] Iran Contra Affair where factions in the CIA and NSA were engaged in this very thing: the drugs, weapons, violence gambit. Drug money is off the books cash which allows plausible denial for governments for their intelligence agencies criminal behavior."[369] While the Taliban had succeeded in bringing opium production to an all-time low, since the American invasion production has skyrocketed, with Afghanistan now providing over 80% of the world's supply.[370] How and where the United States government will next want to use funds obtained from the opium trade is yet to be seen.

President Bush exploited the fears of U.S. citizens in preparing for the invasion of Afghanistan. He accused the Taliban of sheltering and sup-

---

[367] https://www.thenewamerican.com/reviews/opinion/item/24247-fifteen-years-into-t he-afghan-war-do-americans-know-the-truth. Accessed on June 16, 2018.

[368] https://247wallst.com/special-report/2017/02/13/20-companies-profiting-fro m-war/5/; https://www.opensecrets.org/orgs/summary.php?id=d000000104; https://www.opensecrets.org/orgs/summary.php?id=d000000100; https: //www.opensecrets.org/lobby/clientsum.php?id=D000000583&year=2017; https://www.opensecrets.org/orgs/summary.php?id=D000000170id; https://ww w.opensecrets.org/orgs/summary.php?id=D000000175%3Cbr%20%3E%3C/a%3E. Accessed on June 16, 2018.

[369] https://www.ancreport.com/report/us-really-invade-afghanistan/. Accessed on November 12, 2019.

[370] https://www.washingtonpost.com/graphics/2019/investigations/afghanistan-paper s/afghanistan-war-confidential-documents/. Accessed on December 16, 2019.

Table 1 – Defense Industry Profits and Contributions

Company and Profits – 2017	Donations to Politicians – 2018 Election Cycle	Lobbying – 2018 Election Cycle
Lockheed Martin Corp. - Arms sales: $36.44 billion - Total sales: $46.13 billion - Profit: $3.61 billion - Employees: 126,000	$3,065,135	$14,464,290
Boeing - Arms sales: $27.96 billion - Total sales: $96.11 billion - Profit: $5.18 billion - Employees: 161,400	$2,602,429	$16,740,000
BAE Systems - Arms sales: $25.51 billion - Total sales: $27.36 billion - Profit: $1.46 billion - Employees: 82,500		$4,030,000
Raytheon - Arms sales: $21.78 billion - Total sales: $23.25 billion - Profit: $2.07 billion - Employees: 61,000	$1,991,219	$5,080,000
Northrop Grumman Corp. - Arms sales: $20.06 billion - Total sales: $23.26 billion - Profit: $2.0 billion - Employees: 65,000	$4,277,968	$11,990,000

plying terrorists, and demanded that they surrender all al Qaeda leaders to the U.S. When the Taliban refused to abide by the U.S.'s exact terms, Bush started the so-called global war on terrorism. Since then, Presidents Barack Obama and Donald Trump have continued this deadly war-making in this beleaguered country.

Chapter 24: Iraq (2003–2011)

As we saw in Chapter 22 on the Gulf War, the U.S. supported the regime of Saddam Hussein for years, making it the fourth largest military power in the world. Of course, this was only until it fell into disfavor, at which point an invasion and overthrow of the government was required. This would eliminate the troublesome Hussein, and also open Iraq's vast oil reserves for U.S. exploitation.

Yet, as mentioned before, U.S. intervention anywhere in the Middle East can usually be traced to one of two sources: oil or Israel. In the case of the Iraq War, both were factors, and which was predominant can be argued from either perspective. Writer Danny Postel, after saying that the war was "conceived in Washington, but its inspiration came from Tel Aviv," continued: "Not all imperial projects are about economic predation: some simply aim to destroy political enemies."[371] Iraq was not a political enemy to the United States; it wasn't involved in the September 11 attacks, and the U.S. obtained oil from Iraq whenever it wanted. But Israel saw Iraq as an enemy, and, again according to Postel: "But in taking out Saddam Hussein, the U.S. destroyed one of *Israel's* political enemies. In so doing, [John] Mearsheimer) and [Stephen] Walt argue, it undermined American national interests."[372]

What did the war do for Israel? As much as 77% of oil imported to Israel comes from Iraq.[373] This compares to about 5% of U.S. oil coming from Iraq.[374]

Why would the United States overthrow a sovereign government to benefit another country, when doing so greatly increased terrorist recruiting and seriously damaged the U.S.'s international reputation? The Bush Administration was loaded with neocon Zionists. The following is a partial list of influential members of that administration:

---

[371] https://inthesetimes.com/article/17626/what_the_Iraq_war_teaches_us. Accessed on November 12, 2019.

[372] Ibid.

[373] https://www.jpost.com/Business-and-Innovation/Israel-importing-77-percent-of-its-oil-from-Iraqi-Kurdistan-report-says-413056. Accessed on November 12, 2019.

[374] https://www.eia.gov/tools/faqs/faq.php?id=727&t=6. – Accessed on November 12, 2019.

- Ari Fleischer, official White House spokesman, who reportedly holds Israeli citizenship.

- Richard Perle, a foreign policy advisor, was Bush's Jewish national security campaign advisor. He was later employed by an Israeli weapons firm, Soltam.

- Paul Wolfowitz, Deputy Defense Secretary, Bush's Jewish foreign policy campaign advisor, and a close associate of Richard Perle.

- Douglas Feith, Under Secretary of Defense, and Policy Advisor. He is a pro-Israel extremist, closely associated with the Zionist Organization of America. His small law firm, prior to his appointment, was said, on its website, to represent 'Israeli Armaments Manufacturers'.

- Elliott Abrams, National Security Council Advisor. He had previously been a member of the Reagan Administration, and had a major role in the Iran-Contra scandal. He was one of Reagan's most pro-Israel administration members.

- Dov Zakheim, Under Secretary of Defense. He reportedly holds Israeli citizenship.[375]

- Lewis 'Scooter' Libby, Assistant to the Vice President for National Security Affairs under Dick Cheney. Former British Foreign Secretary Jack Straw once commented, when referring to Libby, "It's a toss-up whether [Libby] is working for the Israelis or the Americans on any given day."[376]

With this cast of characters advising a president not known for his strong intellect, Israel's policies, regardless of what they might mean for the United States, were well represented.

President George W. Bush's performance in gaining U.S. citizenry support for the invasion of Iraq is another clear example of knowingly proclaiming lies as truth to the general public. In his first inaugural address, Bush singled out what he called the 'axis of evil': Iraq, Iran and North Korea. The fact that Iraq was led by a man that the U.S. brought to power decades earlier, Iran hadn't invaded another nation since 1798, and

---

[375]http://www.ilaam.net/Sept11/ZionistLinksBush.html. Accessed on November 12, 2019.

[376]https://www.globalresearch.ca/report-libby-a-long-time-israeli-intelligence-agent /6236. Accessed on November 12, 2019.

North Korea, while a nuclear-armed nation, had shown nothing other than verbal belligerence, meant nothing to Bush and his advisers.

The first to feel his wrath was to be Iraq.

Following the attacks of September 11, 2001, the citizenry was reeling. The 110 stories of the twin towers of the World Trade Center in New York City had fallen, victims to hijacked jetliners. Another such plane had crashed into the Pentagon, and another, intended for who knows where, crashed in a Pennsylvania field after passengers fought the hijackers.

As is typical during anything resembling a 'national emergency,' the citizens of the U.S. rallied behind their previously unpopular president, who only came to office earlier that year due to a Supreme Court ruling and the bizarre Electoral College, having lost the popular vote to former Vice President Al Gore.

With the specter of communism having long since faded, Islam became that which was to be feared, and attributing the September 11 attacks to Muslim-majority nations was not difficult to do. The U.S. would now fight 'terrorism,' a war that promises to be as never-ending, and as fruitless, as the 'war on drugs.' The U.S., according to its government officials, would use its self-proclaimed moral and actual military superiority to defeat this new enemy. A form of democracy unrecognizable as such by any reasonable definition would be forced upon the Iraqi people, whether they wanted it or not.

A year and a day after the attacks on the U.S., Bush stood before the United Nations and said this: "Today, Iraq continues to withhold important information about its nuclear program – weapons design, procurement logs, experiment data, an accounting of nuclear materials and documentation of foreign assistance. Iraq employs capable nuclear scientists and technicians. It retains physical infrastructure needed to build a nuclear weapon."[377] What could be more frightening than an Islamic nation building nuclear weapons? Apparently, in the eyes of Bush, nothing.

Five months later, on February 5, 2003, it was Secretary of State Colin Powell's turn to lie to the United Nations. He told the Security Council that satellite photos showed the presence of active chemical munitions bunkers disguised from inspectors. He further discussed an alleged stockpile of between 100 and 500 tons of chemical weapons. *Deutsche Welle* reported:

---

[377] "We Turn to the Urgent Duty of Protecting Other Lives," *The Washington Times*, September 13, 2002.

> The core of his speech was that Saddam Hussein possessed biological and chemical weapons of mass destruction, that his regime was supporting international terrorism, and that it aimed to build nuclear weapons.

> The presentation culminated in a claim, backed up by detailed illustrations, that in order to evade strict controls by UN weapons inspectors, Iraq had converted a fleet of trucks into mobile chemical and biological weapons labs. We remember Powell's speech primarily because all of these claims turned out to be false.[378]

Outside of the United States, Bush's and Powell's statements didn't hold much water. The U.S. attempted to seek U.N. sanction for an invasion of Iraq, but its allies weren't particularly interested in the next U.S. imperial misadventure. Russian officials said they would use their veto power on the Security Council to prevent any such action. Germany threatened to relocate military installations important to the U.S. out of Kuwait if there was any invasion. Canada urged the U.S. not to act.

Saddam Hussein seemed to be in no mood to risk a U.S. invasion:

> Iraq delivered a letter to the U.N. Secretary General saying Saddam Hussein's government would accept the return of weapons inspectors [without conditions]. The government said it based its decision concerning the return of inspectors on its desire to complete the implementation of the relevant Security Council resolutions and to remove any doubts that Iraq still possesses weapons of mass destruction. The letter also noted that the resolutions called for nations to respect the sovereignty, territorial integrity and political independence of Iraq.[379]

The letter reads, in part, as follows:

> After some States and the public were taken in by this lie, while others remained silent, Iraq confronted them with its consent to the return of the international inspectors after agreeing with you, as representative of the United Nations in New York, on 16 September 2002, and in a press statement issued jointly in Vienna on 30 September/1 October 2002 by an Iraqi technical delegation headed by Amer Al-Saadi, Chief Inspector Hans Blix and Mohamed ElBaradei, Director General of the International Atomic Energy Agency

---

[378] https://www.dw.com/en/the-iraq-war-in-the-beginning-was-the-lie/a-43301338. Accessed on August 24, 2018

[379] Harvey Langholtz, Boris Kondoch et al., *International Peacekeeping: The Yearbook of International Peace Operations – Vol. 9* (Martinus Nijhoff, 2005), 368.

(IAEA). Yet a few hours after Iraq's consent to the return of the inspectors became an established fact, including agreement on 19 October 2002 as the date of their arrival, Colin Powell, the American Secretary of State, declared that he would refuse to have the inspectors go to Iraq.[380]

Wasn't this exactly what the U.S. had demanded? It seemed to satisfy what every nation other than the U.S. wanted. Inspections by the International Atomic Energy Agency (IAEA) began. In a CRS (Congressional Research Service) Report for Congress of October 7, 2003, entitled *Iraq: U.N. Inspections for Weapons of Mass Destruction*, the following was reported:

> From late November 2002 to March 2003, U.N. inspectors combed Iraq looking for weapons of mass destruction (WMD). Under the threat of war from the United States and a unanimous Security Council resolution (1441) [this resolution offered Iraq "a final opportunity to comply with its disarmament obligations"[381]], Iraq was granted a final opportunity to disarm. Many had low expectations for successful inspections. After 6 weeks, inspectors turned up some evidence of undeclared activities, but not enough to convince a majority of the Security Council members that military force was necessary. Nonetheless, on March 19, 2003, U.S. and British forces attacked Iraq to forcibly eliminate its WMD.[382]

As the London *Mirror* reported, "George W. Bush's handpicked legion of arms inspectors, having combed Iraq... failed to come up with a single weapon of mass destruction."[383]

With no weapons of mass destruction, one wonders what reason, other than oil, the U.S. had for invading Iraq. And why did the U.S. military remain in that country for nine years?

An alternative reason was floated to the U.S. citizenry. Iraq needed to be punished for its role in the September 11 attacks on the U.S. But was Iraq implicated in those attacks?

---

[380] https://reliefweb.int/report/iraq/letter-minister-foreign-affairs-iraq-secretary-gener al-s20021242. Accessed on August 25, 2018.

[381] https://www.asil.org/insights/volume/7/issue/12/security-council-resolutio n-1441-iraqs-final-opportunity-comply. Accessed on January 29, 2019.

[382] http://www.fas.org/man/crs/RL31671.pdf. Accessed on November 28, 2012.

[383] "Jonathan Freedland: Robin Cook's Devastating Charge That Blair Went to War When He Knew Iraq Had No Banned Weapons – and Posed No Threat – Blasts a Massive Hole in the Prime Minister's Credibility," *The Mirror* (London, England), October 6, 2003.

U.S. government officials were anxious to make the connection, whether it existed or not. Cheney, on 'Meet the Press' in 2001, said that a meeting between Mohamed Atta, one of the September 11 hijackers, and an Iraqi official in Prague was 'pretty well confirmed'. On September 25 of the following year, National Security Adviser Condoleezza Rice said that "[t]here clearly are contacts between al Qaeda and Iraq ... There clearly is testimony that some of the contacts have been important contacts and there's a relationship there." Two days later, Rumsfeld said the link between al Qaeda and Saddam Hussein was 'bulletproof'.[384]

However, was any of this true? Much of the information provided by U.S. officials was based on that alleged meeting of Atta with an Iraqi official in Prague:

> An investigation by the FBI, however, concluded that there was no convincing evidence that Atta was in Prague at the time of the meeting, and the CIA was doubtful about any meeting of Atta and an Iraqi official. A Congressional report said that 'The CIA has been unable to establish that [Atta] left the United States or entered Europe in April [2001] under his other name or any known alias.'[385]

But this focus on Atta and a meeting that never existed was certainly encouraged by Israel. That nation was, according to the *Los Angeles Times*, "pushing the possibility of an Iraqi connection to the terrorist attacks. It could be in Israel's security interests to see the U.S. take a more aggressive stance against Iraq. Germany's mass-circulation *Bild* newspaper Thursday quoted unidentified Israeli intelligence sources as saying Atta received anthrax spores from Iraqi agents in Prague."[386]

It is worth noting Israel's ongoing and unreasonable concern about its 'security interests'. Although it has one of the most powerful militaries in the world, and is backed by the most powerful, the Israeli government loses no opportunity to express concern over its continued existence. As I wrote for an editorial in *CounterPunch*:

> [A]nything Israel doesn't like is an 'existential' threat to that rogue nation. So if Iran has a nuclear program, Israel is threatened. If anyone dares suggest that the blockade of the Gaza Strip be ended, Israel is threatened. If the International Criminal Court investigates

---

[384] https://www.latimes.com/archives/la-xpm-2001-oct-27-mn-62270-story.html. Accessed on November 12, 2019.

[385] James P. Pfiffner, "Did President Bush Mislead the Country in His Arguments for War with Iraq?" *Presidential Studies Quarterly* 34, no. 1 (2004).

[386] https://www.latimes.com/archives/la-xpm-2001-oct-27-mn-62270-story.html.

'possible' Israeli war crimes, Israel is threatened. For pity's sake, if the international soccer association questions Israel's behavior, Israel is threatened![387]

The U.S. government's 9/11 Commission, established in November of 2002, and which released its report on July 26, 2004, found no connection between al-Qaeda and Iraq. It stated this:

> Responding to a presidential tasking, [special assistant to the president Richard] Clarke's office sent a memo to [National Security Advisor Condoleezza] Rice on September 18, titled 'Survey of Intelligence Information on Any Iraq Involvement in the September 11 Attacks.' Rice's chief staffer on Afghanistan, Zalmay Khalilzad, concurred in its conclusion that only some anecdotal evidence linked Iraq to al Qaeda. The memo found no 'compelling case' that Iraq had either planned or perpetrated the attacks. It passed along a few foreign intelligence reports, including the Czech report alleging an April 2001 Prague meeting between Atta and an Iraqi intelligence officer [discussed in chapter 7] and a Polish report that personnel at the headquarters of Iraqi intelligence in Baghdad were told before September 11 to go on the streets to gauge crowd reaction to an unspecified event. Arguing that the case for links between Iraq and al Qaeda was weak, the memo pointed out that Bin Ladin [sic] resented the secularism of Saddam Hussein's regime. Finally, the memo said, there was no confirmed reporting on Saddam cooperating with Bin Laden on unconventional weapons.[388]

The result of this invasion was that the sovereign nation of Iraq was invaded, its leadership overthrown, its infrastructure destroyed, millions of its people killed, with millions more displaced, some fleeing to refugee camps in neighboring countries. The country erupted in civil war. And in the sixteen years since then, eight of them with U.S. soldiers actively at war, no weapons of mass destruction have ever been found.

One might reasonably ask why Bush didn't delay, in view of the access the United Nations Weapons Inspectors were receiving from Iraq, and the opinion of U.S. allies that there was certainly insufficient evidence to warrant military action. The profit motive is never far from U.S. warmaking. Bush and several of his Cabinet members and advisors have or had strong ties to the oil industry. For example, then Vice President

---

[387] https://www.counterpunch.org/2015/07/31/israeli-missteps-take-a-toll/. Accessed on November 12, 2019.

[388] http://www.gpo.gov/fdsys/pkg/GPO-911REPORT/pdf/GPO-911REPORT.pdf. Accessed on November 28, 2018.

Dick Cheney is the former chairman and CEO of Halliburton. Other advisors with ties to the oil industry include Commerce Secretary Donald Evans, former CEO of Tom Brown, Inc.; Christine Todd Whitman of the Environmental Protection Agency, who has significant holdings in oil wells in Texas and Colorado; Defense Secretary Donald Rumsfeld, with millions of dollars invested in energy-related companies, and National Security Advisor Condoleezza Rice, a member of the board of Chevron, which actually named an oil tanker the *Condoleezza Rice.*

Additionally, according to a study by the Center for Public Integrity, "Of the top 10 lifetime contributors to George W. [Bush]'s war chests, six either come from the oil business, or [had] ties to it."[389] But it isn't just oil-related lobbies that influenced Bush's Administration.

1. Israeli lobbies contribute vast amounts to the campaign coffers of U.S. elected officials, and Israel seeks complete hegemony in the Middle East. With the U.S. destabilizing the other nations there, and continuing to provide Israel with $9 million every day, Israel and the members of Congress which it purchases with those contributions are happy.

2. So-called 'defense' industry lobbyists are also quite generous to U.S. elected officials (see **Table 1 – Defense Industry Profits and Contributions** in Chapter 23 – Afghanistan). U.S. wars enable the country to showcase the latest in killing technology, so that companies within the 'defense' industry have an extravagant means of demonstrating their newest weaponry's capabilities to potential buyers. The U.S. is the world's largest arms dealers, having sold weapons to at least 98 countries between 2013 and 2014.[390]

Once again, a false flag was waved to frighten the U.S. citizenry. With that came all the propaganda about Iraqi links to the September 11 attacks, warning that Muslims are the enemy. Once again, cooler heads, those who recognized the valuable work of the United Nations' weapons inspectors, were ignored in the headlong rush to war. And once again, the U.S.'s reputation was tattered, terrorism increased and the bodies of U.S. victims – men, women and children – continued to pile up.

---

[389]http://www.globalresearch.ca/articles/CAV111A.html. Accessed on November 28, 2012.

[390]https://www.businessinsider.com/top-countries-exporting-weapons-arms-sales -2018-3#1-united-states-10. Accessed on August 25, 2018.

The false flags of terrorism and 9/11, and the potential threat to the U.S. from 'weapons of mass destruction,' were proudly flown in the blood-spattered U.S. breeze. Neither had any truth to them.

Three years after the fact, Powell was asked about his statements at the UN. As the *Telegraph* reported:

> ... Powell tried to explain how the West had made mistakes in the run-up to war. Asked whether the statement about WMD tarnished his reputation, the former general responded: 'Of course it will. It's a blot. I'm the one who presented it on behalf of the United States to the world and [it] will always be a part of my record. It was painful. It's painful now.'[391]

Regardless of Powell's 'pain', the war was based on lies. David Altheide and Jennifer Grimes concluded: "The invasion of Iraq was justified to the American people by a sophisticated propaganda campaign that reflected a think tank's vision for a new foreign policy."[392]

Jeffrey St. Clair, writing in *Counterpunch* thirteen years after the U.S. invasion of Iraq, said this: "The war on Iraq won't be remembered for how it was waged so much as for how it was sold. It was a propaganda war, a war of perception management, where loaded phrases, such as 'weapons of mass destruction' and 'rogue state' were hurled like precision weapons at the target audience: us."[393]

Ray McGovern, who spent 27 years with the CIA, including holding senior positions with that agency, said this regarding the 'intelligence' that was provided to the public to justify the war: "The intelligence was not mistaken; it was fraudulent – and they knew it."[394]

Another false source was an Iraqi chemist living in Germany, Rafid Ahmed Alwan al-Janabi. German intelligence (BND) interrogated him, hoping to gain information about Iraq's chemical weapons program. Al-Janabi, nicknamed 'Curveball,' quickly learned that the more information he gave, the more his living conditions improved: he was provided with an apartment, money, and a German passport. *Deutsche Welle* reported:

---

[391] https://www.telegraph.co.uk/news/worldnews/middleeast/iraq/1498095/Powell-admits-his-Iraq-WMD-claim-is-painful-blot.html. Accessed on August 25, 2018.

[392] https://onlinelibrary.wiley.com/doi/pdf/10.1111/j.1533-8525.2005.00029.x. Accessed on November 7, 2018.

[393] https://www.counterpunch.org/2016/07/08/how-the-iraq-war-was-sold/. Accessed on November 7, 2018.

[394] https://www.dw.com/en/the-iraq-war-in-the-beginning-was-the-lie/a-43301338. Accessed on November 9, 2018.

This continued until the BND tracked down al-Janabi's former boss, who picked apart his web of lies. The German intelligence services then informed their American partners of this development. Nonetheless, there was renewed interest in 'Curveball' after the attacks of September 11, 2001. Citing former BND head August Hanning, the daily newspaper *Die Welt* reported in August 2011 that the Americans had demanded a binding commitment from the Germans in 2001 assuring that Curveball's statements were correct. Hanning refused to provide it, writing instead to the head of the CIA, George Tenet, 'attempts to verify the information have been unsuccessful' and that it 'must therefore be considered unconfirmed'.

Despite other, more explicit warnings about the veracity of Curveball's testimony, it became the centerpiece of Powell's war propaganda. Ray McGovern is certain: 'They didn't care whether Curveball knew what he was talking about. What they had was something they could put on the record, that they could give to these very imaginative and very professional graphics people working for the CIA, and they in turn could render drawings of these nonexistent mobile chemical weapons labs, which of course they did and which Colin Powell featured during his speech.'[395]

This was the launch of the so-called 'war on terrorism.' But has it had the allegedly desired effect? A report from December 12, 2017, stated:

... global terrorist attacks rose dramatically after 2004: There were just over 1,000 in 2004, but almost 17,000 in 2014. The numbers from 2015 and 2016 have remained remarkably high, but below the 2014 peak. The upward pattern holds even when removing attacks in Iraq and Afghanistan.[396]

The cost in human lives has been mentioned above. Additionally, according to Tom Engelhardt,

... the Costs of War Project at Brown University's Watson Institute published an estimate of the taxpayer dollars that will have gone into America's War on Terror from September 12, 2001, through fiscal year 2018. That figure: a cool $5.6 trillion (including the future costs of caring for our war vets). On average, that's at least $23,386 per taxpayer.[397]

---

[395] https://www.dw.com/en/the-iraq-war-in-the-beginning-was-the-lie/a-43301338. Accessed on Nov. 9, 2018.

[396] https://warontherocks.com/2017/12/terrorism-war-terror-look-numbers/. Accessed on August 24, 2018.

[397] http://www.tomdispatch.com/post/176423. Accessed on August 25, 2018.

As we look at this ugly record of lies that the U.S. has used to expand its territory, power and/or influence around the world, we must consider that it is once again using the same tactics to march the nation toward war with Iran.

Chapter 25: Libya (March–October 2011)

The United States has involved itself in the destabilization of the Middle East for several years; the rise in U.S. intervention in that part of the world matches the increase in pro–Israel lobby money donated to the political campaigns of elected U.S. officials. And while the U.S. has a goal of destroying and/or destabilizing any Middle Eastern or North African nation that isn't allied with Israel, there are generally side benefits to the U.S. of their destruction. This was certainly true with Libya.

Professor of international law Francis A. Boyle writes:

> [T]he United States, France, Britain and NATO immediately hijacked a legitimate but very brief 'Arab Spring' in Benghazi in order to promote their own imperial agenda of (1) stealing Libya's oil and gas; (2) reversing the anti-imperial and anticolonial Qaddafi Revolution; (3) re-establishing a neo-colonial outpost on the north coast of Africa and a beachhead on the southern rim of the Mediterranean – right next to the strategically pivotal Egypt – in order to better control and dominate the Maghreb, the southern Med and the Sahel, and (4) from Libya they felt they could then better project their imperial power southwards onto the rest of the African continent.[398]

U.S. imperialism was on very public display as Libya became caught in the crosshairs. But the Israeli connection cannot be discounted either. This wasn't simply a war to better position the U.S. such that it could control northern Africa. Boyle continues:

> [T]he Zionist apparatchiks dominating the Neolib Obama administration had long personally detested Qaddafi because of his strident and uncompromising support for the Palestinians against Israel. There was a strong element of typical Zionist vindictiveness put into operation by the Obama administration and the U.S. news media in their gleeful vendetta against Qaddafi and his family, though the Palestinians had nothing to do with the Nazi Holocaust against the Jews.[399]

---

[398] Francis A. Boyle, *Destroying Libya and World Order: The Three-Decade U.S. Campaign to Terminate the Qaddafi Revolution* (Atlanta: Clarity, 2013), 178.
[399] Ibid.

As an example of Qaddafi's support for the Palestinians, on January 1, 1986, he said this: "I firmly reject the claim that the Palestinian action should be accused of terrorism. The Palestinian action is the most sacred action on earth in this era because it concerns fighting by people who have been wronged".[400]

As early as 2004, U.S. intentions in Libya were clear. On December 13 of that year, at the Arab Strategy Forum in Dubai, Boyle said this: "Libya had always been sitting on those vast pools of oil and gas; and the Libyans could hardly defend themselves against great-power predators. The American neoconservatives had called this phenomenon 'low-hanging fruit'."[401]

It was seven years later, "In 2011 the neoliberals of the Obama administration decided to pluck Libya. As far as U.S. imperialism was concerned, plucking Libya was only a question of timing – when, not if."[402]

> ... The United States government will seek direct military control and domination of the hydrocarbon resource of the Arab and Muslim world until there is no oil and gas left for them to steal, using Israel as its regional 'policeman' towards that end. Oil and Israel were behind both the Bush Sr. and Bush Jr. wars against Iraq. And now Bush Jr. is threatening to attack Syria, Lebanon and Iran in conjunction with the genocidal apartheid regime in Israel. As the oil and gas in the Arab and Muslim world proceed to run out, the United States and Israel will become even more predatory, aggressive, destructive, and genocidal toward Arab and Muslim states and peoples ...[403]

One must ask what conditions were like in Libya under Qaddafi. Some facts are instructive.

Under Qaddafi, according to Michel Chossudovsky,

> The [Libyan Arab Jamahiriya] has had a high standard of living and a robust per capita daily caloric intake of 3144. The country has made strides in public health and, since 1980, child mortality rates have dropped from 70 per thousand live births to 19 in 2009. Life expectancy has risen from 61 to 74 years of age during the same span of years.[404]

---

[400]Brian L. Davis, *Qaddafi, Terrorism, and the Origins of the U.S. Attack on Libya* (New York: Praeger, 1990), 186.

[401]Ibid., 173

[402]Boyle, *Destroying Libya*, 143.

[403]Ibid., 173.

[404]https://www.globalresearch.ca/destroying-a-country-s-standard-of-living-what-libya-had-achieved-what-has-been-destroyed/26686. Accessed on August 29, 2018.

Italian Journalist Yvonne de Vito, who visited Libya before the invasion, described the nation that she saw. She said this: "Libya is considered to be the Switzerland of the African continent and is very rich and schools are free for the people. Hospitals are free for the people. And the conditions for women are much better than in other Arab countries."[405]

De Vito also commented on the many anti-Qaddafi demonstrations that the U.S. media was showing: "Even if all the television stations are showing people fighting and demonstrating against Gaddafi, I personally saw many people demonstrating for Gaddafi. I don't know why so many journalists are not showing this, because they are manipulating the situation."[406]

If conditions in Libya had improved markedly during Qaddafi's tenure as leader, and if there was some significant support for him, as witnessed by Yvonne de Vito, the U.S. needed to invent some reason for the invasion that the U.S. citizenry would buy. Toppling a leader because he supported the human-rights struggles of the Palestinian people would not sit well with the citizenry as more of its members grew sympathetic to Palestine. Declaring that Libya needed to be destroyed to become a puppet of the U.S. so that U.S. economic and strategic interests in Africa could be protected would also not have come up to snuff.

But there were two tried-and-true excuses, never valid but always palatable. The first was to protect the U.S.'s national security, and the second was 'humanitarian aid', the U.S. practice of bombing people to death in order to assist them.

With Libya a small nation on the other side of the world, the myth of needing to bomb it to protect the U.S. would not have flown. But 'humanitarian aid' always sounds appealing, and that was the false flag flown to justify and gain support for the invasion of Libya.

What was happening in Libya that enabled the U.S. to invade for 'humanitarian' purposes? Rebels within the country began fighting the government, which, as one might expect, worked to put down the rebellion. There were reports that government forces were indiscriminate, attacking areas where they thought there might be rebels, and killing innocent civilians in the process. The U.S. sought a United Nations resolution which would allow a U.S.-led, NATO-authorized force to protect civilians, enforce a no-fly zone and an arms embargo, and freeze various Libyan

---

[405] https://www.rt.com/news/interview-libya-nato-intrusion-127/. Accessed on August 29, 2018.

[406] Ibid.

assets. This resolution passed the Security Council on March 17, 2011. Two days later, Libya was invaded.

It should be noted that within four days of the invasion, President Barack Obama secretly approved U.S. aid to the Libyan rebels. On March 23, 2011, the *Pittsburgh Tribune-Review* reported this: "President Obama has signed a secret order authorizing covert U.S. government support for rebel forces seeking to oust Libyan leader Muammar Gadhafi, government officials told Reuters on Wednesday."[407] Needless to say, neither this, nor the extensive bombardment of Libyan territory was permitted under the terms of the UN resolution.

Yet two weeks after that, on March 30, 2011, Assistant Secretary of State Philip Gordon declared: "The military mission of the United States is designed to implement the Security Council resolution, no more and no less ... I mean protecting civilians against attacks from Qaddafi's forces and delivering humanitarian aid."[408]

If humanitarian aid, and not regime change, was the goal, why did the U.S. support the rebels? Would not additional rebel activity only worsen the already deteriorating conditions for the citizens of Libya?

U.S. propaganda, supporting the U.S. involvement in the destruction of Libya, filled the media, with the *New York Times* leading the charge as the unquestioning tool of an imperial government. A June 30, *NYT* article headlined 'Tripoli Refugees Stream into Libya's Mountains', by Kareem Fahim, included this:

> '[P]eople (are) fleeing Tripoli,' hundreds leaving to escape 'the dread-ed People's Guard carr(ying) long lists of wanted men ... Their numbers – more than a hundred families on a recent day alone – suggest a quickening exodus from the capital.' His source – mer-cenary rebels providing falsified information, not verified accounts from independent sources.[409]

This mirrors current 'reports' about Syria (see Chapter 26), wherein U.S. media outlets quote information from the 'Syrian Observatory of Human Rights', an organization consisting of one man, based in Coventry, England. Further,

---

[407]"Covert U.S. Aid to Rebels Reported," *Tribune-Review/Pittsburgh Tribune-Review*, March 31, 2011.

[408]https://foreignpolicy.com/2016/03/22/libya-and-the-myth-of-humanitarian-interve ntion/. Accessed on August 29, 2018.

[409]https://www.globalresearch.ca/war-propaganda-western-media-promotes-nato-ter ror-bombing-of-libya/25492. Accessed on August 29, 2018.

Fahim quoted a man named Ali Mohammed Rahaybi, saying 'he saw signs of resistance to (Gaddafi's) rule everywhere: in graffiti on schools, at occasional demonstrations, and in the flags drawn on neighborhood walls.'

Apparently he didn't notice one million pro-Gaddafi Libyans, rallying in Tripoli for him. No *Times* report covered, or even mentioned, what was too obvious to miss. Instead, Fahim, other *Times* writers, and all major media ones provide managed news propaganda, violating their profession's ethical code that's required to keep their jobs.[410]

Yet this misinformation, printed in the highly respected *New York Times*, went unchallenged in the mainstream media. Boyle writes:

As was true for almost every previous invocation of the doctrine of so-called 'humanitarian intervention' in modern history going all the way back to the mid-19th century, the application of R2P [Responsibility to Protect] to Libya in 2011 was based upon outright lies, falsehoods, propaganda, and half-truths that were systematically manufactured, concocted, and disseminated by the U.S./NATO states, their ground-feeding news media, their sycophantic NGOs, and their prostituted academics and 'intellectuals' ...[411]

The war against Libya was a short one; it ended in October of the year it started. But for the U.S., it was highly successful. The government was overthrown and the infrastructure completely destroyed. The country is now in a state of anarchy. According to Stephen R. Weissman writing in *Presidential Studies Quarterly*:

Although there was a democratic parliamentary election in July 2012, the country quickly succumbed to the rule of lawless militias. These were largely descended from local rebel brigades that benefited from the intervention. In September, an extremist Islamist militia was implicated in the assassination of four Americans, including Ambassador Christopher Stevens, in the former rebel capitol of Benghazi.

Today Libya is widely characterized as a 'failed state'. Rival governments – in the West and in the East – proclaim their legitimacy. But effective political and economic power resides in hundreds of competing militias, including newer Islamic State and tribal formations. In 2014, fighting killed up to 2,500 people. In February 2016,

---

[410]Ibid.

[411]Boyle, *Destroying Libya*, 187.

the Obama administration debated using military force against the Islamic State grouping.

On the international level, the undisciplined outflow of arms, ethnic fighters and Islamic extremists from postwar Libya precipitated an Islamic extremist takeover of half the nation of Mali and strengthened jihadists from North and West Africa to the Egyptian Sinai. The intervention, mainly organized by the North Atlantic Treaty Organization (NATO), aggravated relations between the United States and Russia. The latter continues to denounce alleged Western misuse of the United Nations to force regime change. Recently the chaos in Libya precipitated a breakdown of coastal migration controls, contributing to a risky mass exodus of African and Middle Eastern refugees toward Europe.[412]

Despite all this, the Libyan disaster is seen as a success by the U.S. government. When asked about his worst mistake as president on Fox News, Obama responded, "Probably failing to plan for the day after what I think was the right thing to do in intervening in Libya."[413] A prosperous North African nation not allied with Israel must not be allowed to exist; therefore, its destruction is assured. And in the case of Libya, that destruction is complete.

Did Colonel Qaddafi violate international human rights laws? There is little doubt that he did. But, as Boyle writes, Qaddafi's violations of international law "pale into insignificance before the 50,000 Libyans exterminated in 2011 by the U.S./NATO states and their genocidal surrogate terrorist army proxies."[414]

What was and is the cost for Libya? In addition to at least 50,000 Libyans that were killed, the government was completely destroyed and, as of this writing, its 6,000,000 people live with constant violence, poverty, uncertainty and grave hardships. This is what U.S. 'humanitarian aid' brought to once-prosperous and peaceful Libya.

---

[412]Stephen R. Weissman, "Presidential Deception in Foreign Policy Making: Military Intervention in Libya 2011," *Presidential Studies Quarterly* 46, no. 3 (2016).

[413]"Obama: Failing 'The Day After' in Libya Worst Mistake of Presidency," *Hindustan Times* (New Delhi, India), April 12, 2016.

[414]Boyle, *Destroying Libya*, 187.

Chapter 26: Syria (2011–Present)

Since beginning in 2011, the chaos in Syria has been the product of U.S interference. The U.S. and some of its allies, including Israel, have trained, armed and fully supported so-called 'rebel' groups that have caused unspeakable suffering there. Due to the fact that the U.S. would like to present the conflict as a simple case of oppressed people rebelling against a repressive government, not much reporting is done on the reality. But the government of Bashar al-Assad was elected in what international bodies all said were fair and democratic elections in 2014, and he has the overwhelming support of Syrian citizens.

Nevertheless, the U.S. continues. It supports the White Helmets, a heavily armed terrorist propaganda group; the Free Syrian Army, another 'rebel group', along with many others. It accepts without question pronouncements from the Syrian Observatory for Human Rights, a one-man operation based in the United Kingdom.

Why Syria? Why would the U.S. add fuel to the burning fires of the Middle East, when Syria has in no way threatened the U.S.?

James P. Rubin, Assistant Secretary of State for Public Affairs in the Clinton Administration and a close associate of Hillary Clinton, wrote to Clinton in 2012, advising her on Syria. Part of the email, which she then forwarded to undisclosed persons, reads as follows:

> As you will see from the attached piece, I believe that action on Syria will forestall the biggest danger on the horizon, that Israel launches a surprise attack on Iran's nuclear facilities. Although the pressure has now eased for a variety of reasons, it will return. Action by Washington on Syria, on the other hand, I believe will eliminate much of the urgency for Israeli action. In other words, a more aggressive policy on Syria will eliminate the best case the republican's [sic] have going into the November election, will ease substantially the pressure on Israel to attack Iran and possibly spark a wider war in the Middle East, and finally would be the right stance on Syria going forward.[415]

---

[415] https://foia.state.gov/searchapp/DOCUMENTS/HRCEmail_NovWeb/293/DOC_0C05794497/C05794497.pdf. Accessed on August 16, 2018.

This shows that Rubin's concern, apparently shared by Clinton since she forwarded this attachment to others, was twofold: 1) to prevent Israel from invading Iran, and 2) for political expediency going into an election. For these reasons, the autonomous, legitimate government of Syria was to be destroyed, with hundreds of thousands, and possibly millions of its people killed.

Such reasons would be unlikely to succeed in convincing the U.S. populace to support a war in Syria. Since there was no legitimate reason for such interference by the U.S. or any of its allies, which false flag could be sent up the flagpole? The choice was unoriginal, but successful, and has been recycled several times over the course of the war. In 2013, the U.S. accused Syria of launching a chemical attack against its own citizens. President Barack Obama said that the Syrian government had thus crossed a red line.

That a chemical attack occurred is difficult to dispute. What is unclear, however, is who was responsible. The *Washington Times* reported:

> Testimony from victims strongly suggests it was the rebels, not the Syrian government, that used Sarin nerve gas during a recent incident in the revolution-wracked nation, a senior U.N. diplomat said in 2013.
>
> Carla del Ponte, a member of the U.N. Independent International Commission of Inquiry on Syria, told Swiss TV there were 'strong, concrete suspicions but not yet incontrovertible proof,' that rebels seeking to oust Syrian strongman Bashar al-Assad had used the nerve agent.
>
> But she said her panel had not yet seen any evidence of Syrian government forces using chemical weapons, according to the BBC, but she added that more investigation was needed.[416]

Such facts are not of interest to the U.S. government.

On April 4, 2017, Syria was again accused of launching a chemical attack on its own people. Three days later, the U.S. launched 59 Tomahawk missiles on Syria, allegedly in direct response to the Syrian attack. However, the evidence for this attack was even less credible than the 2013 incident. In February of 2018, Secretary of Defense James Mattis said that there

---

[416]https://www.washingtontimes.com/news/2013/may/6/syrian-rebels-used-sarin-ner ve-gas-not-assads-regi/. Accessed on November 10, 2018.

was "no evidence" that Syria had used chemical weapons, either in April of 2017, or in 2013.[417]

This startling news was not widely reported; certainly, it didn't get nearly the publicity that the original, and false, accusation received. Notice that the U.S. did not await any confirmation; the accusation was sufficient to justify, in the minds of U.S. government officials, retaliatory measures. Even from the start, there were questions about Syria's guilt, as reported in *Newsweek*:

> Serious, experienced chemical weapons experts and investigators such as Hans Blix, Scott Ritter, Gareth Porter and Theodore Postol have all cast doubt on 'official' American narratives regarding President Al-Assad employing Sarin.
>
> These analysts have all focused on the technical aspects of the two attacks and found them not to be consistent with the use of nation-state quality Sarin munitions.[418]

The U.S. response might be somewhat – if just barely – understandable, if the U.S. responded uniformly to alleged chemical weapons attacks. But the U.S. uses its justifications selectively. Turkey and the Kurdish militia, both allied with the U.S., were accused of using chemical weapons early in 2018, but as Whitney Webb wrote in early 2018 for *MintPress News*, "it seems that the U.S. is willing to turn a blind eye to such attacks when its allies are implicated".[419] The same can be said of Israel's use of chemical weapons against the Palestinians. Webb continues:

> In these instances, the U.S.' response has been drastically different from its response to alleged chemical weapon attacks where the accused party has been the Syrian government – even when the U.S. has admitted that it has never had evidence of Syria's chemical weapons use. Yet that lack of evidence didn't stop the U.S. from calling for a 'no-fly zone' in Syrian government-held territory after an alleged chemical weapons attack in 2013, and a unilateral attack against Syria after another alleged chemical weapons attack last year.
>
> In the most recent case, an alleged chemical gas attack, which was said to have injured a single person, was blamed on the Syrian

---

[417] http://www.newsweek.com/now-mattis-admits-there-was-no-evidence-assad-using -poison-gas-his-people-801542. Accessed on August 16, 2018

[418] Ibid.

[419] https://www.mintpressnews.com/us-applies-useful-double-standard-alleged-use-che mical-weapons-syria/237846/

government earlier this month. The evidence given was the verbal testimony of members of the White Helmets, long exposed as a 'propaganda construct' and logistics group for the terrorist group al-Nusra. Al-Nusra and other so-called 'rebels' in Syria have also been accused on several occasions of chemical weapons use, but these accusations have also failed to draw a response from the U.S. – even when these groups admitted to using the prohibited weapons.

In contrast, the case in Turkey was documented by both pro-opposition groups and pro-Syrian government groups and there was video footage. However, in this case, the accounts of the U.S.' Kurdish allies are apparently not as trustworthy as those of the al-Nusra-affiliated White Helmets.[420]

Such stories of chemical attacks are not new; they have been promulgated since the start of the problems in Syria, as political analyst Tim Anderson shows:

A steady stream of atrocity stories – 'barrel bombs', chemical weapons, 'industrial scale' killings, dead babies – permeate the western news on Syria. These stories all have two things in common: they paint the Syrian President and the Syrian Army as monsters slaughtering civilians, including children; yet, when tracked back, all the stories come from utterly partisan sources. We are being deceived.[421]

The U.S. and its allies didn't hesitate to tell the most blatant lies about Syria. In 2011, Secretary of State Hillary Clinton proclaimed in an article in Al Jazeera that Basher al-Assad Syria's president, had "lost all legitimacy".[422] Contrast that statement to the following:

"[I]n 2012, western media interviewed three Free Syrian Army (FSA) commanders in Aleppo," Anderson writes. "They all admitted they were hated by the local people and that the Syrian President had the loyalty of most. One said President al-Assad had about '70 percent' support in that mainly Sunni Muslim city. A second said the local people, 'all of them, are loyal to the criminal Bashar, they inform on us.'"[423] And according to a report in the World Tribune, "an internal NATO report estimated that 70% of Syrians supported the President, 20% were neutral and 10% supported the rebels."[424] This evidence was not widely reported in the

---

[420]Ibid.

[421]Anderson, *Dirty War*, 11.

[422]Ibid., 13.

[423]Ibid.

[424]Ibid.

U.S., but Clinton's statement about the Syrian president having 'lost all legitimacy' was, and her statement was even more damaging because it carried the weight of her position in the Obama administration.

The propaganda campaign even involved the 'reputable' organization, Human Rights Watch. Its head, Kenneth Roth, according to Anderson, "has even been exposed posting photos of devastated Gaza and Kobane, falsely claiming that both showed Aleppo after 'Assad's barrel bombing.'"[425]

Civilian death rates are also very difficult to estimate. They are often provided by the 'Syrian Observatory for Human Rights'; the Syrian Network for Human Rights, also based in England; and the Violation Documentation Center, based in Turkey. Anderson comments: "[T]hey are all partisan voices, sectarian Islamists committed to overthrow of the secular state and highly motivated to vilify and lie about the Syrian Army."[426]

What has the U.S.'s involvement been in Syria? As stated above, it was not supporting a Syrian people's movement to overthrow their government. Since at least 2013, the U.S. has been arming, supporting and training what are essentially mercenaries doing the work the U.S., through the Central Intelligence Agency, hired them to do. This program, which the Trump administration officially ended in 2017, "began in 2013 as part of efforts by the administration of then-President Barack Obama to overthrow Assad, but produced little success".[427]

What has been the result? The number of deaths is unknown. The reason, according to the *New York Times*:

> [T]he United Nations, which released regular reports on the death toll during the first years of the war, gave its last estimate in 2016 — when it relied on 2014 data, in part — and said that it was virtually impossible to verify how many had died.
>
> At that time, a United Nations official said 400,000 people had been killed.[428]

Since that time, the U.S. has bombed areas of the country where thousands more people have been killed. The death toll may reach, or exceed, 1,000,000. What did these innocent people die for? In July 2018, Steven

---

[425] Ibid., 16.

[426] Ibid., 15.

[427] https://www.reuters.com/article/us-mideast-crisis-usa-syria/trump-ends-cia-arms-support-for-anti-assad-syria-rebels-u-s-officials-idUSKBN1A42KC.

[428] https://www.nytimes.com/2018/04/13/world/middleeast/syria-death-toll.html. Accessed on August 16, 2018.

Cook wrote an article titled "The Syrian War Is Over, and America Lost" in *Foreign Policy*, in which he said the following:

> Syrian regime forces hoisted their flag above the southern town of Daraa and celebrated. Although there is more bloodletting to come, the symbolism was hard to miss. The uprising that began in that town on March 6, 2011, has finally been crushed, and the civil war that has engulfed the country and destabilized parts of the Middle East as well as Europe will be over sooner rather than later. Bashar al-Assad, the man who was supposed to fall in 'a matter of time,' has prevailed with the help of Russia, Iran, and Hezbollah ...[429]

Syria continues to be a troubled nation, with the U.S. withdrawing some, but not all of its soldiers. Yet Trump is far from forgetting about Syria. On October 30, 2019,

> ... the President said that he is not only keeping American forces in Syria to 'secure' its oil fields, he is willing to go to war over them. 'We may have to fight for the oil. It's O.K.,' he said. 'Maybe somebody else wants the oil, in which case they have a hell of a fight. But there's massive amounts of oil.' The United States, he added, should be able to take some of Syria's oil. 'What I intend to do, perhaps, is make a deal with an ExxonMobil or one of our great companies to go in there and do it properly,' he said. The goal would be to 'spread out the wealth.'[430]

Trump sees Syria as merely a future colony, one to be exploited for the rich. Yet this plan will not sit well with Turkey, Russia or Iran, each of which is, or is becoming, a major power broker in the Middle East. But Trump has little grasp of history, world politics or diplomacy; his next steps in Syria could be catastrophic.

---

[429] https://foreignpolicy.com/2018/07/23/the-syrian-war-is-over-and-america-lost/. Accessed on August 16, 2018.

[430] https://www.newyorker.com/news/our-columnists/trumps-baffling-plan-to-pillage-syrias-oil. Accessed on November 12, 2019.

Chapter 27: Yemen (2015–Present)

The U.S. war on Yemen differs from many of its other interventions. There was no one incident (e.g. Gulf of Tonkin, Chapter 15; or weapons of mass destruction, Chapter 24). There was no need to invent a reason to bomb Yemen, because it happened gradually and secretly, without the public's knowledge. When it finally came into the consciousness of the U.S. citizenry, it wasn't new, and was lumped in with the country's other 'national security' imperialist ventures.

Yemen is a nation with a population of about 24,000,000 people, located at the southern tip of the Arabian Peninsula. As Middle East expert Jeremy M. Sharp stated:

> The country's rugged terrain and geographic isolation, strong tribal social structure, and sparsely settled population has historically made it difficult to centrally govern (and conquer), a feature that has promoted a more pluralistic political environment, but that also has hampered socioeconomic development.[431]

Following the abortive Arab Spring uprisings, Yemen negotiated what was expected to be a peaceful political solution. Columnist Gerald Feierstein summarized the agreement:

In November 2011, Yemen's major political parties, with the support of the United States and the international community, signed the Gulf initiative that included provisions for the:

- Replacement of the government of former President Ali Abdallah Salih,

- Election of a new interim president, and

- Establishment of a two-year roadmap for new presidential and parliamentary elections to include the creation of a National Dialogue as a forum to address Yemen's problems.[432]

---

[431] Jeremy M. Sharp, "Yemen: Background and U.S. Relations," *Current Politics and Economics of the Middle East* 2, no. 1 (2011).

[432] Gerald Feierstein, "Is There a Path out of the Yemen Conflict?: Why It Matters," *Prism: A Journal of the Center for Complex Operations* 7, no. 1 (2017).

For the next two years, things proceeded smoothly, with Abd Rabuh Mansur Hadi being elected interim president, and the Yemeni military restructuring their operations. However, all was not well:

> Developments outside of the initiative, however, were ominous and proved fatal to the transition process. Comprised equally of members drawn from Ali Abdallah Salih's General People's Congress and the opposition Joint Meeting Parties, under the leadership of Prime Minister Mohammed Basindwa, the interim government was weak, dysfunctional, and riven by party and personal rivalries. Governance and security collapsed, while corruption surged to new levels. Sabotage and insurrection around the country brought economic activity to a halt as the capital, Sanaa, and other urban centers were plunged into darkness for days and weeks at a time.[433]

The powerful Huthi tribe[434] – although included in most, but not all, of the activities leading to this agreement – boycotted the 2012 election of Abd Rabuh Mansur Hadi, and wouldn't withdraw from their armed encampment in Sanaa. Following their successful siege of the town of Dammaj, they defeated another force in Amran. At this point, former President Ali Abdallah Salih, who'd previously had poor relations with the Huthis, joined his forces with theirs.

By 2014, a new political agreement was signed, creating a new government under Prime Minister Khalid al-Bahah. This agreement collapsed in early 2015, and Hadi fled to Saudi Arabia.

All this might have had only minimal importance to the United States, had the Huthis not been closely aligned with Iran, and "hostile to key U.S. goals and objectives".[435] In March of 2015, it was decided by the U.S. and Saudi Arabia that Saudi Arabia would intervene to keep the Huthis from occupying Yemen. Additionally, Saudi Arabia would attempt to stabilize Aden and the surrounding area, to enable the return of Hadi and the re-establishment of a government under him. To date, Saudi Arabia has been unable to accomplish this goal.

Note that in all this there is no consideration for the wishes of the Yemeni people. The concepts of self-government and self-determination are nowhere to be found. Granted, the country has serious problems, but Saudi and U.S. interference has not been helpful.

In October 2016, according to *Vox*:

---

[433]Ibid.

[434]Alternately spelled 'Houthi'. Both spellings are used herein, depending on the source from which the information was obtained.

[435]Ibid.

... the United States bombed Yemen's Houthi militants for the first time, launching cruise missiles at three Houthi-controlled radar installations. The strikes were billed as limited retaliation: Twice in the past week, missiles have been fired from Houthi-controlled territory at US warships in the area (which they luckily missed).[436]

U.S. warships had no business being where they were; the Houthi 'militants' were defending their nation from foreign invaders who have wrought unspeakable damage and suffering to the Yemeni people. And this 'first time' bombing Yemen is deceptive; since at least 2015, the U.S. has "been quietly participating in a Saudi-led war against the Houthis, providing valuable logistical support for Saudi Arabia's airstrikes".[437]

What is the U.S. supporting in Yemen? The *Vox* report continues: "Saudi airstrikes have struck civilian targets like marketplaces and funeral homes. Their warships have blockaded Yemeni ports, helping to create a humanitarian catastrophe in which children are literally starving to death."[438]

Propaganda about the war mainly focuses on the 'assistance' that Saudi Arabia is attempting to provide to Yemen, which Houthi rebels are thwarting. A few examples are informative:

- Irina Tsukerman, writing in the pro-Israel publication, *Mosaic*, said this: "It was the Houthis, not the Saudis, who first imposed a humanitarian blockade against Yemen. They then used humanitarian-aid shipments to their own population as a disguise for smuggled weapons, which ultimately led to many deaths from starvation. The Saudis were forced to impose their own naval blockade as a defensive measure to counter ballistic-missile strikes and increased attacks on coalition [forces] on the ground—yet the Houthis have succeeded in painting the kingdom as the villain."[439]

  Daniel Larison, writing in *The American Conservative*, disputes these pronouncements:

  > The Houthis are responsible for impeding aid deliveries in territory they control, but they have neither the means nor

---

[436] https://www.vox.com/world/2016/10/14/13269580/us-bombing-yemen-houthis. Accessed on September 6, 2018.

[437] Ibid.

[438] Ibid.

[439] https://mosaicmagazine.com/picks/2018/04/irans-brutal-war-in-yemen-threatens-the-security-of-the-entire-middle-east/. Accessed on September 9, 2018.

the inclination to blockade their own country. The accusation
is self-refuting and an obvious lie. The sea and air blockade of
the country was imposed by the coalition at the outset of the
Saudi-led intervention. The blockade is the principal cause of
the country's humanitarian crisis, and the responsibility for
it rests entirely with the Saudi-led coalition and its Western
backers.

The coalition was not 'forced' to do this, but chose to do
it from the beginning of their war. The coalition blockade
predates any missile attacks on Saudi Arabia and was not
imposed because of them, so that is another lie.

It is exceptionally dishonest to label the conflict 'Iran's war'
when Iranian involvement has been and remains negligible
for the last three years. Tsukerman asserts that 'Tehran is
building a naval base in Yemen,' but that is also false.[440]

- U.S. Secretary of State Mike Pompeo said this on May 21, 2018:
  "In Yemen, Iran's support for the Houthi militia fuels a conflict that
  continues to starve the Yemeni people and hold them under the
  threat of terror." Daniel Larison also addressed these lies: "What
  Pompeo doesn't mention here is that the conflict was escalated by
  the Saudi coalition with U.S. backing that continues to this day.
  The people of Yemen are being starved in large part because of the
  coalition blockade that the U.S. supports. Yemeni civilians are most
  often terrorized by indiscriminate coalition bombings of their cities
  and towns."[441]

- In December 2017, *The Listening Post* reported: "There's little reporting of the behind-the-scenes roles Britain and the United States
  are playing in this conflict – underwriting the Saudis with arms, expertise and diplomatic cover. There are a lot of angles to this story
  – including the alleged role Iran is playing in Yemen, an angle long
  on allegations and short on proof."[442]

- A ceasefire in the fighting in the important port city of Hodeidah
  went into effect in early July 2018: "The ceasefire probably came
  about because the western-backed coalition needed time to lick its

---

[440] https://www.theamericanconservative.com/larison/the-war-on-yemen-and-pro-sau
di-propaganda-in-the-west/. Accessed on September 6, 2018.

[441] https://www.theamericanconservative.com/larison/the-war-on-yemen-and-pompe
os-propaganda/. Accessed on September 6, 2018.

[442] https://www.aljazeera.com/programmes/listeningpost/2017/12/covering-yemen-sal
eh-saudi-media-171209082634258.html. Accessed on September 6, 2018.

wounds amid ferocious resistance, which saw an Emirati ship destroyed and missiles hitting Riyadh for the first time. However, the coalition's western backers will no doubt demand that it fights on after determining a propaganda mechanism for blaming everything on the Houthis."[443]

Iran's involvement in Yemen, although minimal, has enraged the U.S. Feierstein further commented on this aspect of the conflict:

> For the Government of Iran, the [Saudi and U.S.] Coalition's inability to defeat the insurgents and restore the legitimate government in Yemen is a significant win. Iranian support for the Huthis comes at very little cost in contrast to the financial, human and reputational damage suffered by the Coalition.[444]

Please note that the 'legitimate' government described in the above quotation is a Saudi-ruled, U.S. puppet.

As indicated, the propaganda surrounding the Yemen war is based on a few false premises, each of which works in the favor of the U.S. government:

1. *The Huthis are causing mass starvation, and so the U.S. has 'no choice' but to intervene.* As shown above, it isn't the Huthis who have initiated the blockade and prevented the Yemeni people from obtaining food, thus starving to death tens of thousands of people, with millions more on the brink of starvation. The 'Coalition' – Saudi Arabia and the U.S. – is directly responsible for this atrocity.

2. *The Huthis are insurgents, and the U.S. must help the legitimate government.* It must be remembered that one person's 'insurgent' is another one's freedom fighter. The Huthis are defending their nation against foreign invasion and what they see as an illegal government.

3. *Iran, which the U.S. has bizarrely described as the world's foremost sponsor of terrorism, is heavily involved in Yemen, and the U.S. must defeat this insidious threat.* It must be remembered that the U.S., which accuses Iran of terrorism, is currently bombing seven countries, and has been at war for nearly two decades with Afghanistan. Just in this millennium, the U.S. has destroyed Libya and Iraq, is

---

[443] https://www.middleeasteye.net/columns/confronting-threat-independent-yemen -121085297. Accessed on September 6, 2018.
[444] Feierstein, "Is There a Path."

decimating Afghanistan, attempting to destroy Syria (unsuccess-fully, but at a terrible cost to the Syrian people), in addition to helping plot the overthrow of the Venezuelan government. Iran has not invaded another nation since 1798.

False flags and propaganda are on full display regarding the U.S.'s brutal onslaught of Yemen.

Chapter 28: Iran (1979–Present)

As of this writing, the U.S. has not invaded Iran. However, under the administration of President Donald Trump, that nation is now firmly in the U.S.'s crosshairs. A variety of false flags are being raised, and the propaganda machine is in overdrive. There is ever-increasing U.S. aggression against Iran.

On January 3, 2020, a U.S. bomb successfully targeted General Qassam Soleimani, the head of the Quds Force of the Islamic Revolutionary Guard Corps. The General was a revered figure in Iran, and his assassination was condemned around the world as a violation of international law and a dangerous and unnecessary escalation of tensions between the two nations. Iran responded by bombing a U.S. base in Iraq; the Iranian government could not allow such a brazen act against a top military commander to go unchallenged. Additional responses may still be performed. Iran is in a position, due to its geographic location and its role as a Middle East power, to retaliate in ways doubtless not anticipated by the short-sighted President Donald Trump, who is said to have personally ordered this criminal act.

But U.S. aggression against Iran is not new.

In 1953, the CIA overthrew the democratically elected government of Prime Minister Mohammad Mosaddegh, and installed the brutal Shah of Iran as monarch. For the next twenty-six years he oppressed the people of Iran, until he was overthrown in 1979, against the wishes of the United States. That revolution established the Islamic Republic of Iran, which the U.S. has opposed since its inception.

Iran has not invaded another country since 1798. The Iranian government, since the Islamic Revolution, has worked to strengthen its military and improve the living standards of its people.

Yet the U.S. government is in the pocket of Iran's sworn enemy, the apartheid nation of Israel. Millions upon millions of dollars in campaign contributions from pro-Israel lobbies flow into the coffers of U.S. officials seeking election or re-election. Expensive and luxurious 'fact-finding' trips to Israel are provided to these officials. Thus, thoughts of equality, human rights and international law are pushed aside, as doing whatever is required to maintain these political contributions and other political benefits comes to the forefront.

The U.S. has also financed terrorist rebel groups in Iran's ally, Syria, from at least 2011 to the present (see Chapter 26). Iran's Revolutionary Guard Corps has been successful in assisting the Syrian government in expelling them. Syria, in the view of the U.S., must be destroyed as the U.S. destroyed Libya (see chapter 25) and Iraq (see Chapter 24), so that Israel retains complete hegemony in the Middle East. And that is why Iran must be destroyed, according to the U.S.

In the midst of this simmering conflict, in 2015, Iran signed an agreement with the U.S., Russia, China, Germany, Britain, France and the European Union, known as the Joint Comprehensive Plan of Action (JCPOA). The purpose of this was to regulate Iran's nuclear program; in exchange, crippling sanctions that the U.S. and other nations had issued against Iran would be removed.

It must be noted that Iran's spokespeople had always said that their nation's nuclear program was for peaceful purposes. But with Israel's Prime Minister Benjamin Netanyahu proclaiming annually that Iran was anywhere from a few weeks to a few months away from developing nuclear weapons, the U.S. took the lead in endorsing that view. Thus, the JCPOA was negotiated and signed by President Barack Obama.

In view of this, some peculiar statements have been made; we will look at a few.

In February of 2017, the U.S. Secretary of Defense, James Mattis, said this: "As far as Iran goes, this is the single biggest state sponsor of terrorism in the world." At the time Mattis made that statement, the U.S. was bombing seven countries. It was working to destabilize and overthrow the government of Syria. Since the end of World War II, it has invaded, destabilized, overthrown or worked to overthrow the governments of the following countries. Syria (1949), Iran (1953), Guatemala (1954), Tibet (1955), Indonesia (1958), Cuba (1959), Democratic Republic of the Congo (1960–1965), South Vietnam (1963), Brazil (1964), Chile (1964–1973), Ghana (1966), Afghanistan (1979–1989), Turkey (1980), Poland (1980 –1981), Nicaragua (1981–1990), Cambodia (1969–1975), Angola (1980s), Philippines (1986), Iraq (1992–1996; 2003–2011), Venezuela (2002; 2012– present), Afghanistan (2001–present), Palestine (2006–present), Somalia (2006–2007), Iran (2005–present), Libya (2011), Syria (2011–present).[445]

---

[445]Some countries are listed multiple times due to repeated attempts at overthrow by the U.S.

Then U.S. Ambassador to the United Nations Nikki Haley made this statement in October 2017: "Iran hides behind its assertion of technical compliance with the nuclear deal while it brazenly violates the other limits of its behavior." Iran is not hiding behind its own assertion of compliance with the JCPOA; the agreement specifies that United Nations inspectors must certify compliance, which they have done consistently since the agreement was signed. Even Trump agreed that Iran was in compliance. And what of Iran violating "the other limits of its behavior"? This statement simply makes no sense.

Secretary of State Mike Pompeo, on his first trip abroad in his new role, said this: "Iran destabilizes this entire region." Currently, the U.S. is bombing Afghanistan, Iraq, Libya, Somalia, Syria, and Yemen. Iran is helping to defend Syria against U.S. bombs and U.S.-trained jihadists. It would appear that the facts contradict Pompeo's statement; it is, after all, the U.S. that is destabilizing the entire region.

Additionally, Israel is bombing Syria, selecting Iranian military sites, as it also continues to occupy Palestine and oppress the Palestinians. Yet Pompeo only accused Iran of 'destabilizing' the region.

Trump has repeatedly called the JCPOA "the worst deal ever". It's interesting that, despite the recent U.S. violation of the agreement, all the other signatories said that they would maintain their part of it (however, most of them quickly bowed to U.S. pressure, and ceased to honor their agreements). They have all expressed dismay at the U.S.'s actions, and proclaimed that they will work together to assure that Iran continues to reap the financial benefits of the agreement, while it complies with it. Yet Trump has threatened to sanction any country that continues to do business with Iran, even though those very countries are among the U.S.'s oldest and most trusted allies.

In September of 2018, then U.S. Secretary of Defense James Mattis, at that time the last remaining member of the Trump team that opposed his aggression towards Iran, was about to enter the revolving door of Trump's cabinet:

> Back in late June, *MintPress News* reported on related concerns that Mattis would soon be the next high-profile Trump administration official to be shown the door after the firings of National Security Adviser H.R. McMaster and Secretary of State Rex Tillerson. As *MintPress* noted at the time, both McMaster and Tillerson lost their jobs because of their opposition to Trump's aggressive Iran policy as well as his extreme pro-Israel policy, both of which have

since been championed by their replacements, John Bolton and Mike Pompeo, respectively.

Mattis is the last remaining high-ranking member of the Trump cabinet who has publicly opposed the President's Iran policy, particularly the U.S.' unilateral withdrawal from the Joint Comprehensive Plan of Action (JCPOA), also known as the Iran nuclear deal.[446]

The departure of Mattis escalated Trump's aggression and war-mongering towards Iran. He has increased sanctions and issued threats every time Iran legitimately exercises its military force in its own defense. The U.S. government also condemns Iran's increasing uranium enrichment activities, done in accordance with the JCPOA, under the terms that are allowed if other signatories do not maintain the agreement. Since the U.S. was the first to violate it, and then threatened sanctions against the other signatories unless they did likewise, it is the height of hypocrisy for Trump to criticize and threaten Iran for increasing nuclear enrichment.

Iran is allied with Russia, and that alliance seems to have been strengthened by both countries' successful efforts to defeat U.S.-supported terrorist groups in Syria. In September 2018, Russian President Vladimir Putin met with the Ayatollah Khamenei and Iranian Vice President Eshaq Jahangiri, to discuss a wide range of issues, including U.S. hostility towards Iran, specifically the U.S. withdrawal from the JCPOA, and a strengthening of economic cooperation. It is highly unlikely that Russia would countenance a U.S. invasion of its ally, Iran. The potential, then, for a much wider and deadlier war, should the U.S. invade Iran, is very real. Israel, of course, would support the U.S. position, and that rogue nation might launch nuclear missiles, the result of which would be catastrophic for the entire planet.

Trump & Co. continue to rattle their sabers in Iran's direction, repeating the lie of Iranian 'terror', as they continue to devastate the world with their own. How successful this propaganda will be remains, at this writing, to be seen.

---

[446]https://www.mintpressnews.com/trump-actively-discussing-mattis-replacement-loo king-for-cooperative-iran-hawk/248930/. Accessed on September 11, 2018.

Chapter 29: Anti-Communist Interventions, and Dictators Supported by the U.S.

The preceding chapters all discuss major or 'lesser' U.S. wars waged against innocent people for the U.S.'s own purposes. Each discusses the lies that were told before and during the war, and the propaganda campaigns that were used.

The list of countries that the U.S. didn't invade – but in which they worked to either overthrow democratically-elected governments, or to support brutally repressive dictators – is long. For some, like Palestine, it isn't its own dictator that the U.S. supports, but its brutal occupier, Israel. Some of these countries were destabilized at one point and invaded at another. Some experienced multiple 'interventions' by the United States.

Others, such as Laos and Vietnam, were invaded in order to prevent a communist government from coming to power.

We will review some of the countries that have been so brutalized by the U.S. here.

Guatemala (1920–1954)

Throughout much of the twentieth century, Guatemala experienced political instability, with multiple and frequent changes of leadership. In 1920, Guatemalan dictator Estrada Cabrera was overthrown, ending his 22-year reign. A few months later, a second coup occurred, which put General Jose Orellana into power. The U.S. objected; it was much more amenable to Jorge Ubico. As Orellana tried to control the government, historian Kenneth Grieb writes, U.S. representatives in Guatemala

> ... caucused with various political leaders and members of the Assembly during the subsequent days, participating in the political confrontations and employing the full weight of American power to assure that the Orellanistas were excluded from the new government.[447]

---

[447]Kenneth J. Grieb, "American Involvement in the Rise of Jorge Ubico," *Caribbean Studies* 10, no. 1 (Apr. 1970), 5–21.

Ubico was an obvious choice for the U.S.: "His reorganization of the area's security forces and orders to execute all suspected bandits gained him a reputation for efficiency and cruelty."[448] Further, "American representatives were highly impressed by Ubico's accomplishments." [449] Charge de Affairs Stanley Hawkes noted "that the general was 'favorably inclined towards the United States'."[450]

In 1931, with the situation quickly deteriorating, the U.S. rushed the nation into an election, ostensibly based on "a desire to regularize the situation as rapidly as possible."[451] Jorge Ubico was victorious. Installed as president with much help from the United States, Ubico was known for his cruelty and oppressive policies. During his reign, according to historian Stephen M. Streeter, "he exempted the United Fruit Company from all taxes... permitted the United States to establish a military base in Guatemala, and he invited U.S. military advisors to direct the Escuael Politecnica, the nation's major military academy."[452]

Despite U.S. backing, his brutal regime eventually "provoked a popular insurrection led by students, middle-class intellectuals, professionals, and junior army officers."[453] On July 1, 1944, Ubico was forced from office and fled the country. The U.S. expected his successor to be General Federico Ponce Vaides, from whom Washington expected no resistance. Yet, Ponce Vaides did not rule for long; the revolution that had ousted Ubico only grew, and within less than four months, Ponce Vaides, too, fled the country. The leaders of the revolution, Captain Jacobo Arbenz Guzman and Major Francisco Arana, along with a lawyer, Jorge Toriello, formed a new government with a promise to hold elections by the end of the year. This represented a significant departure from the Ubico years. Streeter writes:

> Ubico and his predecessors had willingly sacrificed Guatemala's sovereignty to enrich themselves. The leaders of the 1944 revolution, by contrast, were true patriots who wanted to reverse Guatemala's economic dependence on the United States.[454]

---

[448]Ibid.

[449]Ibid.

[450]Ibid.

[451]Ibid.

[452]Stephen M. Streeter, *Managing the Counterrevolution: The United States and Guatemala, 1954–1961*, 12.

[453]Ibid.

[454]Ibid., 13.

One might think that the U.S. would have supported the new government of Guatemala and its peoples' self-determination. This, however, was not the case: "Washington eventually come to oppose Guatemalan nationalism under the guise of anticommunism, but the historical setting suggests that that opposition stemmed from U.S. economic and strategic interest rather than from confusion of the political orientation of the Guatemalan revolution."[455]

Following a period of relative stability and economic growth, Jacobo Arbenz Guzman won the presidency in the 1950 election. He promised, during the campaign, to continue the socioeconomic reforms of his predecessor (Juan Jose Arevalo, who was not legally allowed to run for another term), reforms which "the CIA disdainfully refers to (these reforms) in a memorandum as 'an intensely nationalistic program of progress colored by the touchy, anti-foreign inferiority complex of the 'Banana Republic.'"[456]

One of the projects that Arevalo began that Arbenz continued was land reform. U.S. specialist Greg Grandin said that this was the first and only time when, in Guatemala, "a significant part of the state authority was used to promote the interests of the nation's masses."[457]

The first attempts to overthrow the government were made under President Harry S. Truman. Efforts were renewed by President Dwight D. Eisenhower, when he authorized the PBSUCCESS operation, with "a $2.7 million [about $25 million in 2018 dollars] budget for 'psychological warfare and political action' and 'subversion'."[458]

Sadly for the people of Guatemala, this project was successful. In an article on the disinformation campaign against Arbenz, Roberto Garcia Ferreira writes:

> After several military coup attempts and an intensive national and international campaign by the Eisenhower administration against President Arbenz, a small force of exiles and mercenaries invaded from Honduras and penetrated a few miles into the country. Air raids by planes operated by CIA pilots created terror and confusion, while U.S. diplomatic pressure for Arbenz's ousting was applied locally and internationally. The end of Guatemala's 'democratic spring' was approaching.[459]

---

[455] Ibid.

[456] Peter Kornbluh, "Licensed to Kill," *The Nation*, June 16, 1997, 5.

[457] Greg Grandin, "Pensar globalmente, actuar localmente," cited in Roberto Garcia Ferreira, "The CIA and Jacobo Arbenz: History of a Disinformation Campaign," *Journal of Third World Studies* 25, no. 2 (2008).

[458] Ferreira, "The CIA and Jacobo Arbenz."

[459] Ibid.

Arbenz and his top aides had been able to flee the country, but after the C.I.A put Castillo Armas in power, hundreds of Guatemalans were rounded up and some killed. Between 1954 and 1990, human rights groups estimate successive military regimes have murdered more than 100,000 civilians.[460]

A timeline produced for a PBS report on Guatemala details the following:

> The U.S. Central Intelligence Agency backed a coup commanded by Colonel Carlos Castillo Armas against the democratically-elected president, Jacobo Arbenz. He was considered a communist threat, especially after legalizing the communist party and moving to nationalize the plantations of the United Fruit Company.
>
> Following the coup, Castillo was declared president, and set about reversing land reforms that benefited poor farmers. He also removed voting rights for illiterate Guatemalans.[461]

Yet overthrowing Arbenz and installing a cruel dictator wasn't enough; Arbenz's entire legacy that inspired much of Latin America had to be destroyed. Ferreira continues:

> [T]he CIA documentation alerts us to how much the agency continued to dedicate itself covertly to destroying the public image of the president after he was toppled. Arbenz was considered a political figure of the first order of importance within the Latin American spectrum, a fact corroborated in the historiographic literature. For that reason, the CIA seems to have taken an immediately vigilant attitude toward Arbenz.[462]

Guatemala had six presidents in the next 10 years, continuing the chaos that scarred the nation prior to the Arbenz presidency.

The contemptuous manner in which the U.S. government considered the aspirations of the Guatemalan people and their leader's efforts to improve their lives tells much about U.S. motivations.

Today, the current president, Jimmy Morales, had no experience in government before running for president; he had worked previously as a television comedian. His election in October 2015 was strikingly similar

---

[460]Ibid.

[461]https://www.pbs.org/newshour/health/latin_america-jan-june11-timeline_03-07. Accessed on November 24, 2018.

[462]Ferreira, "The CIA and Jacobo Arbenz."

to that of Donald Trump in the U.S. in 2016; Morales' major opponent was a former first lady, Sandra Torres, wife of Alvaro Colom Caballeros, who was closely associated with the oligarchy.

What are conditions like today in Guatemala? Amnesty International's 2017/2018 report on that nation provides this summary:

> Thousands continued to flee the country to escape high levels of inequality and violence. Human rights defenders, in particular those working on land, territorial and environmental issues, were at great risk and faced smear campaigns. Impunity and corruption persisted, undermining public trust in local authorities and hindering access to justice. Recent progress to consolidate the criminal justice system and the rule of law was challenged. High-profile cases of past crimes under international law remained stalled.[463]

This is the situation that the 'freedom-loving' United States brought to the people of Guatemala.

Albania (1946–1951)

Following World War II, when anti-communist fervor was ascending, the U.S. and the United Kingdom embarked on a plan to prevent Soviet influence within its Eastern European satellite nations. As Richard Trahair summarized the situation, "Albania was considered to be one of the first nations – the others would fall like dominoes – to be freed from Russian domination."[464] This undertaking, begun in 1946, was expected to succeed by 1951.

During World War II, communists from Albania fought fiercely against fascism. After Hitler withdrew in November of 1944, they created the People's Republic of Albania.

The manner in which the U.S. would attempt to destabilize Albania should be familiar, as it has been replicated countless times since then: "The committee's Cold War Subcommittee aimed to loosen Russia's grip on its satellite nations," writes Trahair, "by promoting in each one civil discontent, internal confusion, and political and economic strife."[465] Also

---

[463] https://www.amnesty.org/en/countries/americas/guatemala/report-guatemala/. Accessed on November 24, 2018.

[464] Richard C. S. Trahair, *Encyclopedia of Cold War Espionage, Spies, and Secret Operations* (Westport, CT: Greenwood Press, 2004), 5.

[465] Ibid., 4.

typical, "America and Britain would secretly sponsor a rebellion in Albania and pay for, train, and equip Albanian exiles to effect the rebellion, afterward disclaiming all knowledge of the operation."[466]

How did this start? As Regula and Edward Boorstein write:

> In December 1946, the [U.S] Government adopted guidelines for the conduct of psychological warfare and soon began preparations for other forms of covert action. The establishment of the CIA followed [in 1947].[467]

Albania was one of the first nations in the deadly sights of the CIA. As former CIA director William Colby noted in his memoirs,

> The CIA clandestinely supported the development of an anti-Communist resistance movement in the Ukraine and occasionally by parachute or PT boat delivered agents to the Baltic countries. A major effort to break Albania out of the curtain by stirring up a revolt against the Communist regime there was underway.[468]

> In 1949, Albania began making overtures to the Soviet Union, and the anti-communist U.S. government decided to act. Historian Scott C. Monje said that, as of October 1949, "In coordination with British intelligence, the CIA begins infiltrating anti-Communist rebels into Albania."[469]

Yet the entire undertaking by the U.S. in Albania was unsuccessful. Although rebels were trained in Malta, upon landing in Albania in October of 1949, they were captured or killed. During the next two years, additional U.S.- and U.K.-backed rebels entered the country, only to meet the same fate.

Since that time, Albania has had leftist or left-leaning governments. Yet, strategically, with its long coastline on the Adriatic Sea, it has some importance to the U.S., and the two countries have been allies since 1991.

Palestine (1948–Present)

Conditions in Palestine have been horrific since the bloody birth of Israel. In 1948, the newly-minted United Nations gave over 50% of the nation

---

[466]Ibid., 5.

[467]Regula Boorstein and Edward Boorstein, *Counterrevolution: U.S. Foreign Policy* (New York: International Publishers, 1990), 251.

[468]William Colby and Peter Forbath, *Honorable Men: My Life in the CIA* (New York: Simon and Schuster, 1978), 104.

[469]Scott C. Monje, *The Central Intelligence Agency: A Documentary History* (Westport, CT: Greenwood Press, 2008), xxxi.

of Palestine to establish Israel. Over 750,000 Palestinians were driven from their homes, with no decision in their own displacement, and no recompense. During the original expulsion, at least 10,000 Palestinians were killed. Since that time, tens of thousands more have been killed, with no one held accountable for these deaths.

Genocide is defined as the eradication of a people and their culture; it is clear that what has been happening to the people of Palestine is genocide.

It would seem that this would be the kind of situation that the U.S. government would object to. Indeed, on May 27, 1916, President Woodrow Wilson said, "Every people has a right to choose the sovereignty under which they shall live."[470] For some reason, this has never applied to the Palestinians.

There can be no doubt that Israel is an apartheid regime: it has separate laws for Israeli Jews and Israeli Arabs, and for Israelis and Palestinians; Palestinians cannot travel on Israeli roads; penalties for crimes are far more severe for Arabs than for Israelis accused of the same crime; Palestinians have to endure arbitrarily manned checkpoints within their own country. The list goes on.

The United Nations has issued more resolutions critical of Israeli violations of international law and the human rights of the Palestinians than of all other countries combined. The number would be higher if the United States did not routinely veto such resolutions in the Security Council.

Periodically, Israel bombs the Gaza Strip, an area of land described by many as the largest open-air prison in the world. Over 2,500,000 people reside in an area of 365 square kilometers (141 sq. mi), making the Strip one of the most densely populated areas in the world. After days of bombing, when homes, hospitals, mosques, United Nations refugee centers and press vehicles and buildings are targeted, all in violation of international law, Israel refuses to allow the importation of construction material. The last major bombing was in 2014, when thousands of Palestinian men, women and children were killed.

The Gaza Strip is blockaded by air, sea and land on all sides. Palestinians in Gaza wanting to visit friends or relatives in the West Bank, part of their own country, are not allowed to do so. Leaving the Strip for medical attention which isn't available in Gaza, mainly due to Israeli restrictions on medical imports, is next to impossible.

It would seem that two of the U.S.'s typical reasons for intervention

---

[470] *Congressional Record,* 64th Congress, 1st Session (Washington, DC: U.S. Government Printing Office, 1917), 54, pt 2:1742.

could be invoked in this situation. First, an oppressed people, deprived of the basic human right of self-determination, could certainly use the assistance of the most powerful military in the world to gain their freedom. And second, with unemployment over 40%, and much higher among young people, hospitals destroyed and medicines banned from import by Israel, 90% of the water unfit to drink and food supplies limited, this seems to be the very definition of a humanitarian crisis.

Additionally, following Israel's 54-day bombardment and invasion of the Gaza Strip in 2014, rains caused flooding, which further eroded the quality of drinking water, and increased the risk of disease. In addition, the tens of thousands of people who were rendered homeless by Israel's attack had to find shelter where they could: in buildings still standing that may have been damaged to the point of being unsafe; by quickly assembling make-shift shelters from whatever parts of destroyed buildings they could use; or by crowding in with anyone lucky enough to still have a home. This, it would seem, is the kind of suffering that provides countless photo opportunities for U.S. politicians to showcase their concern for the less fortunate.

However, the U.S. government does not see it that way. Rather, it gives Israel $4 billion annually in aid, more than it gives to any other nation. Recently, U.S. President Donald Trump cut all U.S. aid to United Nations agencies charged with assisting the Palestinian people. And whenever Israel bombs Gaza, which it does frequently (the carpet bombing of the Gaza Strip happens every few years, but bombs drop periodically), U.S. government officials say that Israel has a right to defend itself.

In 2012, then Secretary of State (and later Democratic presidential candidate) Hillary Clinton said this in regard to Syria: "We reject any equivalence between premeditated murders by a government's military machine and the actions of civilians under siege driven to self-defence."[471] It is not unrealistic to consider a brutally occupied nation to be 'under siege'. Would not such a people, as Mrs. Clinton so eloquently expressed, be 'driven to self-defence'? One might think so.

In the last 18 years, 1,242 Israelis have been killed by Palestinians. During that same time, more than10,000 Palestinians have been killed by Israelis. These tolls include 134 Israeli children, and 2,167 Palestinian children.[472]

---

[471] https://www.reuters.com/article/uk-syria-un/u-s-allies-clash-with-russia-on-endin g-syria-violence-idUKBRE82B0RQ20120312.

[472] https://ifamericansknew.org/. Accessed on December 17, 2019.

And what of propaganda? U.S. government officials decry the 'rockets from Gaza raining down on Israel.' Yet Professor Norman Finkelstein, son of Holocaust survivors and an ardent advocate of Palestinian rights, has referred to those rockets as 'enhanced fire works,' nothing at all compared to the deadly, U.S.-provided missiles that Israel drops on Gaza. Those officials also ignore the fact that, during 54 days in the summer of 2014, Israel shot more rockets into Gaza than Gaza had fired into Israel in the previous 14 years.

Some Zionists talk about Israel as 'a land without people for a people without a land,' either ignoring the 750,000 Palestinians who were driven from their homes to make way for the nation of Israel, or demonstrating a shocking racism by not considering Palestinians to be people.

The U.S. has declared Hamas, the democratically-elected government of the Gaza Strip, a 'terrorist' organization. It criticizes Hamas for, among other things, not recognizing the existence of Israel. Yet Israel has been slowly destroying Palestine for decades. Hamas does not have the power to destroy Israel, yet by 'appropriating' more and more Palestinian land for Israeli-only housing, Israel is slowly destroying Palestine.

Why does the U.S. government choose to not only overlook, but even finance, some of the most blatant and brutal human rights violations occurring on the planet today? In the United States, special interest groups and their powerful lobbies, and not the average citizen, comprise the constituency of elected officials. Needing millions of dollars for their election and re-election campaigns, they overlook international law, human rights violations, and even the U.S. Constitution in their quest for campaign dollars. Indeed, current members of the U.S. senate have received $25,754,362.00 in campaign contributions from pro-Israeli lobby groups during their careers.[473] With that much at stake for people who put their high-paying, low-responsibility jobs over everything else, human rights will always take a distant back seat.

Laos (1955–1975)

U.S. interference in Laos did not begin during the Vietnam War. Its ugly history there dates back at least to the 1950s, when Laos was still a French colony. Historian Sami Abouzahr concisely summarizes the situation as follows: "France had ruled the Indochinese states of Laos, Cambo-

---

[473] https://www.opensecrets.org/industries/summary.php?ind=Q05&cycle=All&recipd etail=S&mem=Y. Accessed on December 17, 2019.

dia and Vietnam since the late nineteenth century. The oppressive nature
of French rule helped sow the seeds of rebellion."[474]

The U.S., having been victorious in World War II and emerging as
one of the planet's two super-powers, would now work to order the world
to its liking. The Marshall Plan, the U.S. program to rebuild Europe,
would be key to this endeavor. The appeal of colonization had long since
faded, at least publicly. President Franklin D. Roosevelt and Josef Stalin
had agreed that, after the war, France would not regain its Indochinese
colonies, which were, at that time, occupied by Japan.[475] But following
the Japanese defeat, the three nations were once again French colonies
and the U.S. couldn't criticize French actions in Indochina. According to
Jack Kenny:

> Washington needed French co-operation in the reconstruction of
> Western Europe along U.S. policy lines, and their requirements made
> it impossible for the U.S. to condemn or attempt to alter French
> policy in Indochina. By 1949, the U.S. had become committed to
> keeping Communism out of Southeast Asia within its own Cold War
> strategy. This pushed the U.S. to pour money and aid into the hope-
> less French attempt to keep its imperial possession. By the time the
> French abandoned the effort after the catastrophic defeat at Dien
> Bien Phu (1954), the U.S. was financing 80 percent of the French
> war effort, and had committed itself financially, politically and emo-
> tionally to preventing a Communist victory there.[476]

For France, holding on to Laos, Vietnam and Cambodia "seemed indis-
pensable to French prestige. Imperial power was the link to France's more
glorious past, and the key to moving beyond the humiliation of German
occupation and Vichy collaboration."[477]

As the three nations fought against France, expenses for France kept
mounting, and victory seemed remote. While the Indochinese war continued, the U.S. was adjusting its own foreign policy, shifting from anti-
colonialism to anti-communism. Yet despite its professed anti-colonialism,

---

[474]Sami Abouzahr, "The Tangled Web: America, France and Indochina 1947–50: Sami
Abouzahr Untangles US Policy towards France at the Time of the Marshall Plan
and the War in Indochina," *History Today*, October 2004.

[475]Jack Kenny, "Vietnamese Friend or Foe: U.S. Foreign Policy Has Often Been High-
lighted by Shortsightedness, Disregard of Foreign Concerns, and Regime-Change
Operations-As Shown in the Lead-Up to the Vietnam War," *The New American*,
November 18, 2013

[476]Abouzahr, "Tangled Web."

[477]Ibid.

the U.S. was willing to help a fellow imperialist nation, France, continue to hold onto its colonies.

U.S. financing seemed endless as the country funneled monies that could have gone to rebuilding Europe to France, so it could remain an imperial nation, but none of it staved off the inevitable: the nationalist movements in Laos, Vietnam and Cambodia would be successful.

Once France finally realized the reality that it couldn't hold on to these three nations, the U.S. stepped in, mainly in Vietnam, where Ho Chi Minh was seeking to unite a divided nation. The U.S.'s deadly interference in Vietnam has been detailed (see Chapter 15). But Laos was not ignored, since President Eisenhower had said "that a communist victory in Indochina could cause other nations in the region to fall to the communists like 'a row of dominoes.'"[478]

As U.S. interference and violence increased in Vietnam, the U.S. secretly and illegally expanded the war. Nixon administration officials lied to Congress, and the death toll continued to mount. It wasn't until the late 1960s that these crimes were finally exposed.

Fred Branfman was an international aid worker who went to Laos in 1967. In an article written just after Branfman's death in 2014, William Yardley wrote:

> Determined to immerse himself in the society, he lived with an elderly villager, learned to speak Laotian and became a translator. In time, he met Laotians who told him something startling. There was a second war in their country, a secret American bombing campaign that was devastating remote villages.
>
> It had gone on for years – Air Force bombers attacked parts of Laos controlled by the Communist North Vietnamese, killing thousands of Laotian civilians – but it had been invisible to most Americans.[479]

It wasn't until January 31 to February 2, 1971, that the bombing of Laos started to become known. Those were the days of the Winter Soldier Investigation in Detroit, Michigan. Sponsored by the organization Vietnam Veterans Against the War (VVAW), the event opened with remarks

---

[478] Jack Kenny, "Vietnamese Friend or Foe: U.S. Foreign Policy Has Often Been Highlighted by Shortsightedness, Disregard of Foreign Concerns, and Regime-Change Operations-As Shown in the Lead-Up to the Vietnam War," *The New American*, November 18, 2013.

[479] William Yardley, "Fred Branfman, 72, Is Dead; Exposed U.S. Bombing in Laos," *International New York Times*, October 8, 2014.

by Senator Mark Hatfield of Oregon. The panel discussions covered a
wide range of topics, including Laos.

Even then, in 1971, government influence on the media was strong.
Historian Andrew E. Hunt writes:

> The Winter Soldier Investigation concluded on Tuesday evening,
> February 2, 1971. Veterans went home, and organizers lamented
> the event's sparse media coverage. In fact, the inquiry instantly be-
> came a case study for its failure to attract television and newspaper
> attention. There was much that was newsworthy about the hearings.
> On the first day, panels on the 1st and 3rd Marine Divisions offered
> the first public evidence that American troops were conducting com-
> bat operations in Laos early in 1969, a fact not widely known at the
> time.[480]

One of the veterans testifying was Chris Soares. Part of his testimony
is instructive in several ways:

> The order was, when I left Ashau Valley, where the operation took
> place, on a helicopter—I was given the order by a second lieutenant—
> that if we met any war correspondents in our rear, which is Quang
> Tri, Vandegrift Combat Base, we were not to speak to them at all
> about Operation Dewey Canyon and if approached by any war cor-
> respondents, we were to say nothing. Perhaps just say we weren't in
> Operation Dewey Canyon and our name and serial number if they
> requested so. If they persisted, to go up the chain of command. In
> other words, if a war correspondent had any kind of idea that this
> operation took in Laos, he could not find anything and you end up
> knocking on White House and, of course, he wouldn't be let in. So, in
> a way, the American people perhaps knew about Operation Dewey
> Canyon but certainly did not know that it took place in Laos.[481]

It is clear from this short quotation that, as these soldiers were violating U.S. law by invading Laos, this was not information that was to be
conveyed to the U.S. citizenry. Soares continued:

> I can verify one thing; we lost, I'll be very conservative, at least 50%
> of these 2,000 men in this operation—wounded and killed. My com-
> pany itself which was approximately 115 men, the whole company
> itself, we had about forty replacements waiting in the rear, and I

---

[480] Andrew E. Hunt, *The Turning: A History of Vietnam Veterans against the War* (New
York: New York University Press, 1999), 72.

[481] http://www2.iath.virginia.edu/sixties/HTML_docs/Resources/Primary/Winter_S
oldier/WS_14_3Marine.html. Accessed on November 29, 2018.

was one of the replacements during the operation itself. That goes for body counts. Another thing, too, that's the complete devastation and defoliation in that area. I do not know if it was perhaps of shrapnel from high explosives delivered by air strikes or artillery strikes, but I know that quite a few hundred miles were just stumps or something that looked like stumps sticking out of the ground, and just let me say that that land, there is just nothing left of it.[482]

Soares also disputed the official body count:

MODERATOR. Excuse me, you mentioned the body count of the U.S. casualties. Were these figures accurate? I mean, you said they were conservative, but when the Pentagon gives out the statistics they have their numbers. But do you agree with the numbers they give out?

SOARES. Definitely not. [The] Marine Corps puts out magazine called *Northern Marine*. It says that we killed 1,111 NVA soldiers. Now that's a pretty interesting number. Now the only body I saw is the one I walked over and I saw a hell of a lot of bodies of ours being taken away in one piece or another.[483]

Another soldier, Gordon Stewart, testifying at the Winter Soldier Investigation, said, "Body counts are like football games. They keep a score and as long as the other side has more dead, then it's got to be a success."[484] This, after Soares said that airmen estimated their counts while bombing a field from no lower than 500 feet, going 600 miles per hour, and that the counting of chickens and pigs among the 'dead' was not unusual.

For nine years, from 1964 to 1973, the U.S. bombed Laos. During that time, according to the Legacies of War organization,

... the U.S. dropped more than two million tons of ordnance on Laos during 580,000 bombing missions – equal to a planeload of bombs every 8 minutes, 24-hours a day, for 9 years – making Laos the most heavily bombed country per capita in history.[485]

It is estimated that up to one third of these bombs didn't explode and, since the last bombing, more than 20,000 people have been killed

---

[482]Ibid.

[483]Ibid.

[484]Ibid.

[485]http://legaciesofwar.org/about-laos/secret-war-laos/. Accessed on November 29, 2018.

or injured by them.[486] On the present-day consequences of this legacy, journalist Jane Perlez writes: "Rural people often scavenge for the bombs, believing the metal has value. Children often think they are toys".[487]

What was the result? What did all this bombing, ostensibly to prevent the Laotian people from choosing a communist government, accomplish? Brett Dakin provides an answer:

> The results of the so-called Secret War in Laos, neither disclosed to the American people nor authorized by their representatives in Congress, were devastating. It lasted more than a decade, leading to the deaths of more than 200,000 Laotians, about one-tenth of the country's total population. Nearly twice as many were wounded, and almost a million Laotians were made refugees in their own country.[488]

> When all was said and done, after the United States withdrew, a Communist government quickly assumed power, and rules Laos to this day.[489]

Decades after the United States illegally bombed and invaded Laos to prevent a communist government to take power there, literally decimating the country by killing at least 10% of its citizens (some estimates put the number much higher), a communist government rules, and the killing continues, as innocent men, women and children are destroyed by unexploded ordnance, dropped by the United States.

Ghana (1957–1966)

Ghana, like many African nations, was a colony of Great Britain, and after World War II, sought and gained independence. This came about peacefully, through the work of the Gold Coast Convention, a political party established solely for that purpose. In March 1957, after Kwame Nkrumah was elected the nation's first prime minister, he declared the nation's independence from Britain.

Yet there is no nation so obscure, so distant or so unimportant in terms of strategic, financial or geopolitical importance to the United States that its actions are not scrutinized. According to Charles Quist-Adade:

---

[486]Ibid.

[487]Jane Perlez, "On Rare Laos Trip, Clinton Views War's Legacy ; Victims of Dormant Bombs from Vietnam Era Call for More Action," *International Herald Tribune*, July 12, 2012.

[488]Brett Dakin, "From Spying to Killing: How America's 'Secret War' in Laos Transformed the CIA," *The Washington Monthly*, January-February 2017.

[489]Ibid.

[T]he CIA issued a report on Ghana in December 1957, which was distributed within the American government and intelligence community. The report was right in its prediction. 'The fortunes of Ghana – the first Tropical African country to gain independence – will have a huge impact on the evolution of Africa and Western interests there.'[490]

Nkrumah, who said "we have got to make our little country an example for the rest of Africa,"[491] set out to assure liberty and justice for his people. Within ten years, 31 other countries on the continent had declared their independence.

Nkrumah believed strongly that political and economic independence were both required. In his own book, *Africa Must Unite*, he wrote this:

A country has very restricted economic links with other countries. Its natural resources are developed only insofar as they serve the interests of the colonial power ... In planning national development, the constant fundamental principle, is the need for economic independence.[492]

He set about to achieve this goal, and within ten years, writes Baffour Ankomah, in a retrospective on Nkrumah's accomplishments,

... Ghana had 68 sprawling state-owned factories producing every need of the population – from shoes to textiles, to furniture, to lorry tires, to canned fruits, vegetables and beef; to glass, to radio and TV; to books, to steel, to educated manpower, virtually everything![493]

As Ghana began to prosper, some of Nkrumah's statements and actions sent up red flags in the paranoid U.S. government. In a discussion on political systems, advocating a one-party system, he said: "A one-party system of government is an effective and safe instrument only when it operates in a socialist society."[494] That much-feared word – socialism – is always cause for alarm in U.S. governance.

---

[490] Charles Quist-Adade, "Kwame Nkrumah, the Big Six, and the Fight for Ghana's Independence," *Journal of Pan African Studies* 1, no. 9 (2007)

[491] Ibid.

[492] Ernest Emenyonu (editor), *Politics and Social Justice* (Boydell & Brewer Ltd., 2014), 98.

[493] https://www.ghanaweb.com/GhanaHomePage/NewsArchive/Ghana-celebrates-Africa-rejoices-380934. Accessed on November 22, 2018.

[494] https://www.pambazuka.org/pan-africanism/nkrumah-and-one-party-state. Accessed on February 2, 2019.

He further expressed his intentions to enable Ghana to completely shed the yoke of imperialism, under which its people had suffered for generations. When addressing the Indian Council on World Affairs on December 26, 1958, he said this: "We, in Africa, will evolve forms of government, rather different from the traditional Western pattern, but no less democratic in their protection of the individual and his inalienable rights."[495] For U.S. government officials, only the U.S. model will do, anywhere in the world.

In his book, *Class Struggle in Africa*, he went even further in promoting and endorsing socialism, when he wrote this: "In a socialist state, the government represents the workers and peasants. In a capitalist state, the government represents the exploitative class. The state then, is the expression of the domination of one class over other classes".[496]

But what did the one-party socialist government of Ghana under Nkrumah mean for the people? A few facts are instructive:

> In only nine years, Nkrumah and the CPP [Convention People's Party] built the most modern road network in Ghana, including the Accra-Tema Motorway. Since his overthrow, other governments have not added a single kilometre. The Akosombo hydroelectric project was also constructed under Nkrumah and the CPP government. Dr. K.A. Busia, then leader of the opposition, described the hydroelectric project as a 'communist inspired prestige undertaking'. But this dam created the Volta Lake and it is the primary source of Ghana's electricity forty years later.

> Other infrastructure built under Nkrumah and the CPP provided pipe-born water, housing, schools and hospitals.

> In education, Nkrumah and the CPP achieved more in nine years, than the British did in 100 years of colonial rule; and more than all the successive governments after Nkrumah and CPP. There was free and compulsory education. Free education was provided from primary to university level. Textbooks were supplied free to all pupils in primary, middle, and secondary schools. Night schools for adults, males and females, were created as part of a mass literacy campaign.

> The state farm corporation developed a 20 square mile rubber plantation. Soon after Nkrumah's overthrow, this valuable plantation was given to the Firestone Rubber Company of the USA.

> Even the prison system was improved under Nkrumah and the CPP government. Nkrumah and the CPP built the most humane prison

---

[495]Ibid.
[496]Ibid.

in Ghana, Nsawam Prison, the only prison in Ghana that had recreational facilities, a church, a mosque, and a library. Today, it is overcrowded and antiquated, as all successive governments after Nkrumah have turned a blind eye to the prison situation in the country. In short, Kwame Nkrumah laid the foundations for Ghana's development in every sector of the country.[497]

These were all significant accomplishments for Africa's first independent nation.

As is true with any government leader, even those who are visionary as Nkrumah was, he wasn't faultless. His use of the Prevention Detention Act (which enabled him to detain without charge anyone – in practice, it was usually his political opponents – for up to 5 years) was a grave violation of human rights. Yet if the U.S. has such scruples against laws of this sort, one might ask why the CIA doesn't overthrow Israel (see section on Palestine in this chapter). But overall, objective analysis generally agrees that the Ghanaians were better under Nkrumah than they were previously, or since.

Ankoumah writes:

> Sadly, on 24 February 1966, the work of this African hero, the work that had inspired a continental drive for political liberation and economic empowerment, was cut short in a military coup organized (according to declassified documents released in recent years by the Americans and the British) by the CIA (with support from London) and delivered by local collaborators in Ghana.[498]

Today, Ghana lacks the many advantages that Nkrumah implemented. According to Amnesty International's 2018 report, the following violations of human rights are prevalent:

- Death Penalty: Scores of people on death row, including six officially considered to have mental and intellectual disabilities, faced poor prison conditions. Inmates experienced overcrowding and lack of access to health care and educational and recreational facilities. Many death row inmates reported that they had not received adequate legal representation at their trials. Fewer than one in four death row inmates interviewed by Amnesty International had been

---

[497] https://www.pambazuka.org/pan-africanism/nkrumah-and-one-party-state.

[498] Baffour Ankomah, "Never Again! ... 40 Years after the Coup That Derailed Africa's Progress," *New African*, February 2006.

able to appeal against their conviction or sentence. Few inmates interviewed were aware of how to appeal or access legal aid, while most were unable to pay for private lawyers.[499]

- Justice System: Access to justice remained limited, especially for people from low income or marginalized backgrounds. The Ghana Legal Aid Scheme suffered from funding shortages; just 23 lawyers offering legal aid were available to the country's population of more than 28 million people.

- Right to health: Shackling of people with psychosocial disabilities remained common, particularly in private 'prayer camps' across the country. The practice involved restraining a person using chains or ropes and locking them in a confined space such as a room, shed or cage.[500]

With the current government in Ghana, the U.S. has exactly what it wants. Recently, the two nations signed a military agreement, which caused widespread protests in Ghana. A Ghanaian lecturer, Justice Srem Sai, wrote the following about the agreement:

> The agreement tells you that the army of another country will come into your town. They'll occupy some places, access to which will be controlled by them (not you). They'll import military equipment which even your security agencies can't inspect, let alone authorize. Forget about your tax authorities – they can't even levy. The army will operate the equipment and drive them in your streets without your licence. The laws of your country don't apply to them.
>
> All this means you have no independent means of knowing what they do in your country in order for you to even regulate them. On top of that, no court under the sun can review what they do. And the relationship is such that use of force will not end in your favour.
>
> And there's no foreseeable end to the relationship.[501]

The opposition from the people means nothing to either government; it's difficult to see Nkrumah ever agreeing to this re-colonization of his nation. But thanks to the U.S. he is long gone, and his current successor is willing to do as his imperial commanders demand.

---

[499] https://www.amnesty.org/en/countries/africa/ghana/report-ghana/. Accessed on November 22, 2018.

[500] Ibid.

[501] https://www.myjoyonline.com/news/2018/March-23rd/what-is-in-the-2018-ghana -us-agreement-that-you-cant-find-in-a-1998-document.php.

Indonesia (1958–1965)

In 1965, the U.S. overthrew the democratically elected government of founding Indonesian President Sukarno, following an established pattern that should be very familiar by now: the post–World War II fear of communism infecting nations across the globe.

From the time that Indonesia gained independence from the Netherlands, the Southeast Asian nation was plagued by political instability for several years, due, at least in part, to the diverse makeup of the population. By 1959, according to a CNN report on influential Asian figures by Pramoedya Ananta Toer, "Indonesia had no fewer than 60 political parties and faced the prospect of a new government every few months. Sukarno reorganized the 60 parties into 11—all of which retained their independence."[502] This reorganization was known as 'Guided Democracy,' and Sukarno felt it was required to stabilize his country. Toer writes: "Sukarno was the only Asian leader of the modern era able to unify people of such differing ethnic, cultural and religious backgrounds without shedding a drop of blood."[503]

Among the eleven political parties was the Indonesian Communist Party (PKI). It was a legal political party in that country, was unarmed and "had gained influence through elections and community outreach".[504] But U.S. government leaders feared Indonesia's close association with China and the Soviet Union. And the strength of the PKI was not something the U.S. was willing to countenance, despite the popularity of the party among the people of Indonesia.

The efforts to topple Sukarno began long before 1965. Journalist Vincent Beings writes in an article for *The Atlantic*: "In 1958, the CIA backed armed regional rebellions against the central government, only calling off operations after American pilot Allen Pope was captured while conducting bombing operations that killed Indonesian soldiers and civilians."[505] This was just four years after U.S. Senator Joseph McCarthy's Congressional witch hunts, and while he had finally been disgraced, the enthusiasm for anti-communism that he flamed would remain and impact U.S. foreign policy for decades.

---

[502]http://edition.cnn.com/ASIANOW/time/asia/magazine/1999/990823/sukarno1.html. Accessed on November 27, 2018.

[503]Ibid.

[504]Ibid.

[505]https://www.theatlantic.com/international/archive/2017/10/the-indonesia-documents-and-the-us-agenda/543534/. Accessed on November 27, 2019.

In the fall of 1965, several groups from Britain and the U.S. invested huge amounts of money on an anti-Sukarno propaganda campaign, which "chipped away at Sukarno's regime, undermining his reputation and assisting his enemies in the army."[506] One employee of the British Foreign office, Norman Reddaway, was given 100,000 pounds for this purpose. In 2018 pounds that is 1,880,602.50, or about $2,397,122.50 U.S. dollars.

On September 30 and October 1, 1965, a coup was attempted, in which six military officers were killed. In their scholarly analysis of the coup, Benedict Anderson and Ruth McVey write: "There is only one place in Central Java where a PKI official came out in open support of a takeover, and that was in Surakarta, where Mayor Utomo Ramelan made a brief statement backing the local coup."[507]

The PKI was the largest political party in Indonesia, with at least 3,000,000 members. With the amount of power and influence it had, there was no reason for party members to attempt a coup. But the U.S. used the opportunity to raise another false flag, creating a non-existent link between the group responsible for the assassinations (the Thirtieth of September Movement), and the PKI. Peter Dale Scott argues that the Movement was actually designed and controlled by General Suharto and the CIA for the purpose of getting him into power. Unsurprisingly, with the success of the coup, Suharto was then installed as president. Thus began thirty years of oppression and terror.

Following Suharto's installation as president, the PKI was banned and the U.S. provided to the military a list of names of 5,000 people suspected of being communist, or having sympathies toward communism. Historian John Prados writes:

> Over the next months, tens of thousands died – estimates range from a Suharto government report of 78,000 to an Amnesty International estimate of more than a million deaths. A CIA report in 1968 on 'The Coup That Backfired' baldly termed these events – which crushed the PKI – one of the worst episodes of mass murder of the twentieth century, ranking with Germany's Holocaust against the Jews.[508]

---

[506] https://www.independent.co.uk/arts-entertainment/how-we-destroyed-sukarno-1188448.html. Accessed on November 27, 2019.

[507] Benedict R. O'G.Anderson and Ruth T. McVey, *A Preliminary Analysis of the October 1, 1965 Coup in Indonesia* (Jakarta, Indonesia: Equinox, 2009), 163.

[508] John Prados, *Lost Crusader: The Secret Wars of CIA Director William Colby* (New York: Oxford University Press, 2003), 155.

Some estimates put the number as high as 3,000,000.[509] When Suharto resigned in 1998, *The Progressive* published the following:

> After pushing aside Indonesia's founding president Sukarno in 1965, Suharto and his military killed as many as one million people. The U.S. government gave Suharto a helping hand. The United States also made sure that Suharto's men had enough weapons to do the job. A steady flow of cable traffic between the U.S. embassy in Jakarta and Washington released under the Freedom of Information Act shows conclusively that the United States was well aware of the killings, approved of them, and even sent emergency supplies of small firearms to arm the killers.[510]

This was only the beginning; for three decades, the U.S. supported the brutal, oppressive Suharto regime.

In 1967, William Colby, who later became the head of the CIA, was an attorney representing the corrupt Indonesian general Ibnu Sutowo, head of Pertamina, an Indonesian oil firm Pertamina. Ex-diplomat and prolific author Peter Dale Scott writes:

> The Securities and Exchange Commission (SEC) had filed a stock fraud action against Sutowo for the 'investments' (or payoffs) he was soliciting for his New York restaurant from oil companies doing business with Pertamina. But Sutowo had pleased the big U.S. oil companies by accepting funds from them for the CIA-supported plot to overthrow Indonesian president Sukarno in 1965 through 1967.[511]

As elsewhere, the U.S. didn't hesitate to make a profit from its military interventions:

> Violent U.S.-supported overthrows of democratically elected leaders in the 1960s – such as those in Brazil, Ghana, and Indonesia – were followed by a radical increase of overseas U.S. direct and indirect investment in these same countries, particularly in fossil fuels.[512]

In 1975, U.S. President Gerald Ford and Secretary of State Henry Kissinger advised Suharto that they wouldn't object to Indonesia's invasion of East Timor. Suharto invaded within two days of the Ford/Kissinger visit to Jakarta. This invasion and the subsequent occupation killed at least 200,000 people. The *Progressive* article cited above continues:

---

[509] Ted Sprague, "Indonesia's Forgotten Massacre," *New Internationalist*, October 2011.

[510] "Suharto's Heirs," *The Progressive*, July 1998. Accessed on November 27, 2018.

[511] Peter Dale Scott, *The Road to 9/11: Wealth, Empire, and the Future of America* (Berkeley, CA: University of California Press, 2007), 94.

[512] Ibid., 19.

Suharto was Washington's creature. And it took Washington the longest time to abandon him. Even on the last day of his rule, there was a split within the Administration over whether to call for him to step down or muffle criticism.[513]

Once again, the U.S. overthrew a government that was working for its people, and installed a cruel, murderous, oppressive dictator whom they supported for decades.

Democratic Republic of Congo (Formerly Zaire) (1960–1965)

In 1960, the "young and idealistic" Patrice Lumumba became the Congo's first prime minister after having been active in their struggle for independence from Belgium.[514] The Belgians ruled the Congo for 75 years and were "particularly nasty, as colonizers went," as Stuart Reid put it in *Foreign Affairs*.[515] The transition to independence was not an easy one, and when territorial conflicts arose, Lumumba sought assistance from the Soviet Union. This action, closely watched by the U.S. government, was essentially the issuing of Lumumba's own death warrant. Less than three months after he became prime minister, the U.S. government, orchestrated his overthrow through the CIA; four months later he was beaten, tortured and executed.

To replace Lumumba, the U.S. installed his Army Chief of Staff, Joseph-Desire Mobutu. In an article for *AlterNet,* Nicolas Davies writes:

Mobutu abolished elections and appointed himself president in 1965, and ruled as a dictator for 30 years. He killed political opponents in public hangings, had others tortured to death, and eventually embezzled at least $5 billion while Zaire, as he renamed it, remained one of the poorest countries in the world. But U.S. support for Mobutu continued.[516]

Why is this? By now, the answer should be obvious. As Stephen R. Weissman put it in *The Washington Monthly*, with reference to Mobutu:

---

[513]"Suharto's Heirs."

[514]Rand Richards Cooper, "History As Tragedy: 'Lumumba'," *Commonweal*, October 12, 2001.

[515]Stuart A. Reid, "Congo's Slide into Chaos: How a State Fails," *Foreign Affairs*, January/February 2018.

[516]https://www.alternet.org/world/35-countries-where-us-has-supported-fascists-dru glords-and-terrorists. Accessed on December 7, 2018.

Time and again, the U.S. foreign policy establishment has supported friendly authoritarian leaders, however flawed, based on the assumption that its clients represent the 'only' feasible pro-Western political alternative. As in domestic affairs, political elites and bureaucracies cling to outmoded ideologies and old organizational commitments long after their wisdom has been called into question. But in foreign policy, this tendency is even more pronounced, since the counterbalance of congressional and public accountability is relatively weak.[517]

Despite proclaiming peace and democracy, the U.S. simply did not care about the people of the Congo or their self-determination. For decades, the U.S. was only interested in preventing communism, regardless of the amount of blood that flowed from innocent victims. Former CIA director William Colby praised several such U.S. 'endeavors', including those that installed the brutal Mobutu. John Prados writes:

> ... he pointed to successes in saving Laos through the 1960s, installing a friendly government in Zaire in that decade, and saving Western Europe from communism in the 1940s and 1950s. The validity of these examples could be debated with hindsight, and Colby went on to predict that the Shah of Iran would survive the political upheavals in his country, though a period of repression would be necessary.[518]

There are two interesting points in that last comment: 1) Colby was willing to support 'repression' to maintain a U.S. puppet in power, and 2) his prediction was hardly accurate about the Shah, since he was overthrown just a year after Colby made that prediction.

The idea of preventing 'godless communism' from overtaking any nation was only the prevailing sentiment. Members of the U.S. government are always willing to sacrifice human rights and international law if supporting them might risk the financial benefit for these august persons. Weissman, writing about U.S. policy in Zaire in 1997, when the U.S. had the opportunity to be a force for democracy and justice, said this:

> I was in the room when liberal Senate icon Frank Church (D-Id.) plumped for military aid to Mobutu to gratify Morrison-Knudsen, a home-state company with a big contract in Zaire. And I personally watched the most anti-Mobutu congressman, Mickey Leland

---

[517] Stephen R. Weissman, "Addicted to Mobutu: Why America Can't Learn from Its Foreign Policy Mistakes," *The Washington Monthly*, September 1997.

[518] John Prados, *Lost Crusader: The Secret Wars of CIA Director William Colby* (New York: Oxford University Press, 2003), 336.

(D-Tex.), go limp when approached by Grover Connell, a key con-
tributor who had major business ties to Mobutu.[519]

Mobutu ruled with an iron fist for decades. From a 1997 report in the
Chicago Tribune:

> Over the course of nearly 32 years, Africa's longest-ruling dictator
> built up a horrific human rights record as he created a state of
> controlled anarchy that allowed him and his military to plunder
> with impunity. Victims and human rights activists say it is a record
> of official murder, rape, arbitrary arrest and routine torture at secret
> detention centers.[520]

After the quick departure of Mobutu a year before his death from
prostate cancer, he was succeeded by Laurent Kabila in 1997. Kabila
was assassinated by one of his bodyguards on January 16, 2001, and succeeded by his son, Joseph.[521]

After taking back the name – Zaire – that Mobutu changed in 1997,
Joseph Kabila remained in power until January 2019. What have 17 years
of the U.S.-supported Joseph Kabila meant for the country? Stuart Reid
writes:

> During his 17 years in office, Joseph Kabila has presided over a
> profoundly decrepit state. Every institution to speak of has been
> perverted to serve itself rather than the people, 77 percent of whom
> live on less than $1.90 per day, which the World Bank classifies as
> 'extreme poverty'. Vast parts of the country go ungoverned, with
> armed militias vying for territory and resources in at least a third of
> its provinces. In the past two years, the number of displaced people
> in the country has doubled, to nearly four million.[522]

A study of the number of people who died between 1998 and 2004 was
conducted in 2004: "Total death toll from the conflict was estimated to
be 3.9 million. Mortality rate was higher in unstable eastern provinces,
showing the effect of insecurity. Most deaths were from easily preventable
and treatable illnesses rather than violence."[523] A later study by the

---

[519]Stephen R. Weissman, "Addicted to Mobutu: Why America Can't Learn from Its
Foreign Policy Mistakes," *The Washington Monthly*, September 1997.

[520]https://www.chicagotribune.com/news/ct-xpm-1997-04-29-9704290128-story.html.
Accessed on December 8, 2019.

[521]Ibid.

[522]Reid, "Congo's Slide."

[523]http://conflict.lshtm.ac.uk/media/DRC_mort_2003_2004_Coghlan_Lancet
_2006.pdf. Accessed on December 7, 2018.

International Rescue Committee, considering deaths up to 2010, indicates the number to be 5.4 million.[524]

And what of Congo today? While one can never know how the nation would have progressed had revolutionary leader Patrice Lumumba been allowed to rule, we can see where the trajectory of U.S. interference took the nation. Amnesty International's 2017/2018 report on the Democratic Republic of the Congo states as follows:

> The human rights situation further deteriorated. Violence in the Kasaï region left thousands dead, at least 1 million internally displaced, and caused more than 35,000 people to flee for neighbouring Angola. In the east, armed groups and government forces continued to target civilians and engage in illegal exploitation of natural resources with impunity. Police, intelligence services and courts continued to crack down on the rights to freedom of expression, association and peaceful assembly. Human rights defenders and journalists were harassed, intimidated, arbitrarily arrested, expelled or killed.[525]

Additionally, child labor is a serious problem in Congo:

> More than half of the world's supply of cobalt comes from the Democratic Republic of Congo, 20 percent of which is mined from artisanal areas in the southern part of the country, according to the *Guardian*. A 2012 UNICEF report estimated that about 40,000 children work in these mines where the conditions are said to be dangerous.[526]

Children as young as seven years old work long hours in these mines daily.

For the U.S., this is all acceptable, as long as the country doesn't turn to communism.

Brazil (1961–1964)

The people of Brazil, like those in every other country on the planet, have a desire for self-determination. Yet self-determination for any nation is only acceptable if the selected government meets the requirements of the

---

[524]http://news.bbc.co.uk/2/hi/africa/8471147.stm. Accessed on December 7, 2018.

[525]https://www.amnesty.org/en/countries/africa/democratic-republic-of-the-congo/report-democratic-republic-of-the-congo/. Accessed on December 7, 2018.

[526]Bamzi Banchiri, "Was the Cobalt in Your Phone's Battery Mined by a Child?" *The Christian Science Monitor*, January 19, 2016.

United States. If the people of Brazil didn't know this before, they learned this hard lesson in the early 1960s.

In 1961, Joao Belchior Marques Goulart became the twenty-fourth president of Brazil. Upon his election, the CIA "carefully scrutinized the lists of Goulart's cabinet and staff appointments, checking for dangerous leftists," according to historian Ruth Leacock.

> It was able to report that Goulard had appointed one Communist Party member, Raul Ryff, to his staff as private secretary. Several other appointees – the justice minister, the chief of police in Brasilia, a general in command of the Vila Militar (a strategic garrison near Rio de Janeiro) – were put down as procommunists.[527]

All this sent up red flags in the halls of U.S. governance.

Goulart's cabinet appointees were, in actuality, quite centrist. Ryff, the alleged Communist Party member, had, in fact, been a member briefly in his youth. The other insinuations were just as oblique.

U.S. State Department officials finally concluded that the new government in Brazil tended to be acceptably conservative. However, the CIA wasn't to be thwarted:

> ... CIA analysts joined the political analysts of the embassy in Rio in arguing that the 'emerging pattern' of Goulart's appointments was 'significantly weighted in favor of the Communists.' In addition, they cautioned that 'we may be witnessing the early stages of an attempted slow-motion coup in which Goulart, wittingly or unwittingly, is paving the way for effective Communist infiltration designed as a prelude to an eventual takeover.'[528]

Yet U.S. interference in Brazil came down not to a fear of communism, but economics. Shortly after Goulart came to power, in February of 1962, the state government of Rio Grande do Sul, under Governor Leonel Brizola, expropriated a subsidiary of ITT that was based in Brazil. This "triggered a massive reaction in the American business community and in Congress."[529]

In 1959, Brizola had taken over properties of AMFORP (American and Foreign Power, an electric utility company) with little fanfare after AMFORP's contract expired.

---

[527]Ruth Leacock, *Requiem for Revolution: The United States and Brazil, 1961–1969* (Kent, OH: Kent State University Press, 1990), 82.
[528]Ibid., 82–83.
[529]Ibid., 82.

This new and overblown reaction to the current 'expropriation' was at least partly the result of propaganda by ITT. As a communications company, it knew how to get its message across to the public. Company officials advised an ever-willing press that this was "another blatant instance of irresponsible seizure of American-owned property."[530] The response to this exceeded all expectations. A year later, after a very lucrative settlement for ITT had been reached, Harold S. Geneen, the CEO, remarked that the entire situation had been "exaggerated out of all proportion to what was seized – a $7.3 million company that was running in the red."[531]

The response in the U.S. was so extreme that Goulart concluded that the company, in conjunction with some of his political enemies, was orchestrating a campaign to damage the prospects of his planned visit to Washington, D.C., in April.

The Brazilian people were no less astonished than their president. The *Correio da Manha* newspaper suggested that this particular subsidy of ITT "must be owned primarily by widows and orphans, with the remaining shares held by members of Congress."[532]

As the 1962 elections approached, the U.S. wasn't about to allow a democratically elected government in power in Brazil if it wasn't going to toe the U.S. party line. The U.S. Embassy in Brazil became the channel by which the U.S. government funded groups supporting its chosen candidate. Leonel Brizola, brother-in-law to President Goulart, was interviewed by the *Diario de Noticias* for his run for Congress, on May 8, 1962. In that interview, he said this:

> The United States Embassy is moving around funds that are at its disposal in the Bank of Brazil and entering into direct understandings with Brazilian politicians. The Embassy is being transformed into a type of Mecca towards which mayors, public and private groups, all move directly, looking for the recommendations and stamp of approval of the Ambassador and American officials. In a short time, if these strange customs continue, we will have the American Embassy transformed into a super-ministry, eclipsing the Cabinet itself, becoming the sole center for the distribution of funds in the nation.[533]

In order to defeat Goulart, the U.S. spent at least $20 million ($167 million in 2018 values). Yet his effort was unsuccessful; Goulart was

---

[530]Ibid., 87.
[531]Ibid.
[532]*Correio da Manha,* February 21, 1962.
[533]Leacock, *Requiem for Revolution,* 119.

victorious, and had every intention of keeping his campaign promises, which included the nationalization of U.S. industries.

U.S. training of terrorists had already begun under Kennedy's 'Alliance for Progress' program. Under this initiative, thousands of military offices from throughout Latin America were instructed in so-called anticommunism and anti-terrorist activities: "The ostensible goal was to 'professionalize' the military, so it could stick to its job of fighting terrorism, which usually meant protecting oligarchies against peasants and laborers."[534] With Goulart having been painted by the CIA with the communist brush, and with the economic interests of U.S. business owners with companies in Brazil threatened, it was time for him to go.

By spring of 1964, things reached a crisis. On April 1, Goulart was overthrown by the military, which then took control of the government. After the fact, William Doughty, Jr., the director of the AIFLD (American Institute for Free Labor Development, a CIA vehicle to infiltrate labor unions), said that he had assisted in planning the coup for months. A labor leader with ties to the U.S. State Department, Victor Reuther, is on record saying:

> What happened in Brazil on April 1 did not just happen – it was planned ... months in advance. Many of the trade union leaders – some of whom were actually trained in our institute – were involved in the revolution and overthrow of the Goulart regime.[535]

What was the U.S.'s role, precisely? "The United States stood over the coup-revolution of 1964," writes Robert Wesson, "although [whether] as fairy godmother, midwife, or practically mother is controversial".[536]

What did the overthrow of their democratically elected government mean for the people of Brazil? For the next twenty-one years, when the nation was ruled by the military, the government issued seventeen 'Institutional Acts', to reinforce the power of the president, with the intention of controlling the politics of Brazil. These included the following:

- The power to restrict the political right of citizens and legislators to enact laws.

---

[534]Michael Stohl and George A. Lopez, (editors), *Terrible beyond Endurance?: The Foreign Policy of State Terrorism* (New York: Greenwood Press, 1988), 91.

[535]Cited in Warner Poelchau (editor), *White Paper Whitewash: Interviews with Philip Agee on the CIA and El Salvador* (New York: Deep Cover Books, 1981), 42.

[536]Robert Wesson, *The United States and Brazil: Limits of U.S. Influence* (New York: Praeger, 1981), 38.

- The abolition of all existing political parties.

- The jurisdiction of military courts to try citizens, if they were accused of crimes that threatened 'national security'.

During this twenty-year period, there was much economic turmoil and political unrest, with extra-judicial executions being legal. Torture was prevalent. A Brazilian study released in late 2014 showed that the U.S. and the United Kingdom had both trained Brazilian officials responsible for 'interrogations' in torture techniques.[537] While the report states that 'only' 191 people were killed during that time, and 243 'disappeared', with over 200 never having been found, torture was the most frequent tool of oppression.

The report further states: "Under the military dictatorship, repression and the elimination of political opposition was becoming the policy of the state, conceived and implemented based on decisions by the president of the republic and military ministers".[538]

Yet with Goulart out of the way, Brazil was once again secure for U.S. business, and the communist 'threat' was defeated. The U.S. government didn't care about the abject suffering of the people, as long as its own geopolitical goals were met.

Chile (1964–1973)

The nation of Chile has a long history of democracy. It "once boasted a longer history of stable democratic rule than most of its neighbors and much of Western Europe," as Pamela Constable and Arturo Valenzuela put it in *Foreign Affairs*.[539] The rise of socialist Salvador Allende heralded the end of this, not because of him or socialism, but because of the U.S.'s intense fear and hatred of communism.

Allende's history with the U.S. is interesting. He ran for president three times unsuccessfully (1952, 1958 and 1964), before his successful election in 1970. Increasingly, during his campaigns, he drew more U.S. attention. As the 1964 election approached, the U.S. was determined to stop him. The CIA supported the U.S.-backed candidate, Christian Democrat Eduardo Frei; the Johnson Administration "viewed the Christian Democrats

---

[537] https://www.theguardian.com/world/2014/dec/10/brazil-president-weeps-report-military-dictatorship-abuses.

[538] Ibid.

[539] https://www.foreignaffairs.com/articles/chile/1989-12-01/chiles-return-democracy. Accessed on November 16, 2018.

as a critical antidote to Cuban communism."[540] The CIA was most generous: "CIA support for Frei alone was double the amount per voter that the Goldwater and Johnson campaigns together spent in the United States that same year."[541] Their efforts to defeat him at that time were successful

But Allende was nothing if not persistent, and in 1970 he was successful. The U.S. president at that time, Richard Nixon, was a rabid anti-communist, and his National Security Advisor, Henry Kissinger, was no less so. As Constable and Valenzuela observe, "[the] Nixon administration was appalled at the rise of Allende. Henry Kissinger, Nixon's national security advisor, remarked impatiently, 'I don't see why we need to stand idly by and watch a country go communist due to the irresponsibility of its own people.'"[542] Washington was faced "with a troubling prospect: the inauguration of an avowed Marxist as the democratically elected leader of a Latin American nation."[543]

Apparently, the concept of self-determination didn't apply to the Chileans.

Once the election was over and – to the surprise and consternation of the CIA and the White House – Allende was victorious, efforts to prevent him from taking power began in the U.S. immediately. The U.S. used two paths, knowns as Track I and Track II. When a candidate for president in Chile is elected by less than a majority, as Allende was, he must be elected by the legislature. Traditionally, the candidate with the plurality of votes is elected. Under Track I, the U.S. attempted to bribe Chilean Congress members to vote against him. This effort proved unsuccessful. Under Track II – begun on September 15 – Richard Helms was under orders from Nixon to foment a military coup.[544] Despite this, Allende became president on October 24.

---

[540] Ibid., 22.

[541] Ibid., 22–23.

[542] Pamela Constable and Arturo Valenzuela, *A Nation of Enemies: Chile under Pinochet* (New York: W. W. Norton, 1991), 23.

[543] Mark Atwood Lawrence, "History from Below – The United States and Latin America in the Nixon Years," in *Nixon in the World: American Foreign Relations, 1969–1977*, edited by Fredrik Logevall and Andrew Preston (New York: Oxford University Press, 2008), 277.

[544] Stephen D. Krasner, *Defending the National Interest: Raw Materials Investments and U.S. Foreign Policy* (Princeton, NY: Princeton University Press, 1978), 306.

At this point, Nixon decided to "make the economy scream."[545] The following lists some of the methods used:

- An end to bilateral assistance.

- Aid grants reduced from $35 million in 1969 to $1.5 million in 1971.

- Export-Import Bank credits reduced from $234 million in 1967, to $29 million in 1969, to zero in 1971.

- U.S. opposition to loans from international lending organizations; this caused a reduction from $46 million in 1970 to $2 million in 1971.[546]

It wasn't only economic pressure that was brought to bear:

> Between 1970 and Allende's overthrow in September 1973, [the U.S.] spent $8 million [$52 million in 2018 dollars]. This money was used to support the National and Christian Democratic parties, to place stories in the mass media, and occasionally to finance private interest groups.[547]

Following Allende's overthrow, General Augusto Pinochet came to power, and ruled for 17 years. His legacy was summed up in a news report after his death: "Truth commissions set up after Chile's return to democracy concluded that Pinochet forces tortured some 29,000 people and killed more than 3,000."[548]

Another stark difference between Allende and Pinochet is seen in their view of political parties. Upon his election, "Allende pledged to respect, among other things, the rights of all political parties."[549] When Pinochet came to power, "[p]olitical parties were declared in indefinite recess. Leftist political parties were banned altogether."[550]

But this was not the only change:

---

[545] Note by Helms, "Meeting with the President on Chile at 1525," Sept. 15, 1970, cited in Kornbluh, *Pinochet File*, 36.

[546] Krasner, 308.

[547] Ibid.

[548] Benjamin Witte-Lebhar, "Chile's Dictatorship-Era Spy Chief Manuel Contreras Dead at 86," *NotiSur – South American Political and Economic Affairs*, August 28, 2015.

[549] Mark Ensalaco, *Chile under Pinochet: Recovering the Truth* (Philadelphia: University of Pennsylvania Press, 2000), 14.

[550] Ibid., 50.

The Chilean state was militarized, and Pinochet managed to fuse the offices of armed forces commander-in-chief and chief executive to become dictator of Chile. The judicial system was marginalized, with the acquiescence of the magistrates of the Supreme Court, and with catastrophic consequences for human rights.[551]

This is the result of U.S. interference; this is the consequence of the U.S. government's irrational fear of socialism. No one can say what Chile would have experienced had Allende served a full term as president. But decades-long democracy in Chile ended with his overthrow by the U.S. government, and the immediate ascendancy of the brutal Augusto Pinochet.

Uruguay (1967–1985)

As in the case of many other nations, it might be difficult to determine why the U.S. focused its attention on Uruguay in the latter half of the twentieth century. As Jeffrey J. Ryan writes in a chapter in a volume focusing on U.S. foreign policy in Latin America:

> With a total national population smaller than most capital cities in the region, a near complete lack of critical resources, and a geostrategic importance that was marginal at best, one would hardly expect Washington to divert much of its finite energies or foreign aid resources there. Yet when viewed through the magnifying glass of Cold War strategy in general, and the hemispheric National Security Doctrine in particular, Uruguay was transformed from a provincial backwater to a frontline state in the continental struggle against communist subversion.[552]

Similar to developments in Chile, when the democratic government of Uruguay began moving too far to the left to please the mighty United States, something needed to be done. The will of the people must not be allowed to stand in the way of U.S. geopolitical goals. The result was U.S. investment in groups and individuals opposed to the government.

Uruguay had a long history of a peaceful, functioning democracy: "As it entered the 1960's, Uruguay had impeccable democratic credentials. In a region where elected civilian rule was often fleeting or elusive, the country was viewed as an oasis of democracy."[553] The military was subject to

---

[551]Ibid.

[552]Jeffrey J. Ryan, "Turning on Their Masters: State Terrorism and Unlearning Democracy in Uruguay," in *When States Kill: Latin America, the U.S., and Technologies of Terror*, edited by Cecilia Menjívar and Néstor Rodríguez (Austin, TX: University of Texas Press, 2005), 282.

[553]Ibid., 279.

civilian authorities and served society in peaceful ways. That was fine with the U.S. government, until some indications of growing interest in Marxism began to appear.

Starting in the late 1950s and continuing for several years, the Uruguayan economy faltered badly. Benefits that the citizenry had long since become accustomed to were in danger of being curtailed. Reaction to this was strong:

> In 1967 alone, the country experienced more than 700 strikes. As labor actions by leftist unions escalated, so too did the willingness of the government to resort to the sort of heavy-handed tactics that were all but unknown in Uruguay's recent memory.[554]

This situation – the declining economy and the resultant government reaction to the strikes – brought about the birth of the Movimiento de Liberacion Nacional – Tupamaros (MLN-T, or the Tupamaros), a leftist urban guerrilla movement. Ryan continues:

> Over the next several years, the Tupamaros demonstrated both an impressive tactical capacity and a well-developed sense of guerrilla theater. Their assaults were designed simultaneously to embarrass the regime and bolster their image as crusading and caring idealists. The Robin Hood image cultivated by the MLN-T through humor and creativity enraged the regime. As the guerrillas proved more daring and the regime less competent, Uruguay appeared as a bright red flash on Washington's Cold War radar screen.[555]

The U.S. began by seeking to 'professionalize' the military; prior to this, soldiers would change out of uniform before going home for the evening, "to avoid being mistaken for bus drivers; one of their main tasks was cleaning up litter on beaches."[556] This was not, according to the U.S., how soldiers should be perceived, or what they should be doing. In attempting to strengthen the police and military in Uruguay, the U.S. provided extensive training.

> While the money and materiel provided by the United States was certainly important, most observers point to the foreign training received by the Uruguayan security forces as the most significant external determinant of their transformation from a democratic to

---

[554]Ibid., 280.
[555]Ibid.
[556]Ibid., 279.

a dictatorial orientation. The vast majority of this training was carried out by the United States.[557]

As is typical for the United States, international law had no importance in U.S. dealings with Uruguay: "there is a growing body of data that U.S. advisors were actively engaged in coordinating and possibly even conducting instruction of Uruguayan personnel in advanced torture techniques."[558]

The purpose for all U.S. efforts in Uruguay was made clear in a USAID (United States Agency for International Development) report that said, in part, the following: "Efforts by U.S. officers to impress the Uruguayans of the dangers of Communism and subversion must be continued so as to awaken additional interests, demands, and support for this important function ... [U.S.] strategy aims to reorganize this [intelligence] service and increase the use of modern technology and techniques to detect and apprehend criminal offenders and subversives."[559]

One of the lessons taught by the U.S. was how to make bombs. While it may be perfectly reasonable for an 'anti-terrorism' organization to learn how to diffuse bombs, there was some question raised about the legitimacy of learning to make them: "When asked to account for why such training was either necessary or advisable, ops officials – who had tried to keep the program under wraps – were at a loss."[560] How to diffuse bombs was not part of the instruction; only how to make them. "At least sixteen Uruguayan officials attended this particular course between 1969 and 1973. It is a disturbing coincidence that shortly after these graduates returned home, right-wing death squads began adding dynamite and bomb attacks to their tactical repertoire."[561]

With U.S. support in both funding and training, Uruguay moved from democracy to brutal dictatorship:

> ... although the regime killed or disappeared a fairly small number of people relative to its regional counterparts, it made such extensive use of imprisonment and torture (particularly psychological torture) that by the mid-1970s Uruguay had the most political prisoners per capita of any nation in the world. A more remarkable distinction, however, might be the nearly absolute lack of indicators that

---

[557]Ibid.
[558]Ibid., 286.
[559]Ibid., 284.
[560]Ibid., 285.
[561]Ibid., 286.

Uruguayan democracy was so imperiled. Only a few years before the imposition of state terror, virtually no one would have thought such a nightmare was possible. The country, known as the 'Switzerland of Latin America,' had one of the most long-established, vibrant, and stable democracies in the hemisphere. Moreover, the ultimate agent of this democracy's destruction, the military, was almost comically ill equipped to pose a threat.[562]

All this assistance from the U.S. government finally paid off. The Uruguayan government invoked emergency powers beginning in 1968, and the army began arresting thousands of people with suspected ties to the Tupamaros. By the end of 1972, the Tupamaros basically ceased to exist:

The effectiveness of the emergency power was matched, however, by their abuse. Allegations of torture were commonplace and the security forces also arrested politicians in opposition to the government. Most importantly, the president and military used the emergency powers to consolidate their power before launching a coup in 1973, thus ending Uruguay's democratic government.[563]

Prior to the coup, observes Michael Freeman, Uruguay "had a free press, regular elections, stable and peaceful transfers of power, a social welfare system and high literacy rates."[564]

The U.S. supported the coup that placed Juan Maria Bordaberry in power; he was overthrown by the military in 1976. In 2007 it was reported that

Uruguayan prosecutors moved against former dictator Juan Maria Bordaberry (1972–1976) and his foreign minister Juan Blanco in November, detaining them for the killings of two important members of Congress and others. Police arrested the former dictator in connection with four 'dirty war' killings dating to 1976, officials said on Nov. 17. It constituted a significant step in Uruguay's ongoing efforts to uncover and punish the abuses committed during the country's 1973–1985 dictatorship.[565]

---

[562]Ibid., 279.

[563]Ibid.

[564]Michael Freeman, *Freedom or Security: The Consequences for Democracies Using Emergency Powers to Fight Terror* (Westport, CT: Praeger, 2003), 91.

[565]"Uruguay: Former Dictator Juan Maria Bordaberry Arrested for Murder of Politicians and Guerrillas," *NotiSur – South American Political and Economic Affairs*, January 12, 2007.

The conditions of the nation prior to this time – the vibrant democracy, the reputation as the 'Switzerland of Latin America', free press, etc. – all existed before U.S. 'assistance' to help the Uruguayans rid the nation of suspected communists. Those rights ceased with the U.S.-supported coup.

Cambodia (1969–1975)

The people of Cambodia were the target of U.S. wrath and violence mainly because of their proximity to Vietnam, one of the many nations that the U.S. tried to destroy to prevent a leftist government from taking power.

As the war against the people of Vietnam raged, U.S. President Richard Nixon decided to secretly bomb and invade Cambodia, in violation of international law. This bombing and invasion began on March 17, 1969. The desire for secrecy was so strong that the Nixon administration "required pilots, crews, officers, and men right up the chain of command to falsify their official reports about the air raids flown against Cambodian targets."[566] Congress was also kept in the dark, thus enabling Nixon to order actions that normally required Congressional consent. The fact that he kept the bombing secret from Congress and the U.S. public certainly indicates that he knew he was acting illegally. His deception was intentional:

> The embassy consciously interfered with the work of American journalists in Cambodia by advising the Khmer government to withhold transportation on military aircraft and even, at one point, asking the Cambodian government to expel an American reporter. Congress got the same treatment: 'When the House Foreign Affairs Committee or the Senate Foreign Relations Committee sent teams to report on the war, the embassy was encouraged by Washington to make their work as difficult as possible and to withhold all information they could possibly manage.'[567]

These actions, as historian P. Edward Haley stated, "were all justified by the administration as necessary to disrupt enemy communications and to destroy supply depots in order to protect American troops in South Vietnam and to hasten their withdrawal from the country."[568] The futility

---

[566]P. Edward Haley, *Congress and the Fall of South Vietnam and Cambodia* (Rutherford, NJ: Associated University Presses, 1982), 29.
[567]Ibid. 28.
[568]Ibid. 29.

of this is well known today, but Nixon, a rabid anti-communist, would stop at nothing to defeat communism. It is estimated that, between the start of the bombing, and the final defeat of the U.S. by Vietnam, at least 250,000 Cambodians were killed by American bombs (estimates range as high as half a million). The American bombing in turn inspired additional atrocities by the communist Khmer Rouge, who killed anywhere between 650,000 and 1,400,000 additional Cambodians by 1979.[569]

The repercussions of the decision to bomb Cambodia were far-reaching in the United States. "Two hundred and fifty State Department employees signed a statement condemning the invasion," notes Peter G. Drivas. "Peace Corps workers seized the organization's headquarters and flew Viet Cong colors from its flagpole."[570] The invasion also renewed protests against the Vietnam War, and sparked the Kent State University war protest in which four students were shot and killed by members of the National Guard. Henry Kissinger, who was President Richard Nixon's National Security Advisor at the time, wrote in his memoir that "in the weeks following the Cambodian incursion, 'the very fabric of government was falling apart.'"[571]

In addition to an estimated 26 million explosives (half a million tons)[572] with which Cambodia was bombed during the Vietnam War, as of 2015, "Cambodia has the undesirable distinction of having the highest number of landmines and unexploded ordnance (UXO) in the world".[573] In 2018, it was estimated that the number of UXO in Cambodia was between 3 million and 5 million.[574] It is estimated that 2,000 tons of bombs are contained in Cambodia's waterways, a result of the U.S.'s brutal bombing campaign.[575] In addition to restricting use of vast tracts of land, it has been reported that "[o]ver 64,000 people have been killed or injured by

---

[569] https://sites.tufts.edu/atrocityendings/2015/08/07/cambodia-u-s-bombing-civil-war-khmer-rouge/. Accessed on December 9, 2019.

[570] Peter G. Drivas, "The Cambodian Incursion Revisited," *International Social Science Review* 86, nos. 3–4 (2011).

[571] Ibid.

[572] http://www.seasite.niu.edu/khmer/ledgerwood/landmines.htm. Accessed on February 6, 2019.

[573] "Boomtown Rats: Giant African Rats Will Soon Be Undertaking an Important and Dangerous Job in Cambodia; Locating the Millions of Unexploded Landmines Left over after over 30 Years of Conflict," *Geographical*, September 2015.

[574] https://theculturetrip.com/asia/cambodia/articles/a-guide-to-cambodias-landmines-and-unexploded-ordnance/. Accessed on February 6, 2019.

[575] Ibid.

explosive items since 1979, and there is still an average of one death or injury every week in Cambodia."[576]

This is what the United States wrought. Certainly, Cambodia has had brutal leaders following the end of the U.S. bombing whose atrocities dwarf those committed by the American bombing, but much of the suffering in Cambodia, including suffering today, is the responsibility of the United States and was a direct result of the American bombing campaign. And despite the carnage that the U.S. brought to Cambodia to defeat the Viet Cong in Vietnam, Vietnam was victorious over the U.S. aggressors. Cambodia was nothing more to the U.S. than collateral damage in a losing war.

Myanmar (1970–Present)

Formerly known as Burma, Myanmar is a nation with a diverse population of over fifty million and, like many nations supported by the U.S., human rights for the entire population is only a dream.

The country's current leader is Aung San Suu Kyi, who won the Nobel Peace Prize in 1991, eighteen years before another undeserving leader, U.S. President Barack Obama, won it. Once praised by the world as an 'outstanding example of the power of the powerless', she came to power in 2016 after years of house arrest. Since then, according to the BBC, international leaders who once fawned over her have been

> [o]utraged by the exodus of hundreds of thousands of Rohingya Muslims from Myanmar into neighbouring Bangladesh due to an army crackdown, [and] they have accused her of doing nothing to stop rape, murder and possible genocide by refusing to condemn the powerful military or acknowledge accounts of atrocities.[577]

On October 18, 2018, reports the *Guardian*,

> Marzuki Darusman, chair of the UN fact-finding mission on Myanmar, said thousands of Rohingya were still fleeing to Bangladesh, and the estimated 250,000 to 400,000 who have remained following last year's brutal military campaign in the Buddhist-majority coun-

---

[576]https://www.maginternational.org/what-we-do/where-we-work/cambodia/. Accessed on February 6, 2019.

[577]https://www.bbc.com/news/world-asia-pacific-11685977. Referenced on December 3, 2018.

try 'continue to suffer the most severe' restrictions and repression. 'It is an ongoing genocide.'[578]

The United States has a long and ugly, CIA-sponsored and drug-fueled relationship with Myanmar. After Generalissimo Chiang Kai-shek was driven from China to Taiwan, about 10,000 of his loyalists gathered in Burma, under the leadership of General Li Mi. The plan was to invade China's Yunnan province, by striking it across the northern border of Burma. Jeffrey St. Clair and Alexander Cockburn write:

> But Li Mi's troops were not just warriors in Chiang's cause: they had also taken control of the largest opium poppy fields in Asia. The CAT (Civil Air Transport) pilots working for the CIA carried loads of Li Mi's opium on their return flights to Bangkok, where it was delivered to General Phao Siyanan, head of the Thai secret police and a long-time CIA asset.[579]

Li Mi's army, the Kuomintang (KMT), was armed, fed and paid by the CIA. St. Clair and Cockburn continue:

> For its part, the CIA was more than pleased to see the KMT forces sustained by a stable flow of opium revenue impervious to the whims of Congress or new arrivals in the White House. By the mid-1970s the KMT controlled more than 80 percent of the Golden Triangle opium market. It was a situation that put the newly created Drug Enforcement Agency at odds with the CIA's opium warlords. Invariably, the DEA emerged defeated from these conflicts.[580]

In 1988, when researching her book *Desperados: Latin Drug Lords, U.S. Lawmen, And The War America Can't Win*, Elaine Shannon spoke with dozens of DEA agents. She wrote this: "DEA agents who served in south east Asia in the late 1970s and 1980s said they frequently discovered that they were tracking heroin smugglers who were on the CIA payroll."[581]

The current CIA-drug situation in Myanmar is not known; however, since 2016, ongoing genocide against the Rohingya people has dominated the news about the country. Over 1,000,000 people have been driven from

---

[578] https://www.theguardian.com/world/2018/oct/24/rohingya-genocide-is-still-going-on-says-top-un-investigator. Accessed on December 3, 2018.

[579] https://www.counterpunch.org/2017/12/01/the-us-opium-wars-china-burma-and-the-cia/. Accessed on December 3, 2018.

[580] Ibid.

[581] Elaine Shannon, *Desperados: Latin Drug Lords, U.S. Lawmen, And The War America Can't Win* (iUniverse, 2015).

their homes; most have fled to Bangladesh and other neighboring nations. At least 10,000 have been killed.

A report from 2015 describes conditions for the Rohingya people even before the military crackdown:

> The Rohingya are the most persecuted minority of the world. Their home country Myanmar does not recognise them as citizens. Rohingya are discriminated in many ways. They are attacked by their neighbours and displaced from their homes. As a result, hundreds of thousands live in refugee camps or in exile.[582]

The U.S., never at the forefront of human rights or international law, has taken notice of this situation: "the United States has levelled targeted sanctions against some senior military officials but stopped short of applying broader measures."[583] In an interview with *Frontier*, U.S. Ambassador to Myanmar Scot Marciel was asked about the U.S. response to this genocide. His comments indicate a lukewarm response to this horrifying and unspeakable situation, at best. Some of his answers in the interview are as follows:

> *Frontier*: The Rakhine crisis has obviously placed strain on US-Myanmar relations after several years of strong, warm ties. In this climate, how much more difficult has it been for you as ambassador to engage with the government?
>
> *Marciel*: I always try to go back a little to where we've come over 10 years and I think the trajectory of the relationship has really followed the trajectory of Myanmar ... we made pretty good progress as Myanmar made pretty good progress. But over the last 14 months, since the Rakhine crisis happened, I think the trajectory here has been overall more negative certainly and that's influenced the relationship.
>
> I think we're still able for the most part to talk, we always try to speak very openly with government officials, we always emphasize – when we're talking about Rakhine or something like that – this is all about trying to help Myanmar overcome this challenge in a way that addresses the human and humanitarian crisis and also helps the country move ahead.
>
> *Frontier*: On sanctions, the US has said it only intends to consider targeted measures. Is that still the policy and should Myanmar

---

[582]https://www.dandc.eu/en/article/myanmar-does-not-recognise-rohingya-citizens-n go-expert-elaborates-our-interview. Accessed on December 3, 2018.

[583]https://frontiermyanmar.net/en/pressure-for-tougher-action-is-growing-us-ambas sador-scot-marciel. Accessed on December 3, 2018.

expect further sanctions, including against military companies, from the US?

Marciel: The goal is to try to take action, including through targeted sanctions against individuals and entities directly involved in human rights abuses. The goal is not to punish, but to encourage progress. That said, going forward, much will depend on whether there is progress. The level of concern remains extremely high. Arguably, pressure for tougher action is growing and the way to reduce that pressure is to show progress, which is what we'd all love to see.[584]

One million people displaced; at least 10,000 killed. One might ask why the U.S. response is 'targeted sanctions' and not bombs. Myanmar, formerly Burma, has long assisted the CIA in its covert operations, including when the U.S. was bombing Burma's next-door neighbor, Laos, and its slightly more distant neighbors of Cambodia and Vietnam. The drug trade from and through Myanmar has proven very lucrative in financing CIA operations, as in Afghanistan. Whether or not it is doing so now is not known, but the likelihood that it is, or will be in the future, is strong. The U.S. will not do anything to alienate a country that is so helpful to its criminal, covert operations.

Argentina (1974–1983)

Argentina, like many South American nations, has experienced periods of instability, often either caused or supported by the United States. Argentina's so-called 'Dirty War' falls into the latter category, referring to the period from 1974 to 1983 when Operation Condor was in effect in Argentina, Chile, Uruguay, Bolivia, Paraguay and Brazil. According to J. Patrice McSherry:

> Condor represented a striking new level of coordinated repression among the anticommunist militaries in the region, and its existence was suspected, but undocumented, until fairly recently. Condor enabled the Latin American military states to share intelligence and to hunt down, seize, and execute political opponents in combined operations across borders. Refugees fleeing military coups and repression in their own countries who sought safe havens in neighboring countries were 'disappeared' in combined transnational operations.[585]

---

[584] https://frontiermyanmar.net/en/pressure-for-tougher-action-is-growing-us-ambassador-scot-marciel. Accessed on December 3, 2018.

[585] J. Patrice McSherry, "Operation Condor: Clandestine Inter-American System," *Social Justice* 26, no. 4 (1999).

Any major, coordinated anti-communist activity anywhere on the planet can be traced back somehow to the U.S., and Operation Condor was no exception.

> Condor must be understood within the context of the global anti-communist alliance led by the United States. We now know that top U.S. officials and agencies, including the State Department, the Central Intelligence Agency, and the Defense Department, were fully aware of Condor's formation and its operations from the time it was organized in 1975 (if not earlier).[586]

State Department documents that were declassified in 2003 clearly show that President Nixon's Secretary of State, Henry Kissinger, supported the Argentinian junta's oppression of dissent:

> The newly released documents show that, in October 1976, Kissinger and other high-ranking U.S. officials gave their full support to the Argentine junta and urged them to finish the repression before the U.S. Congress cut military aid. Congress was expected to consider the following January suspending military aid to the dictatorship and blocking a U.S. $8 million credit from the Inter-American Development Bank (IDB) because of human rights violations.[587]

According to an investigative report written by Martin Edwin Andersen and John Dinges, these and other documents

> show that in 1976 Secretary of State Henry Kissinger played a key role in assuring Argentina's military rulers that that their antiterrorist campaign involving the disappearance, torture and assassination of at least 15,000 people – many of whom were not combatants – would not be criticized by the United States on human-rights grounds.[588]

---

[586]Ibid.

[587]"Argentina: Declassified State Department Files Show U.S. Supported Repression during 'Dirty War'," *NotiSur – South American Political and Economic Affairs*, January 9, 2004.

[588]Martin Edwin Andersen and John Dinges, "Kissinger Had a Hand in 'Dirty War': Declassified Documents Reveal the Former Secretary of State Turned a Blind Eye to Human-Rights Violations during Argentina's Crackdown on Terrorism in 1976. (Investigative Report)," *Insight on the News*, January 28, 2002

As Dinges, an assistant professor at Colombia Journalism School, wrote elsewhere: "Kissinger actually encouraged human-rights violations in full consciousness of what was going on."[589]

These documents prove that President Gerald Ford, too, gave his blessing to the harsh tactics used by the junta:

> The Argentine military had begun going after leftists in 1975, before it took power in a coup the following year. From the time the military took over, the junta insisted it had the support of the US, but proof was lacking until now.[590]

Once civilian rule was reinstated in Argentine, several military officers, the very people implementing the crimes the U.S. supported, were charged with the abduction, torture and execution of leftist opponents of the ruling regime. Many were convicted and imprisoned in 1985 (although pardoned in 1989).

What was the result for the people of Argentina? Various studies have been made to determine the number of people killed for their political beliefs, with estimates as low as 16,000, and as high as 30,000. "An equal number survived detention and torture in illegal jails, and more than a half million people were forced into exile."[591]

This is yet another clear example of the U.S. government's disdain for the will of the people and its willingness to do whatever is required to achieve its geopolitical goals, regardless of the death and suffering of countless innocent people.

El Salvador (1979–1982)

In the latter half of the twentieth century, and into the new millennium, El Salvador was one of many nations to suffer due to the by-now familiar anti-communist attitudes of the United States government. In 1990, Max Manwaring, then Professor of Military Strategy at the Strategic Studies Institute of the US Army War College, wrote:

> In the late 1970s, chronic political, economic and social problems created by a self-serving military-supported oligarchy began to generate another crisis in a long list of crises in El Salvador. During that

---

[589]"Argentina: Declassified State Department Files Show U.S. Supported Repression during 'Dirty War'," *NotiSur – South American Political and Economic Affairs*, January 9, 2004

[590]Ibid.

[591]Ibid.

time, General Carlos Humberto Romero came to power, brought by those who thought that he would be able to establish a regime strong enough to protect the interests of the oligarchy and to control the various forces agitating for change. Yet by 1979, the situation was beyond control by repression.[592]

The U.S. appointed itself the mediator between disparate right-wing groups that were striving to remain in power at all costs. President Jimmy Carter encouraged the government to enact land reform. This was a tricky undertaking, because although the U.S. wanted to weaken the entrenched oligarchy, it also wanted the 'economic elite' to be united in efforts to prevent the success of the revolution.[593]

Ironically, the U.S. initially tried to force the government of El Salvador to implement some of the improvements that the leftists were seeking, although the intention was not to benefit the people. Hugh Byrne, author of a comprehensive analysis of El Salvador's civil war, writes:

> In the period between the Sandinista victory in Nicaragua in July 1979 and the reformist military coup in El Salvador in October, U.S. policy makers sought to pressure the Romero government to institute reforms that would undercut the revolutionaries and prevent 'another Nicaragua.'[594]

While the U.S. had a limited role in El Salvador before the coup, it became a major player afterwards, desperate to prevent a leftist government from taking power. However, this put the U.S. in a difficult position:

> In defining the left as the major danger in El Salvador, the Carter administration underemphasized the danger of the right wing and did little to stop the massive violations of human rights during 1980. Although the role of the military in such killings as those of the FDR (Frente Democrático Revolucionario) leaders and the four U.S. church women was well known, the U.S. response was little more than symbolic. Cutting off military aid could weaken the Salvadoran armed forces and lead to what the United States strove to prevent: a leftist victory.[595]

---

[592]Max G. Manwaring, "A Strategic View of Insurgencies: Insights from El Salvador," *McNair Papers*, no. 8 (1990).

[593]Hugh Byrne, *El Salvador's Civil War: A Study of Revolution* (Boulder, CO: Lynne Rienner, 1996), 66.

[594]Ibid., 47.

[595]Ibid., 65.

In the 1980s, a civil war erupted, "one that pitted leftist revolutionaries against the alliance of countries, oligarchs, and generals that had ruled the country for decades – with U.S. support – keeping peasants illiterate and impoverished."[596] The death toll was at least 75,000, mostly civilians. Atrocities abounded. The following are some examples.

In the El Mozote massacre, 1,200 men, women and children were slaughtered. Some were tortured before being executed. Children were ripped from their mothers who were then raped before being executed. Their children were herded into a convent, where soldiers fired through the windows, killing over 100 children; the average age of those victims was six. The slaughter was perpetrated by the infamous Atlacatl Battalion, which received training from the United States. An account of this massacre related by Stanley Meisler is instructive. In the evening, members of the Atlacatl battalion

> ... pounded on the homes and forced everyone to come and lie down on the square in the darkness. After an hour and a half, the villagers were allowed to go back into their homes. 'We were happy then,' Rufina Amaya [the only survivor of the massacre] told [Alma] Guillermoprieto [a stringer for the *New York Times*]. 'The repression is over', we said.

> But before dawn the next day, the soldiers forced everyone back into the square. After a few hours of standing, the soldiers separated the men from the women and children and herded the men into the church. The women and children were put into a single home.

> The soldiers beat and interrogated the men and then led them blindfolded from the church in small groups. At noon, the soldiers pulled young girls and women out of the house and took them to the hills outside the village, where they raped and killed them. The soldiers returned for the older women, marching them in small groups to another house where soldiers waited to shoot them. Some soldiers hesitated about killing children. But their officers berated them. Amaya told [Ray] Bonner [of the *New York Times*] that she heard her nine-year-old son scream, 'Mama, they're killing me. They've killed my sister. They're going to kill me.'

> After the carnage, the Atlacatl Battalion burned down the buildings of El Mozote ...[597]

---

[596] https://www.theatlantic.com/international/archive/2018/01/trump-and-el-salvador/550955/. Accessed on November 19, 2018.

[597] Stanley Meisler, "The Massacre in El Mozote," in *Thinking Clearly: Cases in Journalistic Decision-Making*, edited by Tom Rosenstiel and Amy S. Mitchell (New York: Colombia University Press, 2003), 115.

Todd Greentree, a man who worked at the U.S. embassy at the time, said that the massacre was done by the Atlacatl Battalion,

> ... which had just completed a three-month counterinsurgency training course in the United States. That training was also supposed to instill respect for human rights. The El Mozote operation was the battalion's very first after completing the course.[598]

This wasn't the only atrocity committed by the Atlacatl Battalion after completing its training by the U.S. On August 22, 1982, in El Calabozo, battalion members murdered over 200 men, women and children who had been taken prisoner without any resistance: "According to witnesses, the fugitives were surprised by the Atlacatl Battalion unit. Some of them managed to escape; the rest were rounded up and machinegunned."[599] This was the result of U.S. training.

The international community was shocked by this atrocity, which was denied by the Salvadoran authorities. Meisler writes:

> Despite their claim to have made an investigation, there is absolutely no evidence that such an investigation took place. The El Calabozo massacre was a serious violation of international humanitarian law and international human rights law.[600]

In other areas of the country, the brutal Atlacatl Battalion diligently practiced the murderous trade taught to them by the U.S.

Why was the U.S. government willing to tolerate such atrocious human rights violations? Why would a government that prides itself on its support for human rights and self-determination support such a vicious government? The only reason was the fear and loathing of a government that might possibly be sympathetic towards communism, or that might align with communist countries. For the U.S. government, regardless of whether a Republican or a Democrat is in the White House, being viewed as 'soft' on communism is a political death knell. As a result, any crimes against humanity committed by the U.S. can be justified as protecting people from communism, whether or not they want that protection.

Lastly, what was the result for the people of El Salvador? Did a democratic government come to power? In 1996, two years after the first elections following the end of the long civil war, the Center for Information,

---

[598]Ibid.
[599]Ibid., 145.
[600]Ibid.

Documentation and Research Support (CIDAI) issued a lengthy report. Portions of it follow:

> The war ended with the peace accords, but the structural causes which set it off continue to prevail: the impoverishment and marginalization of the majority of the population continues to be an indisputable reality in post-war El Salvador. And this is despite the very same peace accords, in which some basic socio-economic reforms were set forth but have yet to be carried out, such as the Forum for Economic and Social Consensus-Building (definitively aborted) or the land transfer programs and others to help ex-combatants rejoin civilian life. In other words, the end of the war has not meant the end of structural violence; and although in order to begin eradicating the latter it was necessary to put an end to the former, so far it seems that the end of the civil war has become the ultimate and definitive achievement for the elites who run this country, instead of representing a starting-point for addressing the endogenous factors which set off the civil war in the first place, and in order to make progress toward the social democratization of El Salvador.
>
> ... [P]olitical democratization does not merely consist in the fact that voters can have diverse ideological and political options (basically, left, center and right) on election day, but instead, above and beyond a plurality of options, voters must become citizens and progressively broaden their degrees of involvement in the nation's different socio- political realms. Not only is such citizen involvement not being strengthened in our country, but also – on the contrary – it is increasingly being obstructed by an authoritarian exercise of power, by both the executive and legislative branches.
>
> [Is El Salvador a democracy?] Definitely not. Nor can we speak of a social democracy in even minimum terms, since the socio-economic exclusion of the majority of the population continues to increase; nor can we speak of a consolidated political democracy or one that is on the way to becoming consolidated, when political exclusion, intolerance and anti-pluralism are part of the daily lives of the majority of Salvadorans.
>
> In other words, if tolerance, inclusion and pluralism are not a reality for the majority, then democracy will be nothing more than an empty word, no matter what government and business propaganda say to the contrary.[601]

Again, the United States intervened in a country with no major strategic or military benefit to it, to brutally thwart the will of the people. It

---

[601] http://www.hartford-hwp.com/archives/47/074.html. Accessed on November 20, 2018.

successfully kept the oligarchs, who could be relied upon to do the U.S.'s bidding, in power, while relegating the common men and women to lives of poverty and repression. As it has done throughout its history, successive U.S. governments care nothing for the will of the people around the world, seeking only to increase their own power and profits, no matter the cost to countless innocent men, women and children in foreign lands.

Yugoslavia (1980–1999)

The recent history of Yugoslavia is extremely complex, and the numerous intricacies involved will not be detailed here; such an explanation would require volumes. Suffice it to say, Yugoslavia was a nation consisting of diverse and often rivalling republics, as evidenced by its eventual splintering into the countries of Bosnia, Herzegovina, Croatia, Macedonia, Montenegro and Serbia.

Following World War II, Yugoslavia established a more open socialist society than its neighboring nations. Living standards were very high, and international travel was freely allowed, which in and of itself set the country apart from its communist neighbors.[602]

But issues beneath the surface soon began to erupt. The Yugoslav economy, relying on western loans, proved unstable. As nationalist feeling among Croats and Kosovars increased, the government worked to crush them. The country functioned due to the leadership of Josip Broz, known as Marshall Tito. But his death in 1980 left the country without a clear leader, and nationalist feelings among Croats, Slovenes and Albanians further bubbled to the surface.

Upon the increasingly chaotic void left by Tito's death, Serbian Slobodan Milosevic rose to power, chanting the attractive yet destructive mantra of nationalism. In 1989 he abolished Kosovo's autonomy. This naturally alarmed the Croats and Slovenes, who feared that their rights would be next to be curtailed. "In this way a spiral of competitive and mutually fearful nationalisms began to destroy the country. Politicians fanned the embers of all the old divisions – Serbs versus Croats, Orthodox Christians versus Catholics versus Muslims, and so on."[603]

As these conflicts and rivalries escalated, the U.S. declared that the rest of the world needed to provide 'humanitarian' aid, to prevent the

---

[602]http://www.bbc.co.uk/history/worldwars/wwone/yugoslavia_01.shtml.   Accessed on December 6, 2018.

[603]Ibid.

slaughter that was occurring. To this end, NATO forces, led by the U.S., began bombing cities in Yugoslavia, creating a new humanitarian crisis.

During this 'intervention', accurate information was hard to find. One report on journalism in war authored by John F. Neville said this: "Determining accuracy is hard, few stories are ever complete, and objectivity needs credible sources, especially in Yugoslavia, where it was hard to disentangle propaganda from fact and where the victims had less access to the media than the victimizers."[604]

The role of propaganda in influencing public opinion cannot be discounted. Information provided to the media came mostly from U.S., NATO, UN and EU officials, many who were openly pro-Serbian and anti-Croatian. Anti-Muslim sentiment was also strong among them. The media referred to the Croats as neofascist, insensitive and ultranationalist. The Serbian alliance with the U.S. during World War II was proclaimed, giving credence to the concept that the U.S. must now assist them.

In its many 'interventions', the U.S. looks for reasons to bomb, rather than to talk, and Yugoslavia was no exception. As Stephen Zunes from the Huffington Post commented:

> It's a tragedy that the West squandered a full eight years when preventative diplomacy could have worked. The United States rejected calls for expanding missions set up by the United Nations and the Organization for Security and Cooperation in Europe (OSCE) in Kosovo, or to bring Kosovo constituencies together for negotiations. Waiting for a full-scale armed insurrection to break out before acting has also given oppressed people around the world a very bad message: Nonviolent methods will fail and, in order to get the West to pay attention to your plight, you need to take up arms.[605]

The exact number of dead resulting from the U.S.'s 'humanitarian' efforts in Yugoslavia is unknown. According to Human Rights Watch, "The Yugoslav government has claimed that NATO was responsible for at least 1,200 and as many as 5,000 civilian deaths."[606]

Why did the U.S. decide to become involved? Tariq Ali writes that NATO "assumed that a short, sharp war in the Balkans would rapidly bring Milosevic to his knees, and Kosovo would become the second NATO

---

[604] John F. Neville, *The U.S. Media and Yugoslavia, 1991–1995* (Westport, CT: Praeger, 1998), 38.

[605] https://www.huffingtonpost.com/stephen-zunes/the-us-war-on-yugoslavia_b_211172.html. Accessed on February 6, 2019.

[606] https://www.hrw.org/news/2000/02/07/new-figures-civilian-deaths-kosovo-war. Accessed on December 23, 2019.

protectorate in the region."[607] Yet as Ali puts it: "This has been a war for U.S. hegemony in Europe and the world, the act of a triumphant imperialism designed to rub the face of its old enemy in mud enriched with depleted uranium."[608]

At the time of the U.S. intervention in what was then Yugoslavia, U.S. Secretary of State Madeleine Albright announced the end of long-time U.S. support of that country on March 9, 1998 (quoted in the *Washington Post*, March 31, 1998):

> Referring to the Kosovo issue between the Albanian minority and the Slav majority in Serbia, she declared: 'We must first acknowledge that this crisis is not an internal affair of the FRY (Federal Republic of Yugoslavia, comprising Serbia and Montenegro). The violence is an affront to universal standards of human rights we are pledged to uphold'.[609]

Yet two years earlier, when confronted on the news program *60 Minutes* and asked about an estimated half-million Iraqi children who died as a result of U.S. sanctions, she said that it was worth it.[610] One would think that a universal standard of human rights that any decent person is pledged to uphold would include not killing 500,000 children. Like almost all U.S. government officials, human rights are respected only when convenient.

Was the U.S. justified in bombing Yugoslavia? Gregory Shank writes:

> ... NATO's 'humanitarian bombing' of Kosovo, a province of Serbia (the dominant republic in Yugoslavia), introduced a new geometry of terror, complete with a resurrected Hitler, Holocaust-like images of a people uprooted, papers stripped and sent to camps, charges of genocide and atrocities – in short, a world Europeans and all people of conscience had hoped to consign to the past. Human rights organizations called for immediate action to prevent ethnic cleansing. And the U.S.–NATO alliance outlined the moral imperative to intervene militarily in a civil war taking place in a sovereign state outside the territory of the alliance to prevent crimes against humanity. Never mind that juridically, the bombing is an act of aggression and unjustifiable under international law. The world should never again stand by and 'do nothing' in the face of evil.

---

[607]Tariq Ali, "NATO's Balkan Adventure," *Monthly Review*, June 1999.

[608]Ibid.

[609]David Binder, "Ignorant 'Albright Doctrine' Entangles US in Ancient Disputes," *Insight on the News*, May 4, 1998, 30.

[610]https://www.youtube.com/watch?v=omnskeu-puE. Accessed on December 7, 2018.

Such logic soon began to strain under closer inspection. Slobodan Milosevic's regime has engaged in despicable thuggery, but what sense does it make to destroy a country in order to defend the ethnic rights of one of its minorities, especially since U.S. policy opposed independence for Kosovo?[611]

The monies used to bomb areas of Yugoslavia could certainly have been put to better use: "The cost of a single cruise missile could provide the seeds and tools for 50,000 poor peasants in the Third World to grow their own food for a year."[612] But that is not the U.S. way. The long-term benefits of peace over war are not considered when elected officials are more concerned with ensuring that campaign contributions from military contractors continue than they are with peace and human rights. This is an ongoing pattern in U.S. 'governance', and one unlikely to change soon.

Sudan (1998)

While Congress and the news media focused on President Bill Clinton's tawdry affair with a White House intern, little notice was given to the U.S. bombing of a pharmaceutical plant in Sudan. On August 20, 1998, Clinton ordered the bombing of the Al Shifa factory in Sudan, and sites in Afghanistan, allegedly in retaliation for the bombings of U.S. embassies in Kenya and Tanzania. The sites in Afghanistan and the Al Shifa factory were alleged to have some ties to Osama bin Laden, who was believed responsible for the embassy bombings.

Libertarian journalist Nick Gillespie wrote in *Reason* magazine at the time:

'Our forces ... attacked a factory in Sudan associated with the bin Laden network. The factory was involved in the production of materials for chemical weapons,' explained the president matter-of-factly after the bombing, which injured at least 10 people. Administration officials claimed that a soil sample taken by the Central Intelligence Agency from outside the plant revealed traces of EMPTA, a chemical they said could be used only in the production of VX nerve gas.[613]

---

[611] Gregory Shank, "Commentary: Not a Just War, Just a War – NATO's Humanitarian Bombing Mission," *Social Justice* 26, no. 1 (1999).

[612] Ibid.

[613] Nick Gillespie, "Bombs Away," *Reason*, December 1998.

Yet was this true? The German ambassador, who was familiar with the plant, disputed Clinton's claims.

> The *Los Angeles Times* cited experts who said not only that EMPTA has multiple uses but that apparent traces could have come from a number of other sources. British newspapers such as the *London Observer* reported that the factory lacked airlocks and other chambers necessary for producing chemical weapons.[614]

This would be damning indeed, but that is not the only evidence that the U.S. had no legitimate reason to bomb the factory. The Sudanese government demanded an international inquiry, claiming that the factory was the production site for 50% of the nation's legitimate pharmaceutical drugs. The U.S. government would not allow any independent testing of the CIA soil sample and didn't even know who owned the building until after it had been bombed.[615]

What was the result? What were the consequences of the U.S. bombing of a pharmaceutical factory in Sudan? Nathan Robinson quotes Jonathan Belke of the *Boston Globe* reporting that the attack on the factory "likely exacerbated a medical catastrophe":

> Without the lifesaving medicine it produced, Sudan's death toll from the bombing has continued, quietly, to rise. . . this factory provided affordable medicine for humans and all the locally available veterinary medicine in Sudan. It produced 90 percent of Sudan's major pharmaceutical products. Sanctions against Sudan make it impossible to import adequate amounts of medicines required to cover the serious gap left by the plant's destruction. Thus, tens of thousands of people – many of them children – have suffered and died from malaria, tuberculosis, and other treatable diseases ...[616]

As of this writing, the factory has not been rebuilt.

What was accomplished for the U.S., or anyone else, by the bombing of this factory? There was never any proof that the owner of the building had ties to any terrorists, and all credible evidence indicates that the products made there were medically necessary for people in Sudan. But the U.S. wanted to teach someone a lesson, suspecting that someone in Sudan had bombed U.S. embassies, and in the twisted view of U.S. governance, any

---

[614]Ibid.

[615]Ibid.

[616]https://www.jacobinmag.com/2016/10/bill-clinton-al-shifa-sudan-bombing-khart oum/. Accessed on February 18, 2019.

scapegoat will do. This time, it was the Sudanese who were victimized by U.S. violence.

Colombia (1991–2017)

Under the guise of fighting drug trafficking, combined with allegedly strengthening the Colombian government's internal security structure, the U.S. worked diligently to thwart the will of the people. And as is usual in such situations, it was the people who suffered the most due to U.S. 'assistance.' Professor in International Security and Strategy Doug Stokes writes:

> Throughout the Cold War, Colombia was one of the largest recipients of U.S. counter-insurgency military aid and training. Counter-insurgency – CI for short – was designed to reorient recipient militaries away from a posture of external defence, toward one of 'internal defence' against allegedly Soviet-aligned guerrillas. States that received U.S. CI military aid were told to police their own populations to make sure that 'subversion' did not grow.[617]

The way the U.S. defined 'subversive' activities helps explain the extreme repression that they fostered in many Latin American countries, including Colombia. One manual that was used in the training of CI forces there states that these forces should ask the following questions:

- Are there any legal political organizations which may be front for insurgent activities?

- Is the public education system vulnerable to infiltration by insurgent agents?

- What is the nature of labor organizations; what relationship exists between these organizations, the government, the insurgents?[618]

A variety of instructions and 'information' is provided, including this: "organizations that stress immediate social, political or economic reform may be an indication that the insurgents have gained a significant degree of control".[619]

---

[617] Doug Stokes, "America's Other War: Terrorizing Colombia," *Canadian Dimension*, July–August 2005.

[618] Ibid.

[619] Ibid.

The U.S. has always defined 'insurgents' in its own peculiar way; it defines such people in a country where it *supports* revolution as 'freedom fighters'. To think that there is something 'insurgent' about a people wanting 'social, political or economic reform' – and to consider that so dangerous as to spend countless millions of dollars to combat it – is typical for the U.S. government, as indicated by its support for 'counter-insurgency' in Colombia.

The CIA manual for use in Colombia included a list of 'Insurgent Activity Indicators'. Those indicators include the following:

- Increase in the number of entertainers with a political message.

- Appearance of questionable doctrine in the educational system.

- Appearance of many new members in established organizations like labour organizations.

- Increased student activity against the government and its police ...

- Increase of petitions demanding government redress of grievances.

- Initiation of letter-writing campaigns to newspapers and government officials deploring undesirable conditions and blaming individuals in power.[620]

Part of the U.S. effort in Colombia, at least as far as the public was concerned, included combatting drug trafficking. As heroin addiction increased in the early part of this millennium, U.S. efforts to prevent the flow of the drug from Colombia also increased. However, this may have simply been a smokescreen for the U.S.'s real purpose, that of denying the Colombian people a right to choose their own destiny. Michael L. Evans, a senior analyst for the pro-transparency National Security Archive, writes:

> A 1992 CIA report noted that 'Andean government assertions that increased attacks against the insurgents would affect the drug trade are primarily an attempt to convince the U.S. to allow the use of counter narcotics aid for counterinsurgency operations,' and that 'officials in Lima and Bogota, if given antidrug aid for counterinsurgency purposes, would turn it to pure antiguerrilla operations with little payoff against trafficking.' Indeed, as of 1991 the Colombian army had no apparent intention to attack the drug trade. A

---

[620]Ibid.

Colombian army document obtained by Human Rights Watch indicates that a 1991 reorganization of the Colombia military intelligence system – drawn up with assistance from CIA and DOD officials – made no mention of drugs and instead focused on 'the armed subversion.'[621]

Using counter-drug intelligence for counterinsurgency violates both U.S. and international law. Neither seems to be of any concern to the U.S. government, unless it is some other nation that is violating its own, or international, law.

During much of this time, Pablo Escobar was a wanted drug-trafficker. Organizations in Colombia that received funding and intelligence from the U.S. "systematically eliminated people and property associated with Escobar's network."[622] This included bombings and assassinations of family members and associates.

What has been the result of U.S. interference in Colombia? What has this 'counter-insurgency' done for the Colombian people? According to Project Ploughshares:

In 2017, Colombia's Victim's Unit indicated that approximately 268,000 people have been killed in Colombia's conflict since 1985. It also reported more than 7 million people forcefully displaced, 46,000 forcible disappearances, 30,000 cases of hostage-taking, over 10,000 torture victims, and 10,800 injuries due to anti-personnel mines and unexploded ordnance.

The CIA reported 6.3 million displaced persons.

Death tolls were highest after the 1980s, when paramilitary groups emerged.

Between 1996 and 2005, someone was kidnapped every eight hours on average and someone was hurt or killed by an anti-personnel mine every day in Colombia.[623]

Also, at the end of 2017, 7.7 million Colombians had been displaced over the period that began in 1985.[624] Today, the violence in Colombia continues.

---

[621] Michael L. Evans, "Problems with Current U.S. Policy," *Foreign Policy in Focus*, June 4, 2001.

[622] Ibid.

[623] http://ploughshares.ca/pl_armedconflict/colombia-1964-first-combat-deaths/#D eaths. Accessed on November 19, 2018.

[624] Ibid.

Once again, the self-proclaimed 'City on a Hill', the 'Land of the Free and the Home of the Brave', worked its violent destruction on yet another country, disdaining not only the right of self-determination, but the very lives of the Colombian people.

Venezuela (2018–Present)

The U.S. has long been hostile to this South American country. While U.S. interference in Venezuela dates from before 2018, the focus of this chapter will be its current, violent and unjust meddling in that nation. As the world's fifth largest oil exporter, and holding the largest reserves of oil outside of the Middle East, Venezuela was one of the four top oil suppliers to the U.S. as of 2004. According to Nina Lopez:

> Before (Hugo) Chavez was elected, two political parties representing the white elite and their U.S. friends ruled Venezuela for 40 years. Torture, disappearances and corruption were rife. Only 24 per cent of revenue from its nationalized oil reached state coffers. As a consequence, 80 per cent of the country's population (who are mainly people of African and indigenous descent) are living in poverty despite its oil wealth.[625]

In 1998 and 2000, Hugo Chavez was elected by large majorities. During his early tenure, the nation's constitution was re-written.

> The new Constitution opposes discrimination, recognizes the rights of indigenous people, strengthens workers' rights and, uniquely, recognizes women's unwaged caring work as productive, entitling housewives to social security. These reforms have strengthened grassroots movements inside the country, creating a 'participating democracy' where people themselves act rather than delegate power to a wealthy minority.[626]

What does this 'participating democracy' look like? Pete Dolack writes, in *CounterPunch*:

> The base of the Venezuelan political system are the communal councils. Various political structures designed to organize people at the grassroots level have evolved into a system of communal councils,

---

[625]Nina Lopez, "Dance with Democracy: Renewed US Attempts to Remove President Hugo Chavez from Office," *New Internationalist*, August 2004.
[626]Ibid.

organized on a neighborhood level, which in turn build up to communes and communal cities. These are direct-democracy bodies that identify and solve the problems and deficiencies of their local areas with the direct support and funding of the national government.[627]

The very foundations of the United States give the rights of governing to wealthy, white, male landowners, a system not so far removed from that which obtained in Venezuela for so long. And so Venezuela, which attempted to establish a real democracy – with some success, but mixed results – must not be tolerated. The U.S. government has tried repeatedly to overthrow the government.

One attempt was a U.S.-backed referendum to oust Chavez in 2004. Lopez further comments:

> The referendum to be held on 15 August in Venezuela on whether to oust Hugo Chavez from his Presidential office is the latest attempt by the U.S. Administration and the corporate interests they represent to overthrow a truly popular democratic government.[628]

The U.S. was unsuccessful in thwarting the will of the Venezuelan people at that time. Fifty-eight percent voted against recalling Chavez.

Upon the death of Chavez in 2012, Nicolas Maduro, then the vice-president, became president. In an election held shortly thereafter, Maduro was victorious, albeit by a small margin. He was re-elected in 2017.

While Venezuela certainly faces challenges, and Maduro may be, at least partly, one aspect of the nation's problems, he is the democratically elected leader of that nation. The U.S., however, in January of 2019, recognized Juan Guaido, the President of the National Assembly, as the president of Venezuela, claiming that he is the legitimate leader.

With that, the U.S. then issued heavy sanctions against Venezuela, crippling the economy. The United Nations has agreed to send in 'humanitarian aid,' which the Maduro government has, as of this writing, resisted. Venezuelan Foreign Minister Jorge Arreaza described the situation as follows: "Let's not be so hypocritical in this conversation. There isn't a humanitarian crisis. There is an economy that is subject to a blockade."[629] In explaining this further, Arreaza said this:

---

[627] https://www.counterpunch.org/2019/02/01/sorting-through-the-lies-about-venezuela/. Accessed on February 18, 2019.

[628] Lopez, "Dance with Democracy."

[629] https://www.france24.com/en/20190212-venezuela-un-says-no-aid-crisis. Accessed on February 18, 2019.

A government that is threatening you with use of force, with invasion, with a blockade, that gives orders to other countries for them to block you, do they really want to provide you with humanitarian aid? This is a hostile government that is killing you and then they want to help you out.[630]

A January 28, 2019, press statement issued by Secretary of State Mike Pompeo said that "[t]hese new sanctions do not target the innocent people of Venezuela".[631] However, the *Wall Street Journal*, hardly a bastion of liberal thought, had a different take on the sanctions:

The sanctions could create deeper gasoline shortages in Venezuela. The country's refineries are already operating at a fraction of their capacity, crippled by a lack of spare parts and crude. Venezuela only produced a third of the 190,000 barrels of gasoline it consumed a day as of November, according to Ivan Freites, a leader of the country's oil union. 'Immediately, it's going to hurt the average Venezuelan,' Mr Freites said.[632]

One may recall sanctions against Iraq which killed an estimated 500,000 children, which then Secretary of State Madeleine Albright said was "worth it."[633]

One has to wonder how the U.S. government would have reacted in 2016 when Donald Trump was elected president despite losing the popular vote by a margin of nearly 3,000,000 votes, if the leaders of other nations recognized Hillary Clinton as the 'legitimate' president of the United States. Yet the U.S. government has no problem in recognizing someone other than the duly-elected leader of Venezuela as that nation's president.

In April of 2019 an attempted coup backed by the U.S. government failed, when Guaido failed to win the backing of the military, the Cabinet or the Venezuelan people. Yet as of this writing, the U.S. government continues to say it is willing to end sanctions, on the condition that Maduro leaves the country.

Once again, the U.S. is interfering in the internal affairs of a truly democratic nation. It is difficult to believe that, should the U.S. succeed, the people of Venezuela will fare any better than people did under U.S. puppets in any other nation.

---

[630] Ibid.

[631] https://ee.usembassy.gov/sanctions-venezuela-oil-sector/. Accessed on February 20, 2019.

[632] https://www.globalresearch.ca/whats-the-deal-with-sanctions-in-venezuela-and-whys-it-so-hard-for-media-to-understand/5667880

[633] https://www.youtube.com/watch?v=omnskeu-puE. Accessed on December 7, 2018.

Conclusion

What is to be learned from all this? The U.S. proclaims that it is a beacon of peace and freedom, a model democracy to which all nations aspire. This myth has taken hold among many of its own citizens, despite the solid evidence to the contrary contained herein.

The result of all the U.S.'s interventions has been unspeakable suffering and death; it is estimated that since World War II, the U.S. has killed at least 20,000,000 people, most of them 'non-combatants'; that is, innocent men, women and children. This killing has been done either directly by its bombs, drones and soldiers, or indirectly, such as in the financing of Israel's barbaric occupation and genocide of the Palestinian people, Saudi Arabia's war on Yemen, or through brutal and illegal (under international law) sanctions. As of this writing, conditions in Palestine's Gaza Strip and in Yemen are fast approaching human catastrophe, with mass starvation imminent.

Additionally, as has been shown, unexploded ordnance continues to cause new suffering, especially among children in the many, many nations that the U.S. has bombed.

In July of 2017, Common Dreams reported:

> The U.S. bombing campaign in Iraq and Syria is now the heaviest since the bombing of Vietnam, Cambodia and Laos in the 1960s-70s, with 84,000 bombs and missiles dropped between 2014 and the end of May 2017. That is nearly triple the 29,200 bombs and missiles dropped on Iraq in the "Shock and Awe" campaign of 2003.[634]

The report further states that, in three years of U.S.-led bombing of Iraq and Syria, sources indicate that between 12,000 and 18,000 civilians have been killed, but "[t]hese reports can only be the tip of the iceberg, and the true number of civilians killed could well be more than 100,000, based on typical ratios between reported deaths and actual deaths in previous war-zones."[635]

---

[634] https://www.commondreams.org/views/2017/07/08/us-state-war-july-2017. Accessed on September 11, 2018.
[635] Ibid.

Has this 'war on terror', a war waged by unleashing unspeakable terror against other nations, helped make the world safer?

> What began in 2001 as a misdirected use of military force to punish a group of formerly U.S.-backed jihadis in Afghanistan for the crimes of September 11th has escalated into a global asymmetric war. Every country destroyed or destabilized by U.S. military action is now a breeding ground for terrorism. It would be foolish to believe that this cannot get much, much worse ...[636]

In Afghanistan, where war rages on after nearly two decades, the Taliban is in control of more areas of the country than ever. In Yemen, a humanitarian crisis of almost unfathomable proportions is threatening. Syria seems close to finally fending off U.S. aggression, but at a cost of hundreds of thousands of innocent Syrian lives, and the near-total destruction of that country's infrastructure. One reason for U.S. aggression against Syria was to minimize or decrease Iranian influence in the Middle East; the reverse is what was accomplished.

The U.S. continues to threaten Iran and North Korea, two nations with military strengths unlike any the U.S. has encountered since at least the Vietnam War. Is Donald Trump really willing to risk a nuclear holocaust?

Occasionally, someone will expose U.S. lies and violation of international or domestic law, as Chelsea Manning did in 2010, and Edward Snowden in 2013. Manning was sentenced to 35 years in prison; President Obama shortened that sentence, and she was released from prison in May of 2017. But in February 2019 she was issued a subpoena to testify against WikiLeaks and Julian Assange, which she refused. In March she was held in contempt of court and was put in prison for another two months. Immediately served with another subpoena to testify, she again refused and is currently still in prison.

Snowden was given asylum in Russia, since the international community recognizes that a fair trial for him in the U.S. is impossible.

With a centuries-long history of aggression, can the U.S. be stopped? With an erratic president, one with little grasp of history, foreign policy or even of the basic concept of actions and consequences, can this warmongering, war-waging, violent nation be brought to heel?

In 2000, historian Howard Zinn succinctly described how it can be done:

> Many of us – even old veterans of social movements – had begun to feel helpless as we observed the frightening consolidation of control

---

[636]Ibid.

> by the interests of capital, the giant corporations merging, the American military machine grown to monstrous proportions. But we are forgetting certain facts about power: that the most formidable military machine depends ultimately on the obedience of its soldiers, the most powerful corporation becomes helpless when its workers stop working, when its customers refuse to buy its products. The strike, the boycott, the refusal to serve, the ability to paralyze the functioning of a complex social structure, these remain potent weapons against the most fearsome state of corporate power.[637]

Are the conditions Zinn described in 2000 not still true today, perhaps only more extreme? Six corporations control 90% of the media.[638] The U.S. military budget is larger than the military budgets of the next eight nations combined, while U.S. Congress members blame entitlement programs for the massive federal deficit. In December 2017, Speaker of the House Paul Ryan said: "We're going to have to get back next year at entitlement reform, which is how you tackle the debt and the deficit."[639] He made this comment shortly before Trump signed into law the much-vaunted tax reform bill that is estimated to add one trillion dollars to the national debt by the year 2027, a mere seven years away.

Zinn's belief in the power of the people to make change isn't without evidence:

> Note how General Motors and Ford had to surrender to the strikers of the thirties, how black children marching in Birmingham in 1963 pushed Congress into passing a Civil Rights Act, how the U.S. government, carrying on a war in Vietnam, had to reconsider in the face of draft resistance and desertions en mass, how a garbage workers' strike in New York immobilized a great city, how the threat of a boycott against Texaco for racist policies brought immediate concessions.[640]

The Republican and Democratic Parties cannot be relied upon for change. The GOP has fallen under the spell of Trump and those of his ilk: war-mongering and war-waging imperialists and firm believers in the ugly concept of U.S. 'exceptionalism'. Are the Democrats any different? Their first response to any international crisis is never diplomacy, but bombs.

---

[637] Howard Zinn, "A Flash of the Possible," *The Progressive*, January 2000.

[638] https://www.businessinsider.com/these-6-corporations-control-90-of-the-media-in-america-2012-6.

[639] Robert King, "House Could Be First Up to Tackle Entitlement Reform," *The Examiner* (Washington, D.C.), December 7, 2017.

[640] Zinn, "Flash."

There are few areas where the two parties are aligned, but on war-making and passing legislation to benefit the rich, they are as one.

Third parties have been successfully and almost completely marginalized by the Republicans and Democrats; those two parties now determine who will participate in presidential debates, and by passing legislation, or letting stand the 'Citizens United' Supreme Court ruling removing restrictions on corporate donations to candidates, they have ensured that only those candidates who can prove to the very wealthy that they will do as their corporate handlers bid them, will win elections. Green Party candidates, Socialist Party candidate and others, whose common-sense platforms seek to benefit the many rather than the few, have little chance of participating in the national discourse, wherein the Republican and Democratic candidates pledge their allegiance to apartheid Israel; support massive increases to an already bloated military budget, and decry any attempts at reasonable gun control; all of which demonstrate their disdain for international law and human rights, their dependency on military contractors' campaign contributions, and their cowardice in the face of the gun lobby.

The only solution, as Zinn said, is for the nation to be governed for, by and of the people, as stated in the Declaration of Independence. Elected officials only represent the deep-pocketed special interest groups that have put them there; those are their true constituencies. But strikes of major corporations, refusal of young men to register for the draft, desertion from the military and the refusal to purchase products that help to maintain the status quo are tools in the hands of the people that haven't been used for decades, but are no less effective than they ever were.

As the people wait for a leader to emerge, they continue to suffer from the unspeakable injustices of the U.S. government. Such a leader isn't required; all it takes is one person to begin on social media, and watch the snowball effect.

Hopefully, this will occur before Trump or whoever follows him as president of the United States of America leads the nation and the world into cataclysmic disaster. As Nicolas J.S. Davies writes:

> A huge amount of human suffering could be alleviated and global problems solved if the United States would make a genuine commitment to human rights and the rule of law, as opposed to one it only applies cynically and opportunistically to its enemies, but never to itself or its allies.[641]

---

[641] https://www.alternet.org/world/35-countries-where-us-has-supported-fascists-dru

As has been shown, the United States has a long history of warfare, often against nearly defenseless nations, and almost always for reasons it has invented. And rather than making any attempt to change that trajectory of violence, the military budget continues to expand while funding for social services, the so-called 'safety net', shrinks.

During the chaotic administration of Donald Trump, not only has the military been further glorified, but a weak and spineless Congress has approved funding for a new 'Space Force', effectively weaponizing space. The amount of terror, death and carnage that this will enable the U.S. to wreak on innocent people around the world staggers the imagination.

The country that fears Muslims also worships guns; a study by CNN indicated that, between the years 2001 and 2014, the total number of U.S., citizens killed by terrorism, at home and abroad, totalled 3,142, with nearly 3,000 of those victims dying during the September 11, 2001, attacks. After 2001, the number killed on U.S. soil is twenty-three.[642] And based on this, there is great fear of Muslims in the U.S.

During that same 14-year period, 440,095 citizens died on U.S. soil by firearms. [643] Yet no politicians are screaming about regulating guns. No candidate in the last U.S. presidential election appealed to his or her base by declaring that, under their administration, firearms would be regulated. On April 28, 2017, President Donald Trump spoke to the NRA (National Rifle Association) convention and said this: "only one candidate in the general election came to speak to you, and that candidate is now president of the United States, standing before you. You came through for me, and I'm going to come through for you."[644]

Although a proponent of gun-control prior to entering politics, Trump became an ardent gun-rights supporter afterward. When he refers to the NRA 'coming through' for him, he may be thinking about the $50,000,000 the NRA contributed to his and other Republican campaigns.[645] In the hallowed halls of U.S. governance, money talks.

---

glords-and-terrorists. Accessed on February 13, 2019.

[642] https://www.cato.org/blog/gao-weighs-countering-violent-extremism. Accessed on January 28, 2020.

[643] https://www.cnn.com/2017/10/03/opinions/mass-shootings-white-male-rage-mod an-opinion/index.html. Accessed on January 28, 2020.

[644] https://www.nytimes.com/2017/04/28/us/politics/donald-trump-nra.html. Accessed on January 28, 2020.

[645] https://www.opensecrets.org/news/2016/11/the-nra-placed-big-bets-on-the-2016-e lection-and-won-almost-all-of-them/. Accessed on January 28, 2020.

Can the U.S. be stopped? Sociologist Margaret Mead once said: "Never doubt that a small group of thoughtful, committed, organized citizens can change the world; indeed, it's the only thing that ever has."[646] What can a small and committed group of citizens do? The international organization, 'World Beyond War' (WBW) lists several suggestions. A handful of them follow:

- Work to close military bases. This involves contacting elected officials and making one's vote count.

- Divest from war-profiteering companies. Financial advisors can be told not to invest in war industries.

- Sign WBW's declaration of peace, already signed by tens of thousands of people from around the world.

- Become educated. Learn how war drives the U.S. economy.

- Learn viable alternatives to war. WBW's excellent book, *A Global Security System: An Alternative to War*, which is updated annually, provides the necessary information about how war can, in fact, be prevented.

It has been said that those who are not worried are not paying attention. If we are to save humanity from the most destructive nation in history, we must all act. Complacency is what brought the world to its current situation, enabling the United States to disdain international law, human rights and basic, common human decency. Complacency has been complicit it all its war crimes. A complacent population for generations has looked the other way as the blood of millions and millions of people has been spilled by the United States, most of whom have never presented any risk whatsoever to it.

We will close with on final quotation, this one by Assata Shakur: "Nobody in the world, nobody in history, has ever gotten their freedom by appealing to the moral sense of the people who were oppressing them."[647]

The time to act is now. The suffering must end.

---

[646]"Jennifer Harnish: 'Citizens Are Ideal for Educating Legislators'," *Parks & Recreation*, February 2012, 48.

[647]Wanelisa Xaba, "The Dangers of Liberalism: A Short Reflection on the African National Congress in South Africa," *Yale Human Rights and Development Law Journal* 20 (2019).

Bibliography

Abel, Kerry. "Remembering the War of 1812." *Canadian Parliamentary Review* 35, no. 3 (2012).

Abouzahr, Sami. "The Tangled Web: America, France and Indochina 1947–50: Sami Abouzahr Untangles US Policy towards France at the Time of the Marshall Plan and the War in Indochina." *History Today*, October 2004.

Ali, Tariq. "NATO's Balkan Adventure." *Monthly Review*, June 1999.

Andersen, Martin Edwin and John Dinges. "Kissinger Had a Hand in 'Dirty War': Declassified Documents Reveal the Former Secretary of State Turned a Blind Eye to Human-Rights Violations during Argentina's Crackdown on Terrorism in 1976. (Investigative Report)." *Insight on the News*, January 28, 2002.

Anderson, Benedict R. O'G. and Ruth T. McVey, *A Preliminary Analysis of the October 1, 1965 Coup in Indonesia.* Jakarta, Indonesia: Equinox, 2009.

Anderson, Tim. *The Dirty War on Syria: Washington, Regime Change and Resistance.* Global Research Publishers, 2016.

Ankomah, Baffour. "Never Again! ... 40 Years after the Coup That Derailed Africa's Progress." *New African*, February 2006.

Aranas, Paul F.J. *Smokescreen: The US, NATO and the Illegitimate Use of Force.* New York: Algora, 2012.

"Argentina: Declassified State Department Files Show U.S. Supported Repression during 'Dirty War'." *NotiSur – South American Political and Economic Affairs*, January 9, 2004.

Azzi, Pierre. "Harsh Rule: Recognizing the Taliban." *Harvard International Review*, Spring 1999.

Banchiri, Bamzi. "Was the Cobalt in Your Phone's Battery Mined by a Child?" *The Christian Science Monitor*, January 19, 2016.

Baracco, Luciano. *Nicaragua: The Imagining of a Nation: From Nineteenth-Century Liberals to Twentieth-Century Sandinistas.* New York: Algora, 2005.

Barfield, Thomas. *Afghanistan: A Cultural and Political History.* Princeton University Press, 2010.

Bautista, Veltisezar. *The Filipino Americans: From 1763 to the Present.* Bookhaus, 2002.

Beisel, David R. "Building the Nazi Mindset." *The Journal of Psychohistory* 37, no. 4 (2010).

Bernhard, Nancy. *U.S. Television News and Cold War Propaganda.* New York: Cambridge University Press, 1999.

Bernstein, Barton J. "Reconsidering the Perilous Cuban Missile Crisis 50 Years Later." *Arms Control Today*, October 2012.

Binder, David. "Ignorant 'Albright Doctrine' Entangles US in Ancient Disputes." *Insight on the News*, May 4, 1998.

Black, George. *Triumph of the People: The Sandinista Revolution in Nicaragua*, 1981.

Boorstein, Regula and Edward Boorstein. *Counterrevolution: U.S. Foreign Policy*. New York: International Publishers, 1990.

"Boomtown Rats: Giant African Rats Will Soon Be Undertaking an Important and Dangerous Job in Cambodia; Locating the Millions of Unexploded Landmines Left over after over 30 Years of Conflict." *Geographical*, September 2015.

Boot, Max *The Savage Wars of Peace*. Basic Books, 2014.

Boyle, Francis A. *Destroying Libya and World Order: The Three-Decade U.S. Campaign to Terminate the Qaddafi Revolution*. Atlanta: Clarity, 2013.

Brewer, Susan A. *Why America Fights: Patriotism and War Propaganda from the Philippines to Iraq*. New York: Oxford University Press, 2009.

Brumberg, Stephan F. "New York City Schools March Off to War. The Nature and Extent of Participating of the City Schools in the Great War, April 1917–June 1918." *Urban Education* 24, no. 4 (1990).

Brzezinski, Zbigniew. *The Grand Chessboard: American Primacy and its Geostrategic Imperatives*. Basis Books, 1998.

Byrne, Hugh. *El Salvador's Civil War: A Study of Revolution*. Boulder, CO: Lynne Rienner, 1996.

Casey, Steven. *Selling the Korean War: Propaganda, Politics, and Public Opinion in the United States, 1950–1953*. New York: Oxford University Press, 2008.

Cave, Damien. "U.S. Investigates Visit to Cuba by Jay-Z and Beyonce." *International Herald Tribune*, April 10, 2013.

Chambers, John Whiteclay. *The Oxford Companion to American Military History*. New York: Oxford University Press, 1999.

Chiasson, Lloyd Jr. *The Press in Time of Crisis*. Westport: Greenwood Publishing Group, 1995.

Christensen, Carol and Thomas. *The U.S.–Mexican War*. Bay Books, 1998.

Colby, William and Peter Forbath. *Honorable Men: My Life in the CIA*. New York: Simon and Schuster, 1978.

Coleman, Aaron N. "'A Second Bounaparty?': A Reexamination of Alexander Hamilton during the Franco-American Crisis, 1796–1801." *Journal of the Early Republic* 28, no. 2 (2008).

Collins, Ross F. *Children, War and Propaganda*. Peter Lange, Inc., 2011.

Congressional Record, 64th Congress, 1st Session. Washington, DC: U.S. Government Printing Office, 1917.

Constable, Pamela and Arturo Valenzuela. *A Nation of Enemies: Chile under Pinochet*. New York: W. W. Norton, 1991.

Cooper, Rand Richards. "History as Tragedy: 'Lumumba?'" *Commonweal*, October 12, 2001.

Copeland, David A. *Debating the Issues in Colonial Newspapers: Primary Documents on Events of the Period.* Greenwod; 2000.

"Covert U.S. Aid to Rebels Reported." *Pittsburgh Tribune-Review*, March 31, 2011.

Cowen, David J. "Financing the War of 1812." *Financial History*, Fall 2012.

Cox, Isaac Joslin. *Nicaragua and the United States, 1909–1927.* Boston: World Peace Foundation, 1927.

Curtis, George Ticknor. *Life of Daniel Webster Vol. 2.* Forgotten Books, 2012.

Dakin, Brett. "From Spying to Killing: How America's 'Secret War' in Laos Transformed the CIA." *The Washington Monthly*, January-February 2017.

Davis, Anne Marie. "United States Foreign Policy Objectives and Grenada's Territorial Integrity." *The Journal of Negro History* 79, no. 1 (1994).

Davis, Brian L. *Qaddafi, Terrorism, and the Origins of the U.S. Attack on Libya.* New York: Praeger, 1990.

Deichmann Edwards, Wendy J. "Forging an Ideology for American Missions: Josiah Strong and Manifest Destiny." In *North American Foreign Missions, 1810–1914: Theology, Theory, and Policy*, edited by Wilbert R. Shenk. Grand Rapids, MI: William B. Eerdmans, 2004.

Drivas, Peter G. "The Cambodian Incursion Revisited." *International Social Science Review* 86, nos. 3–4 (2011).

Elder, Grant. *Wiki vs NWO (New World Order): Moving to Collaboration from Domination.* Friesen Press, 2014.

Emenyonu, Ernest (editor). *Politics and Social Justice.* Boydell & Brewer Ltd., 2014.

Ensalaco, Mark. *Chile under Pinochet: Recovering the Truth.* Philadelphia: University of Pennsylvania Press, 2000.

Evans, Michael L. "Problems with Current U.S. Policy." *Foreign Policy in Focus*, June 4, 2001.

Farhi, Paul. "Caught in Conspiracy Crosshairs." *Winnipeg Free Press*, December 10, 2016.

Feierstein, Gerald. "Is There a Path out of the Yemen Conflict?: Why It Matters." *Prism: A Journal of the Center for Complex Operations* 7, no. 1 (2017).

Ferreira, Roberto Garcia. "The CIA and Jacobo Arbenz: History of a Disinformation Campaign." *Journal of Third World Studies* 25, no. 2 (2008).

Feuer, A. B. *The Santiago Campaign of 1898: A Soldier's View of the Spanish-American War.* Praeger, 1993.

Findling, John E. *Close Neighbors, Distant Friends: United States–Central American Relations.* New York: Greenwood Press, 1987.

Fisher, Louis. "When Wars Begin: Misleading Statements by Presidents." *Presidential Studies Quarterly* 40, no. 1 (2010).

Foos, Paul. *A Short, Offhand, Killing Affair: Soldiers and Social Conflict during the Mexican-American War*. University of North Carolina Press, 2003.

Fowler, Will. *Santa Anna of Mexico*. Lincoln, NE: University of Nebraska Press, 2007.

Freeman, Michael. *Freedom or Security: The Consequences for Democracies Using Emergency Powers to Fight Terror*. Westport, CT: Praeger, 2003.

Fridell, Ron. *Dictatorship*. New York: Marshall Cavendish Benchmark, 2007.

Fussel, Paul. *Wartime. Understanding and Behavior in the Second World War*. New York and Oxford: Oxford University Press, 1989.

Gilderhus, Mark T. "The Monroe Doctrine: Meanings and Implications." *Presidential Studies Quarterly* 36, no. 1 (2006).

Gillespie, Nick. "Bombs Away." *Reason*, December 1998.

Gleijeses, Piero. *Visions of Freedom: Havana, Washington, Pretoria and the Struggle for Southern Africa, 1976–1991*. Chapel Hill, NC: University of North Carolina Press, 2013.

Grieb, Kenneth J. "American Involvement in the Rise of Jorge Ubico." *Caribbean Studies* 10, no. 1 (April 1970).

Grunig, James E. "Public Relations and International Affairs: Effects, Ethics and Responsibility." *Journal of International Affairs* 47, no. 1 (1993).

Gutting, Glenn E. "The Alamo: An Illustrated History." *Military Review* 80, no. 3 (2000).

Hagan, John. *Who Are the Criminals?: The Politics of Crime Policy from the Age of Roosevelt to the Age of Reagan*. Princeton, NJ: Princeton University Press, 2010.

Haley, P. Edward. *Congress and the Fall of South Vietnam and Cambodia*. Rutherford, NJ: Associated University Presses, 1982.

Hallenbeck, Ralph A. *Military Force as an Instrument of U.S. Foreign Policy: Intervention in Lebanon, August 1982–February 1984*. New York: Praeger Publishers, 1991.

Han, Vo Xuan. *Oil, The Persian Gulf States, and the United States*. Palgrave MacMillan, 1994.

Hannigan, Robert E. *The New World Power: American Foreign Policy, 1898–1917*. Philadelphia: University of Pennsylvania Press, 2002.

Herman, Edward S. "The Media's Role in U.S. Foreign Policy." *Journal of International Affairs* 47, no. 1 (1993).

Herring, George C. *From Colony to Superpower: U.S. Foreign Relations since 1776*. New York: Oxford University Press, 2008.

Horten, Gerd. *Radio Goes to War: The Cultural Politics of Propaganda during World War II*. Berkeley, CA: University of California Press, 2002.

Hunt, Andrew E. *The Turning: A History of Vietnam Veterans against the War*. New York: New York University Press, 1999.

"In War, Some Facts Less Factual; Some US Assertions from the Last War on Iraq Still Appear Dubious." *The Christian Science Monitor*, September 6, 2002.

Jaher, Frederic Cople. *Doubters and Dissenters: Cataclysmic Thought in America, 1885–1918*. Free Press of Glencoe, 1974.

Jamieson, Kathleen Hall and Paul Waldman. *The Press Effect: Politicians, Journalists, and the Stories That Shape the Political World*. New York: Oxford University Press, 2004.

Jeansonne, Glen and David Luhrssen. *War on the Silver Screen: Shaping America's Perception of History*. Lincoln, NE: Potomac Books, 2014.

"Jennifer Harnish: 'Citizens Are Ideal for Educating Legislators.'" *Parks & Recreation*, February 2012.

Jian, Chen. *China's Road to the Korean War: The Making of the Sino-American Confrontation*. Columbia University Press, 1996.

Johansen, Bruce Elliott (editor). *The Encyclopedia of Native American Legal Tradition*. Greenwood Press, 1998.

"Jonathan Freedland: Robin Cook's Devastating Charge That Blair Went to War When He Knew Iraq Had No Banned Weapons – and Posed No Threat – Blasts a Massive Hole in the Prime Minister's Credibility." *The Mirror* (London, England), October 6, 2003.

Johns, Christina Jacqueline and P. Ward Johnson. *State Crime, the Media, and the Invasion of Panama*. Westport, CT: Praeger Publishers, 1994.

Jones, Wilbur Devereux. *The American Problem in British Diplomacy, 1841–1861*. University of Georgia Press, 1974.

Keenan, Jerry. *Encyclopedia of the Spanish-American and Philippine-American Wars*. Santa Barbara: ABC-CLIO, 2001.

Kelly, John H. "Lebanon: 1982–1984." In *U.S. and Russian Policymaking With Respect to the Use of Force*. Edited by Jeremy R. Azrael and Emil A. Payin. RAND Corporation, 1996. https://www.rand.org/pubs/conf_-proceedings/CF129/CF-129-chapter6.html

Kenny, Jack. "Vietnamese Friend or Foe: U.S. Foreign Policy Has Often Been Highlighted by Shortsightedness, Disregard of Foreign Concerns, and Regime-Change Operations – As Shown in the Lead-Up to the Vietnam War." *The New American*, November 18, 2013.

Kenny, Kevin. *Peaceable Kingdom Lost: The Paxton Boys and the Destruction of William Penn's Holy Experiment*. New York: Oxford University Press, 2009.

King, Robert. "House Could Be First Up to Tackle Entitlement Reform." *The Examiner (Washington, D.C.)*, December 7, 2017.

Kingsbury, Celia Malone. *For Home and Country: World War I Propaganda on the Home Front*. Lincoln, NE: University of Nebraska Press, 2010.

Knight, Melvin M. *The Americans in Santo Domingo*. New York: Vanguard Press, 1928.

Kolb, Richard K. "First Foreign Fight." *VFW Magazine*, June/July 1998.

Kornbluh, Peter. "Licensed to Kill." *The Nation*, June 16, 1997.

—. *The Pinochet File: A Declassified Dossier on Atrocity and Accountability*. New York: The New Press, 2013.

Krasner, Stephen D. *Defending the National Interest: Raw Materials Investments and U.S. Foreign Policy.* Princeton, NY: Princeton University Press, 1978.

Kunczik, Michael. *Images of Nations and International Public Relations.* Mahwah, NJ: Lawrence Erlbaum Associates, 1997.

Langholtz Harvey, Boris Kondoch, *et al. International Peacekeeping: The Yearbook of International Peace Operations – Vol. 9.* Martinus Nijhoff, 2005.

Larson, Cedric and James R. Mock. *Words That Won the War: The Story of the Committee on Public Information.* New York, 1968.

Lasensky, Scott and Kerem Levitas. "Modern History and Politics: Crisis and Crossfire: The United States and the Middle East since 1945." *The Middle East Journal* 60, no. 3 (2006).

Lawrence, Mark Atwood. "History from Below – The United States and Latin America in the Nixon Years." In *Nixon in the World: American Foreign Relations, 1969–1977.* Edited by Fredrik Logevall and Andrew Preston. New York: Oxford University Press, 2008.

Leacock, Ruth. *Requiem for Revolution: The United States and Brazil, 1961–1969.* Kent, OH: Kent State University Press, 1990.

Loewen, J. W. *Teaching What Really Happened: How To Avoid The Tyranny Of Textbooks And Get Students Excited About Doing History.* New York: Teachers College Press, 2010.

Lopez, Nina. "Dance with Democracy: Renewed US Attempts to Remove President Hugo Chavez from Office." *New Internationalist,* August 2004.

Lumley, Frederick E. *The Propaganda Menace.* New York: Century, 1933.

Manning, Martin J. and Clarence R. Wyatt. *Encyclopedia of Media and Propaganda in Wartime America.* Volume 1. ABC-CLIO, 2010.

Manwaring, Max G. "A Strategic View of Insurgencies: Insights from El Salvador." *McNair Papers,* no. 8 (1990).

McManus, John F. "Lebanon: A Case of U.S. Subversion." *The New American,* August 21, 2006.

McSherry, J. Patrice. "Operation Condor: Clandestine Inter-American System." *Social Justice* 26, no. 4 (1999).

Meeks, Brian. *Caribbean Revolutions and Revolutionary Theory: An Assessment of Cuba, Nicaragua and Grenada.* Barbados: University of the West Indies Press, 2001.

Meisler, Stanley. "The Massacre in El Mozote." In *Thinking Clearly: Cases in Journalistic Decision-Making.* Edited by Tom Rosenstiel and Amy S. Mitchell. New York: Colombia University Press, 2003.

Monje, Scott C. *The Central Intelligence Agency: A Documentary History.* Westport, CT: Greenwood Press, 2008.

Morgenstern, George. "The Actual Road to Pearl Harbor." In *Perpetual War for Perpetual Peace: A Critical Examination of the Foreign Policy of Franklin Delano Roosevelt and Its Aftermath.* Edited by Harry Elmer Barnes. Caldwell, ID: Caxton Printers, 1953.

—. *Pearl Harbor: The Story of the Secret War*. New York: Devin-Adair, 1947.

Neville, John F. *The U.S. Media and Yugoslavia, 1991–1995*. Westport, CT: Praeger, 1998.

"Obama: Failing 'The Day After' in Libya Worst Mistake of Presidency." *Hindustan Times* (New Delhi, India), April 12, 2016.

Offner, John L. *An Unwanted War: The Diplomacy of the United States and Spain over Cuba, 1895–1898*. Chapel Hill, NC: University of North Carolina Press, 1992.

"On CIA, Once More: 'Abolish the Damned Thing' (Editorial)." *National Catholic Reporter*, September 6, 1996.

Osgood, Kenneth and Andrew K. Frank (editors). *Selling War in a Media Age: The Presidency and Public Opinion in the American Century*. Gainesville, FL: University Press of Florida, 2010.

Pach, Chester. "The Reagan Doctrine: Principle, Pragmatism, and Policy." *Presidential Studies Quarterly* 36, no. 1 (2006).

Peace, Roger. "The Anti-Contra-War Campaign: Organizational Dynamics of a Decentralized Movement." *International Journal of Peace Studies* 13, no. 1 (2008).

Peguero, Valentina. *The Militarization of Culture in the Dominican Republic, from the Captains General to General Trujillo*. Studies in War, Society, and the Military. Lincoln, NE: University of Nebraska Press, 2004.

Perlez, Jane. "On Rare Laos Trip, Clinton Views War's Legacy; Victims of Dormant Bombs from Vietnam Era Call for More Action." *International Herald Tribune*, July 12, 2012.

Pfiffner, James P. "Did President Bush Mislead the Country in His Arguments for War with Iraq?" *Presidential Studies Quarterly* 34, no. 1 (2004)

Poelchau, Warner (editor). *White Paper Whitewash: Interviews with Philip Agee on the CIA and El Salvador*. New York: Deep Cover Books, 1981.

Ponsonby, Arthur. *Falsehood in War-Time*. Kessinger Publishing, Llc., 2010.

Porter, Gareth. *Perils of Dominance: Imbalance of Power and the Road to War in Vietnam*. Berkeley, CA: University of California Press, 2005.

Prados, John. *Lost Crusader: The Secret Wars of CIA Director William Colby*. New York: Oxford University Press, 2003.

"Probing a Slaughter: A U.S. Assault on Iraqi Troops Was 'A Grouse Shoot' but Was It an Excessive Use of Force?" *Newsweek*, May 29, 2000.

Prucha, Francis Paul (editor). *Documents of United States Indian Policy*. 3rd ed. Lincoln, NE: University of Nebraska Press, 2000.

Pulley, R. "The United States and the Trujillo Dictatorship, 1933–1940: The High Price of Caribbean Stability." *Caribbean Studies* 5, no. 3 (1965), 22–31. http://www.jstor.org/stable/25611893.

Quist-Adade, Charles. "Kwame Nkrumah, the Big Six, and the Fight for Ghana's Independence." *Journal of Pan African Studies* 1, no. 9 (2007).

Reid, Stuart A. "Congo's Slide into Chaos: How a State Fails." *Foreign Affairs*, January/February 2018.

Rezun, Miron. *Saddam Hussein's Gulf Wars: Ambivalent Stakes in the Middle East.* Praeger, 1992.

Rickover, Hyman George. *How the Battleship Maine was Destroyed.* University of Michigan Library, 1976.

Roschwalb S. A. "The Hill & Knowlton cases: A brief on the controversy." *Public Relations Review* (1994).

Rosenbaum, Herbert D. and Alexej Ugrinsky. *Jimmy Carter: Foreign Policy and Post-Presidential Years.* Praeger, 1993.

Rosenfeld, Harvey. *Diary of a Dirty Little War: The Spanish–American War of 1898.* Praeger, 2000.

Ross, Stewart Halsey. *Propaganda for War: How the United States was Conditioned to Fight the Great War of 1914–1918.* Progressive Press, 2009.

Rowse, Ted. "Kuwaitgate." *The Washington Monthly*, September 1992. http://www.questia.com/read/1G1-12529902/kuwaitgate.

Ryan, Jeffrey J. "Turning on Their Masters: State Terrorism and Unlearning Democracy in Uruguay." In *When States Kill: Latin America, the U.S., and Technologies of Terror.* Edited by Cecilia Menjívar and Néstor Rodríguez. Austin, TX: University of Texas Press, 2005.

Schiff, Ze'ev and Ehud Ya'ari. *Israel's Lebanon War.* Edited and translated by Ina Friedman. New York: Simon and Schuster, 1984. http://www.isreview.org/issues/50/Lebanon1982.shtml.

Schmidt, Donald E. *The Folly of War: American Foreign Policy, 1898–2005.* New York: Algora, 2005.

Schmidt, Hans. *The United States Occupation of Haiti, 1915–1934.* New Brunswick, NJ: Rutgers University Press, 1995.

Schmults, Robert C. "Bloodshed and Blame in Angola." *Insight on the News*, March 1, 1993.

Schoultz, Lars. *That Infernal Little Cuban Republic: The United States and the Cuban Revolution.* Chapel Hill, NC: University of North Carolina Press, 2009.

Scott, Peter Dale. *The Road to 9/11: Wealth, Empire, and the Future of America.* Berkeley, CA: University of California Press, 2007.

Seib, Philip. *Campaigns and Conscience: The Ethics of Political Journalism.* Westport, CT: Praeger, 1994.

Shannon, Elaine. *Desperados: Latin Drug Lords, U.S. Lawmen, And The War America Can't Win.* iUniverse, 2015.

Shank, Gregory. "Commentary: Not a Just War, Just a War – NATO's Humanitarian Bombing Mission." *Social Justice* 26, no. 1 (1999).

Sharp, Jeremy M., "Yemen: Background and U.S. Relations." *Current Politics and Economics of the Middle East* 2, no. 1 (2011).

Shipler, David. "The massacre brings on a crisis of faith for Israelis; mourning, anger, and moral outrage." *New York Times*, September 26, 1982. Quoted in http://www.isreview.org/issues/50/Lebanon1982.shtml.

Simons. Geoff. *Iraq: From Sumner to Saddam.* Palgrave Macmillan, 1996.

Sprague, Ted. "Indonesia's Forgotten Massacre." *New Internationalist*, October 2011.

Starkey, Marion L. *A Little Rebellion.* New York: Alfred A. Knopf, 1955.

Stohl, Michael and George A. Lopez (editors). *Terrible beyond Endurance?: The Foreign Policy of State Terrorism.* New York: Greenwood Press, 1988.

Stokes, Doug. "America's Other War: Terrorizing Colombia." *Canadian Dimension,* July-August 2005.

Streeter, Stephen M. *Managing the Counterrevolution: The United States and Guatemala, 1954–1961.* Athens, GA: University of Ohio Press, 2000.

"Suharto's Heirs." *The Progressive,* July 1998.

Szatmary, David P. *Shays' Rebellion: The Making of an Agrarian Insurrection.* Ann Arbor, MI: University of Massachusetts Press, 1980.

Taylor, Alan. "Remaking Americans: Louisiana, Upper Canada, and Texas." In *Contested Spaces of Early America.* Edited by Juliana Barr and Edward Countryman. Philadelphia: University of Pennsylvania Press, 2014.

Tillman, Ellen D. *Dollar Diplomacy by Force: Nation-Building and Resistance in the Dominican Republic.* Chapel Hill, NC: University of North Carolina Press, 2016.

Trahair, Richard C. S. *Encyclopedia of Cold War Espionage, Spies, and Secret Operations.* Westport, CT: Greenwood Press, 2004.

Transcript, meeting of the CPSU CC Politburo, 13 November 1986. Cold War International History Project. http://www.wilsoncenter.org/index.cfm?topic_id=1409&fuseaction=library.document&id=340.

Tucker, Spencer C. and Frank T. Reuter. *Injured Honor: The Chesapeake-Leopard Affair, June 22, 1807.* Naval Institute Press, 1996.

Tvedten, Inge. *Angola: Struggle for Peace and Reconstruction.* Boulder, CO: Westview Press, 1997.

"Uruguay: Former Dictator Juan Maria Bordaberry Arrested for Murder of Politicians and Guerrillas." *NotiSur – South American Political and Economic Affairs,* January 12, 2007.

Vandervort, Bruce. *Indian Wars of Canada, Mexico, and the United States, 1812–1900.* New York: Routledge, 2005.

Vidal, Gore. *Dreaming War: Blood for Oil and the Cheney-Bush Junta.* Thunder's Mouth Press, 2002.

Ward, Harry M. *The War for Independence and the Transformation of American Society.* New York: Routledge, 1999.

"We Turn to the Urgent Duty of Protecting Other Lives." *The Washington Times,* September 13, 2002.

Weissman, Stephen R. "Addicted to Mobutu: Why America Can't Learn from Its Foreign Policy Mistakes." *The Washington Monthly,* September 1997.

—. "Presidential Deception in Foreign Policy Making: Military Intervention in Libya 2011." *Presidential Studies Quarterly* 46, no. 3 (2016).

Welch, Richard E. Jr. *Response to Imperialism.* The University of North Carolina Press, 1987.

Wesson, Robert. *The United States and Brazil: Limits of U.S. Influence.* New York: Praeger, 1981.

Wilkerson, Marcus M. *Public Opinion and the Spanish–American War: A Study in War Propaganda.* Baton Rouge: Louisiana State University Press, 1932.

Windrich, Elaine. *The Cold War Guerrilla: Jonas Savimbi, the U. S. Media, and the Angolan War.* New York: Greenwood Press, 1992.

Witte-Lebhar, Benjamin. "Chile's Dictatorship-Era Spy Chief Manuel Contreras Dead at 86." *NotiSur – South American Political and Economic Affairs,* August 28, 2015.

Xaba, Wanelisa. "The Dangers of Liberalism: A Short Reflection on the African National Congress in South Africa." *Yale Human Rights and Development Law Journal* 20 (2019).

Yardley, William. "Fred Branfman, 72, Is Dead; Exposed U.S. Bombing in Laos." *International New York Times,* October 8, 2014.

Yates, A. "Intervention in the Dominican Republic 1965–1966." In *The Savage Wars of Peace: Toward a New Paradigm of Peace Operations.* Edited by John T. Fishel. Boulder, CO: Westview Press, 1998.

Zinn, Howard. "A Flash of the Possible." *The Progressive,* January 2000.

—. *A People's History of the United States.* Harper Collins, 2003.

Zunes, Stephen. "U.S. Role in Lebanon Debacle." *Foreign Policy in Focus,* May 18, 2007.

Index

About the Author

Robert Fantina is an activist and journalist, working for peace and social justice. A U.S. citizen, he moved to Canada shortly after the 2004 presidential election, and now holds dual citizenship. He is currently active in supporting the human rights struggles of the Palestinian people, and is the past Canadian coordinator of World Beyond War. He serves on the boards of Canadians for Palestinian Rights, and Canadians for Justice in Kashmir.

He is the author of several books, including *Desertion and the American Soldier: 1776–2006*; *Empire, Racism and Genocide: A History of U.S. Foreign Policy*; *Look Not Unto the Morrow*, a Vietnam-era, anti-war story; and *Occupied Palestine: Israel, the U.S. and International Law*.

His writing appears regularly on Counterpunch, Global Research and several other sites.

Mr. Fantina now resides in Kitchener, Ontario.